17th and 32nd Service Battalions
NORTHUMBERLAND FUSILIERS
(N.E.R.) Pioneers 1914-1919

FROM THE AUTHOR

To All who Served in the 17th Northumberland Fusiliers (N.E.R.) Pioneers

WHEN Major Shenton Cole did me the honour of asking me to write this book, I undertook the task with great pleasure, having very pleasant memories of some months spent with you making light railways through the muddy wastes of " The Salient."

I have tried to produce a book which will give pleasure to those whose doings it records. I have attempted to include as many as possible of the little incidents which went to make up our lives in those days, some very hard, others very pleasant, as well as to do justice to the greater achievements. In order to get the real battalion flavour, I have as far as possible used the actual words of the diaries and letters, which have been so kindly lent me by many members of the N.E.R. Pioneers. I have only filled in the gaps so as to make a consecutive narrative, and have added here and there details gleaned from the official War Diaries which were necessary to complete the record.

This book has taken a long time making, and let me assure you it would never have been completed if Major Cole had not been a most determined man with a most equable temper. Major Cole got me the materials which I have woven into this book. To my frequent peevish demands for more information he invariably returned soft answers, and after patient search found someone who could supply my needs, and he has devoted a great deal of his spare time and given much thought to the many troublesome tasks connected with book production.

Your thanks are also due to the many former members of the battalion whose diaries and letters have supplied the greater part of my material. Captain Sadler, R.S.M. Randall, Lance-Corporal Theakstone, Private Nicholson all lent me good diaries. Lance-Corporal T. W. Clapham, besides writing a very useful summary of his diary covering the whole period of the war, supplied me with many well-worded descriptions of those incidents of which I asked for more details. Lieutenant Drury's contribution amounted to a great many pages, from which I culled many useful passages. Others who have helped are Lance-Sergeant N. A. Liddell, Q.M.S. Horsley, Lieutenant Pickering, Captain Robertson, Lance-Corporal J. Caminada, Captain Watson, M.C., Sergeant Welsh, Lieutenant Smith and one or two more. Lieutenant-Colonel Fyffe and Major Leonard Thompson have given me help as regards the 32nd Battalion, and we have to thank Mr. A. Brewis for his assistance in the preparation of Appendix III which gives a brief summary of the history of the regiment. Lastly there is Captain P. B. Glendinning, who has drawn the maps which, whatever the critics may say about my share of the book, will, I am sure, earn high praise from all.

I have drawn on the " Encyclopædia Brittanica " for information regarding phases of the war not included in the official documents open to my inspection.

I have been asked by the Editor to acknowledge the great help he has received from Mr. W. T. Mayne, Managing Director of the Northumberland Press Limited, who has spared no pains to produce the book satisfactorily and cheaply.

As regards the book, I hope you'll like it; if you are pleased I shall be satisfied, whatever others may say. I really value your opinion, for we became friends in the mud and muck round Bridge Four and Burnt Farm in 1917, and in writing this book I have got to know you better and admire you still more, so farewell and the best of luck to you all.

J. Shakespear.

FOREWORD

I AM glad to take the opportunity afforded me by Major-General Sir Eric Geddes, my first Director-General of Transportation in the British Armies in France, to write a brief Foreword to this history of the 17th Service Battalion Northumberland Fusiliers, in evidence both of my appreciation of the work which the battalion did, and of my admiration for the spirit in which that work was undertaken and carried through.

That work and that spirit, the nature and character of which are set out clearly and dramatically in the pages of this book, are largely typical of the varied experiences and sterling qualities of the pioneer battalions of Britain's new armies in the Great War; though the special knowledge possessed by the N.E.R. Pioneers as railway troops made the different duties they were called upon to perform even more varied in their case than in most.

It seems to me very right and proper, from the widest point of view as well as from that of the individual battalion, that the details of the daily life of an essential yet little advertised constituent of a modern army should be put on record. I welcome the chance this Foreword gives me to pay my own tribute to the splendid service at all times so loyally and devotedly rendered by the pioneer battalions that fought under my command.

Haig, F.M.

BEMERSYDE,
    13*th November*, 1925.

CONTENTS

	PAGE
FROM THE AUTHOR	iii
FOREWORD. By Field-Marshal Earl Haig, K.T., G.C.B., O.M., G.C.V.O., K.C.I.E.	v
INTRODUCTION. By the Right Hon. Sir Eric Geddes, G.C.B., G.B.E., K.C.B.	xiii

CHAPTER I

THE RAISING OF THE BATTALION

Outbreak of war—Insufficiency of preparations—W.O. turns to Local Authorities—N.E.R. offers a battalion—Magnificent response to recruiting circular—Completeness of arrangements for housing and equipping battalion—Rapid organization and training—Guarding the coast—Hardships cheerfully borne—Spy hunts—Return to Hull—Training continued—Battalion moves to Catterick—Joins 32nd Division as Pioneers—Moves to Codford—Then to France 1

CHAPTER II

EARLY EXPERIENCES IN FRANCE

Landing in France—The move to Meaulte—First experiences in the line—A " green bunch "—Work and play while preparing for the great attack of 1st July—Bathing—Billets—Leave—Final arrangements—Lieutenant-Colonel Pears invalided—Returns to command on 30th June   15

CHAPTER III

THE FIRST BATTLE OF THE SOMME

The task of the 32nd Division on 1st July—The arrangements for the attack—The task of the battalion—Summary of results of first day's attacks—Doings of 32nd Division—The battalion's doings—" The inestimable value of the opening of Sanda Sap "—On first development of the " green bunch "—Progress of battle—Brief relief—Back to the fight attached to 12th Division—32nd Division returns to the line—Battalion rejoins—Second spell of attack 30

CHAPTER IV

OUR FIRST MOVE NORTH

Withdrawn from Somme—March to Bailleul-les-Pernes—Refitting—Move to Loos—Lieutenant-Colonel Pears leaves battalion—His death—Battalion attached to 16th Division—Good work in front line—Move to Le Preol—Rejoin 32nd Division—Sudden move to Acq and back—Battalion detached from 32nd Division for railway work—Moves back to Somme area 43

CHAPTER V

RAILWAY WORK ON THE SOMME AND AT BERGUETTE

Battalion joins Group Five of Railway Construction Engineers—Work on Beausart Aveluy line—Capture of Thiépval—Work on railway in shelled area—Rapid progress of work—Camp shelled—Casualties—Battalion converted into Railway Pioneer Battalion—Line completed into Pozières under shell fire—Taking of Beaumont Hamel—Construction of broad gauge line from Aveluy to Acheux—Christmas festivities—" A " Company moves to Candas—Battalion moves to Isbergues—Construction of light railway workshops—Size and importance of work—Departure amid tears of Mademoiselles 51

CHAPTER VI

FIVE MONTHS IN THE SALIENT

Move to " The Salient "—Poperinghe in 1917—Work on the Great Midland Railway—Difficulties of work—Interruptions by the enemy—Shells and bombs—The crossing of the Yser Canal—Cheerful co-operation with other units—Battalion put on to light railways—Rough job for " A " on Dickebusch—Battle Wood line—" D's " experiences of a " safe job "—Preparation for attack on St. Julien—Formation of 18th Corps light railway column—Composition of column—Organization—Programme of work—The advance on 31st July—Hard work and rapid progress—Some heavy casualties—Daily routine of work in shelled area—Battalion to revert to 32nd Division 61

CHAPTER VII

THE MOVE TO NIEUPORT

Move to Nieuport—Re-organization as Divisional Pioneers—Work and play in new area—Re-training of Lewis Gunners—" Spit and polish "—Back again to the Salient under 18th Corps—Battalion re-transformed into Railway Construction Unit 72

CHAPTER VIII

MORE "SALIENT," THEN EXPERIENCES WITH AUSSIES

Work on light railways round Langemarck—Association with 7th Battalion Canadian Railway Troops—Work much interfered with by enemy—Casualties—Christmas, 1917, a great feast—Fritz assists at "Soccer" match—Life in "Pop"—Fun, frolics, and funerals—Shells better than bombs—Increased activity of enemy in March—Effect of enemy's great offensive—Sudden transfer of battalion to 1st Australian Division—The joys of "Stand to"—Stopping the Boche—Fortifying front line—Trenches near Pradelles and Strazeele—Hun bolt shot—Battalion attached to 52nd Division 78

CHAPTER IX

NEUVILLE ST. VAAST AND THE FINAL ADVANCE

Battalion as Pioneers of 52nd Division—Work in Willerval sector—P.U.O.—Breaking up of "D" Company—Battalion re-converted to Divisional Pioneers—More "spit and polish"—Back into line Pont du Jour-Thelus—Division into G.H.Q. reserve—The turn of the tide—Division to 6th Corps—Attack of 23rd August, 1918—Work of battalion—Importance of repairing roads, etc.—Breaking the Hindenburg line—Great work of battalion on lines of communication—Division relieved, but not Pioneers—Division back again—Takes Bullecourt—Work of battalion in new advance—Division relieved, but not Pioneers—Heavy work on roads—Death of Major Martin—His career—Division takes over Moevres sector—Heavy fighting—On the Canal du Nord—Attack of 27th September—Battalion's work canal crossings—In fighting round Cambrai—Division relieved 7th October—Battalion has week's rest—Attached to 6th Corps round Douai—Rejoins 52nd Division 29th October 87

CHAPTER X

FINALE

The position of affairs 27th October—Division takes over from 12th Division along Jard Canal—Strength of enemy's position—Rôle of 52nd Division—Operations of adjacent divisions—The flight of the enemy, crossing of Scheldt and Jard Canal—Rapid advance of division—Enemy caught at Jurbise on 10th November—The Pioneers' great share in the advance—The Armistice—Parades—Sports—Education—Demobilization—Return home—Colour deposited in Newcastle Cathedral 100

EMBARKATION ROLL OF OFFICERS AND DRAFTS 109

LIST OF OFFICERS WHO PASSED THROUGH 17TH BATTALION SEPT. '14—SEPT. '15 112

ROLL OF MEN WHO SERVED WITH THE 17TH (S.) BATTALION NORTHUMBERLAND FUSILIERS PIONEERS 1914-1919 113

Contents

APPENDIX I
Congratulatory Messages 167

APPENDIX II
The 32nd Northumberland Fusiliers 169

APPENDIX III
A Brief Outline of the Regiment's History 170

APPENDIX IV
The Construction of the Berguette Light Railway Depot . . 173

APPENDIX V
The Battlefields Re-visited 175

APPENDIX VI
Potted Pioneering 178

APPENDIX VII
The Unveiling of the York War Memorial 179

APPENDIX VIII
Constitution and Rules of the N.E.R. Pioneers' Association . . 180

LIST OF ILLUSTRATIONS

Frontispiece. THE RIGHT HON. SIR ERIC GEDDES, G.C.B., G.B.E., K.C.B.

PLATE
- I. OFFICERS, WARRANT OFFICERS AND SERGEANTS OF THE BATTALION, KING GEORGE DOCK, HULL.
- II. INSPECTION OF THE BATTALION BY THE N.E.R. DIRECTORS, FEBRUARY, 1915.
- III. GENERAL VIEWS AT KING GEORGE DOCK, HULL.
- IV. GENERAL VIEWS AT KING GEORGE DOCK, HULL.
- V. GENERAL VIEWS AT EASINGTON AND BARDON MOOR.
- VI. OFFICERS, WARRANT OFFICERS AND SERGEANTS OF THE BATTALION, CODFORD CAMP, SALISBURY PLAIN.
- VII. BATTALION ON EVE OF DEPARTURE FROM CODFORD CAMP.
- VIII. BOUZINCOURT, NORTHUMBERLAND AVENUE AND PIONEERS ROAD.
- IX. BECOURT CHÂTEAU, ALBERT, MOUQUET FARM.
- X. VIEWS ON THE SOMME FRONT.
- XI. CONEY STREET DUG-OUTS AND ACHEUX WOOD.
- XII. ANNEQUIN, LENS AND NEUVILLE ST. VAAST.
- XIII. WOODCOTE HOUSE AND VIEWS OF THE SALIENT.
- XIV. BURNT FARM AND WATERLOO DUMP.
- XV. NIEUPORT.
- XVI. RAILWAY BRIDGE OVER YSER AND STEENBEEK.
- XVII. VIEWS OF YPRES AND POPERINGHE.
- XVIII. NEUVILLE ST. VAAST AND OTHER VIEWS.
- XIX. QUÉANT, PRONVILLE AND CROISELLES.
- XX. CANAL DU NORD, BOURLON WOOD AND CANTAING.
- XXI. ESCAULT CANAL AND MASNAY ST. JEAN.
- XXII. RETURN OF CADRE AND LAYING UP OF COLOURS.
- XXIII. UNVEILING OF WAR MEMORIAL, YORK, JUNE 14TH, 1924.
- XXIV. WARRANT OFFICERS AND N.C.O.'S OF 32ND NORTHUMBERLAND FUSILIERS.
- XXV. TYPES OF UNIFORM WORN BY THE NORTHUMBERLAND FUSILIERS.
- XXVI. GENERAL VIEWS.
- XXVII. LIFE STORY OF A PIONEER ON ACTIVE SERVICE.
- XXVIII. LIFE STORY OF A PIONEER ON ACTIVE SERVICE—*continued*.
- XXIX. RANGE CONSTRUCTION—BARDON MOOR.

INTRODUCTION

I AM glad that a history of the N.E.R. Battalion has been written, and especially glad that one so well qualified for the work as Lieutenant-Colonel Shakespear, whose battalion, the 18th Northumberland Fusiliers, served with the 17th during the operations preceding the third battle of Ypres in August, 1917, has been able to undertake the task, his close association with and intimate knowledge of the N.E.R. Battalion having put him into a position of writing the history with a more personal note than would have been possible without that close association.

Our thanks are also due to our friends Major H. S. Cole, who has organized the preparation of the history, and to Captain Glendinning, to whom we are indebted for the excellent maps included in it.

The N.E.R. Battalion, formed in the first days of the war, is, I think, unique in being the only complete battalion raised out of the employees in one Company—an origin which it maintained throughout of the war.

In its earliest childhood, during its recruiting, training and equipment at King George's Dock, I was more closely associated with it than during the later stages of its training and its early days in France, but I am proud to remember that when the battalion had reached the full status of manhood among the gallant British Armies in France, I came into intimate contact with it again and it fulfilled under my command in France what I had hoped for it in the days of its infancy and early training at King George's Dock, Hull.

It was in August, 1914, that I went to the War Office and offered to the Director of Movements a fully trained unit of skilled civilian railwaymen of all grades. I was told that the military railway personnel were competent to deal with the situation in France and that railway units were not wanted. The military machine at that time was not prepared to accept civilian specialist organizations in its ranks, but that offer of an N.E.R. Battalion was, I believe, the first step towards the great civilian transportation machine into which it eventually came and which provided movement to the great armies under Sir Douglas Haig, as he then was, and which, in his own words written in May, 1917, supplied " that ' mobility ' which will enable us to out-manoeuvre the enemy and enable me to bring a superior force of guns and men at the *decisive moment* to the *decisive point*, before the enemy can take counter-measures."

I thought then, and I still think, that having regard to the very large proportion of skilled men in its ranks, the men of the North-Eastern Railway Battalion should have been Royal Engineers and not Northumberland Fusiliers. Their fate was otherwise, however, and they became one of the very finest of the pioneer battalions, and from their earliest days in Hull until the end of the war, won golden opinions and high praise wherever they served.

One name must come to the minds of us all as the greatest factor in contributing to the uniformly high reputation of the N.E.R. Battalion in whatever work it performed, and we must be conscious of a deep debt of gratitude to him, coupled with regret that he did not live to bring the battalion home at the end of the war—that is the name of Lieutenant-Colonel Pears.

I know that every officer and man who served under him will appreciate now the enormous satisfaction which I felt in 1914 when I ran across my old friend of the early 'nineties in India—Captain Pears of the Cameronians—and how glad I was to get him, first as Adjutant and then as Commanding Officer, for the battalion, which owes him so much.

Among so many fine officers it is invidious to select the names of others—names which will come readily to the minds of us all.

After the period of training of the battalion at Catterick Bridge in June and July, 1915, I was no longer able to continue my close connection with the battalion, but I never lost my keen interest in its fortunes, and in September, 1916, I came across it again. It was at Querrieux at the Fourth Army Headquarters, and I was talking to General Rawlinson in the garden of the château in which he lived. A heavily laden ammunition train clanked along a railway almost at the foot of the garden, and as I was then reporting on transportation to the Commander-in-Chief, our talk was on railway construction. He told me that railways could be built in record time by these wonderful pioneer battalions which were coming out, but that particular railway had been built by what he thought was one of the finest, if not the finest, pioneer battalion in the Army; that it had been done in record time and that officers and men had worked like Trojans. No praise could have been higher.

I asked casually which pioneer battalion it was, and he told me the 17th Northumberland Fusiliers. It was not difficult to explain why that pioneer battalion could build railways as well as Royal Engineers, and I told him the reason!

In the winter of 1916-17, railway construction in France began in earnest. Sir Douglas Haig said to me about that time that war was made up of three elements—men, munitions and movement. He had the men and the munitions, but he had not got the movement, and he set to work with the calm determination characteristic of him, to provide that " movement."

The figures of railway construction are interesting and have a bearing upon the history of the N.E.R. Battalion. The broad gauge construction by British railway troops in 1914 was $1\frac{1}{2}$ miles; in 1915, 103 miles; in 1916, 417 miles; in 1917, 800 miles; and in 1918, 1,300 miles, and it was on November 4th, 1916, that the 17th Northumberland Fusiliers was officially converted to a railway pioneer battalion.

Their railway construction work, like their work in and behind the trenches, is something to be proud of, as is all work well done, but their complete construction of the light railway shops at Berguette and their construction of what was called the " Great Midland Railway " to the Yser Canal and the crossing of the Yser Canal, stand out as brilliant achievements; and in July, 1917, Lieutenant-Colonel King, who then commanded the 17th Northumberland Fusiliers, was appointed to command the light railway advance of the 18th Corps, with 4,000 men under him, including the 18th Northumberland Fusiliers commanded by Lieutenant-Colonel Shakespear, and the whole area was handed over to the 7th Canadian Railway Troops on the 30th August, 1917.

Thereafter, the great railway construction formations having been organized, the N.E.R. Battalion, on account of its fine reputation as a fighting unit, went back to its old Division and served brilliantly until the call for further railways took it back to the worst part of the salient round Langemarck. When, in April, 1918, the German drive took place, it was again in the front line, and finally, as Pioneers to the 52nd Division, concluded the war and received high praise for its fine work in aiding the pursuit of the retiring enemy.

The record of the N.E.R. Battalion is one unbroken record of work well done, and unlike the proverbial " Jack of all Trades " it was master of all. It represented the North-Eastern Railway with great distinction, and its record adds to the laurels of the famous Northumberland Fusiliers.

ALBOURNE,
November, 1925.

PLATE I.

OFFICERS, WARRANT OFFICERS, AND SERGEANTS.
KING GEORGE DOCK.—HULL.

Inspection of the Battalion by the N.E.R. Directors. February 19th, 1915.

PLATE II.

PLATE III.

THE BAND. THE SIGNALLERS.

ONE OF THE FOUR LARGE DORMITORIES. A & B COMPANIES' DINING HALL.

KING GEORGE DOCK—HULL.

THE USE OF THE BUTT

INSPECTION OF TRANSPORT BY SIR A. KAYE BUTTERWORTH AND Lt. COL. E.C. GEDDES. ST GEORGES DAY 1915

THE CHARGE

THE MINATURE RIFLE RANGE

KING GEORGE DOCK — HULL.

PLATE IV.

CHAPTER I

THE RAISING OF THE BATTALION

BEFORE the war had lasted a month, it became evident that the machinery at the disposal of the Army Council was insufficient to cope with the recruiting, equipment and housing of the vast number of troops that would be needed to bring it to a successful conclusion. This was only to be expected. The country, through its representatives in Parliament, had strictly limited the number of troops to be maintained in time of peace and also the amount of equipment to be held ready against the time of war. When it became a question of, in as short a time as possible, raising and equipping thousands, where hundreds had been provided for, it was only natural that the machinery provided should be found inadequate. In this dilemma the Army Council turned, not in vain, to Local Authorities for help.

On the 4th August, 1914, there were seven battalions of Northumberland Fusiliers (two Regular, one Reserve, and four Territorial); by the end of the month eight more were in process of formation, a performance which reflects great credit on the recruiting agency of the Regular Army and also on the patriotism of the men of Northumberland and the adjoining counties.

Within a few days of the commencement of the war over two thousand men from the North-Eastern Railway had joined the Army and Navy, and when the Army Council's desire for assistance in raising men became known to the management of the railway, it was felt that the opportunity should be seized to give other railwaymen the chance of serving with their friends in a special North-Eastern Battalion. The management, therefore, issued a circular[1] on the 8th September calling on all who wished to serve together to fill in and return the slip which was attached.

---

[1] The circular stated that the company was prepared to make adequate provision for wives, families and dependents; to keep men's positions open for them; to pay their contributions to Superannuation and Pension Funds, and to provide accommodation for the families of men who were occupying company's houses. These terms threw a considerable expense on the company, but the sacrifice was cheerfully made for the common good.

How the call was received is shown by the two following extracts from diaries of N.E.R. men. One writes:

"When the war broke out several of my chums, who were Army Reserve men, were called upon to go to their respective regiments. One by one they went, and I felt 'Oh! I must go myself.' As I had a strong fancy for the Yeomanry, I took to riding a good bit at nights at home after my work hours. I tried to join them at Darlington, but could not get enlisted there, so went up to Newcastle, as I heard they were stationed in camp at Gosforth Park. However, the day I went to Newcastle the Yeomanry left and went to Castle Eden. At the same time it came to my notice that Sir Eric Geddes was raising a battalion of men drawn from the N.E.R. This was to give any pals the opportunity of joining the Army together. I thought this was very nice, and got my chum, Harry Craggs, the only chum I had at home, to join with me. This was on 11th September, 1914. . . . How well I remember leaving home with a full box of clothes mother had so carefully put in for me, she being so particular as to my having plenty of underclothes to change in case of my getting wet some time. Many a time afterwards I have smiled to myself when out in France, wet through, with no change to put on, and no chance of getting any."

How the situation struck another stout fellow is shown by the following extract:

"A nation of shopkeepers, can they become a nation of soldiers? —and a nation of soldiers, Tom, John, Bill, Fred—and myself; what of myself?—a valuer, a soldier! What can I do? Why, I cannot even load a rifle! Warned! Warned! but asleep— business and pleasure, work and play. Hard work, the foundation of a life's career, good and sound, but not a single idea, not the smallest means of holding and keeping my house, my work, my pleasure should any enemy come to take them away. Why!—there should be hundreds, thousands like myself—fools. The hours wasted, the chances missed, without in the least cutting down work or pleasure, but the bill is presented and must be paid—and so, cursing the missed chance, I determined to enlist to-day."

Whether all felt equally sorry for lost opportunities is doubtful, but to all the case appeared urgent, and so, though it was stated on the circular that approximately 1,100 men were needed, almost by return of post came back close upon 3,000 offers to join when called upon.

On 11th September came the formal sanction to the formation of the battalion to be styled 17th Northumberland Fusiliers, and recruiting started on the 14th.

The first Commanding Officer was Colonel D. B. Preston of

Askham Bryan, near York, late of the Garrison Artillery. The battalion owed much to his energy and to the careful grounding he gave all ranks in the early days of their training. He received much assistance from Major W. D. Rudyard, District Engineer N.E.R., who, among other jobs, acted as first President of the Officers' Mess. The would-be recruit was examined by Dr. J. G. McBride, the Company's Medical Inspector, and if he hopped and coughed satisfactorily and was found to be not less than 5 feet 6 inches in height and not less than $35\frac{1}{2}$ round the chest, he was passed on to Major H. A. Watson, the Company's General Superintendent, who attested him, his documents being completed by Mr. S. T. Burgoyne and a staff of clerks from various offices. Within a very few days the battalion was up to strength.

To get recruits in those brave days was an easy matter, but to house, equip and feed them was more difficult. The North-Eastern Railway was, however, in a better position in this respect than many other Local Authorities which were struggling with the problem at that time. The management was fortunate in having ready to hand very suitable accommodation for the battalion.

At Hull on the 26th June previous, His Majesty had opened the King George Dock. This was the joint property of the North-Eastern Railway and the Hull and Barnsley Railway Companies. The latter company gladly agreed to two large warehouses in the dock being fitted up as barracks for the battalion. This was carried out in record time by the Architects' Department, under Mr. A. Pollard, the Deputy Architect, and Mr. Lorrenz, Clerk of the Works.

The Stores Department provided the uniform, kit and necessaries for the recruits, and the speed with which the men were fully equipped showed that Mr. E. H. Clark and his chief clerk, Mr. R. C. Richardson, were men of resource and energy, for such things were hard to come by in the autumn of 1914.

In those early days the feeding of the battalion was in the efficient hands of Captain J. Bywell, V.D., late Quartermaster 3rd V.D. Northumberland Fusiliers, assisted by the Catering Department of the Hull and Netherlands Steamship Company, Quartermaster-Sergeant I. Clark of the N.E.R. Police Force, and Mr. F. H. Layton, Passenger Manager's Office.

Certainly the battalion was lucky in being raised by a company which was so well provided with the means to carry out the task, and had under its control such competent men to make use of those means, chief among whom was the late Deputy General Manager of the Railway, Lieutenant-Colonel E. C. Geddes, who, in the absence in London of Sir A. K. Butterworth, the General

Manager, was the guiding spirit and the motive power in the raising of the battalion. Although Sir Eric Geddes had soon more important matters to think of, he never lost sight of the battalion, and was always ready to give a helping hand when one was needed. Sir Eric's brother, Professor Auckland C. Geddes, of the McGill University, lost no time in coming from Canada to join the battalion, bringing with him several members of the University O.T.C., who did good service in the battalion.[1]

The Professor joined with the rank of Major and took command of " C " Company, but was soon appointed Second-in-Command. The instruction of officers was largely in his hands, and the high standard of efficiency attained by the battalion was to a great extent due to Major Geddes' forceful teaching. Space will not allow of a detailed description of the quarters provided for the battalion in King George Dock being given, but the illustrations will show those who were not there that it might well have been worse off, and will remind those who were there of not unpleasant days. The battalion soon found that it had many friends. From all parts of the railway system came presents, magazines, books, cards, note-paper and writing materials, every conceivable kind of indoor game, and several footballs.

The recreation-room, which measured 200 feet by 70 feet, was provided with every sort of suitable convenience, including a billiard table and harmonium. A study of the account given of the accommodation provided for the battalion which was published by the *North-Eastern Railway Magazine* will convince anyone that the management did its best to make the men comfortable, and very few, if any, of the units so hastily raised in 1914 were as well housed and equipped in every way.

Still, of course, to many of the lads coming from comfortable homes, the accommodation was rough and the food strange. " This (the dormitory) was in the upper story of the grain warehouse and had been boarded off, but, for all that, was very draughty." " It is rather a trying experience going to bed in company with about five hundred men—some more or less ' merry '—especially after being used to home life, and in addition having to sleep in blankets on a bag filled with straw. My first night lives long in my memory." " I made my first acquaintance with Army stew soon after we had placed our luggage in the dormitory. . . . Since then I have become extremely well acquainted with stew, as it seems to be the staple midday meal of the Army."

So smoothly did the machinery work that the first detachment

---

[1] Second-Lieutenants G. S. S. Gordon, G. V. Douglas, G. F. Mucklow, and L. Locock.

arrived at the new quarters on 22nd September, only eleven days after the order to raise the battalion had been received, and by the 1st October the whole battalion was assembled there. It did not take long to shake down. Though there were some old soldiers from whom to select non-commissioned officers, many had to be chosen from the raw recruits. Drill began on the rough ballast just in front of the warehouse, but a field was obtained at Saltend to which the battalion was marched every morning. The three or four mile tramp soon got off superfluous fat and made everyone feel fit.

The monotony of " Shun," " Stand at ease," forming fours, turnings and other mysteries which beset the path of those who would be soldiers was broken by physical training and bayonet fighting, which were more amusing; the former was, perhaps, more entertaining to the spectators than to the performers. To musketry they were introduced early, the dull weariness of the standing load being alleviated by visits to the miniature rifle range which had been provided in the barrack, or to the open air range within the dock enclosure. For sake of old times, let us run through the day's routine: 5.30 a.m., réveillé. Up, dress, wash with cold water, roll up bedding, rush to dining-room for coffee and biscuits. 6.30 a.m., fall in on parade. 7.45, breakfast, after which Orderly Corporals distributed letters. 9 a.m. to 12.30, parade, then dinner, followed by further parade till tea at 4.30 p.m., after which you were free, unless warned for some duty, till the evening roll-call, which was soon followed by " Lights out." The following interchange of views is reported to have taken place in these early days. " No. 1330, you are warned for guard to-night, see that you turn out smart, and that your equipment and rifle are clean." " Sorry, Sergeant, but I shan't be able to work late to-night—theatre, you know, two seats. Sorry, of course, and all that, but really——" " There, there, my lad, stow it. You ain't wearing red tabs yet. Just you hand over those tickets; I'll look after the lady and tell her what a fine soldier you are, while you serve your King and Country."

" Of course, at first, we had no khaki, but wore our civilian clothes with an armlet on the left arm. We looked a motley crew, and this was especially apparent on route marches." Even the Company Sergeant-Major, that awesome being, who had to be addressed as " Sir," while you stood strictly to attention, is said to have appeared with a dirty muffler round his neck and wearing clothes which had seen very much better days. " What a difference though when he got his uniform! " Pending the arrival of khaki, blue jerseys were issued, which made a great improvement in the men's appearance. " I was among the first to get a suit of khaki, and went home on the following Sunday feeling quite proud of myself."

By the 2nd December, eighty days after the first recruit had been enlisted, the battalion was completely equipped, a record of which all concerned may be justly proud.

Prior to the completion of its equipment, the battalion was suddenly moved. Without warning, the men found themselves confined to barracks and the posting of letters strictly prohibited. Kit-bags were issued and elaborate instructions given as to the filling of them. Evidently something was up. The various knowing ones had different ideas as to what it was. Some said Egypt was our destination, others had other notions, and each was sure his was correct. Lengthy discussions and heated arguments filled in the time. Fond husbands and love-sick swains overcame the scruples of the butcher's man and other favoured ones who could get out of barracks, and got letters posted. Just when the excitement was growing too great, the battalion found itself entrained at 2 p.m. on 18th November for an unknown destination, and two hours later was detraining at Patrington.

" Then came the billeting stunt—our first. Some were put into schools, and I remember our Sergeant taking us up the street and the civies shouting from the doors, ' Here, I'll take two, three, four in here,' and that's how we were issued out for the night. I myself got a nice house with a nice young lady to look after us. We thought how lucky we were.

" Alas! our satisfaction was short-lived, for at 7 a.m. we left and marched ten miles to Easington, where we got a short rest, then most of us, I know the whole of ' C ' Company, were taken two miles farther ahead to Kilnsea.[1] What a place to come to—Kilnsea! Surely, the edge of beyond! Such a dreary look—the sea on each side of this narrow neck of land and coming quite close to the roadway! That night some of us were put on sentry go, in pairs, doing two hours on and four off. What a night it was—raining, sleet, snow, and wind, and oh, how dark! and we had no idea where we were."

But to others, even that short night of pleasant anticipations at Patrington was debarred, for No. 11 Platoon marched off straight to Easington, arriving there long after dark. The whole platoon was by this time in a highly excited state, thinking the Germans had landed on the east coast, and expecting them to jump

---

[1] From another source I learn No. 9 Platoon was billeted in Skeffling that night.

out of every hedge. After a two hours' halt, during which the lucky ones found kindly inhabitants who provided them with a meal, No. 11 was broken up into sections of seven men, each under command of the oldest soldier, a tried veteran of at most ten weeks' service, and despatched to guard the coast. It was a wearying job, and the night was bitterly cold. However, morning came at last and No. 11 marched back to Easington and had breakfast at the Platoon Officer's expense.

The battalion remained in that inhospitable region about three months. It was scattered over a large area, the men being billeted in all sorts of buildings; a fisherman's hut, the roof of which was an old boat, held forty men for one night. Another night was passed in the "' Black Hole,' a small room where twenty-five of us tried to obtain some rest." Later the writer was luckier, for "in Easington village I was lucky enough to be allotted to a house where I got a feather bed to sleep on. The occupant of the house was an old lady—' a lone woman' as she put it—who specified that the soldiers billeted in her house should not be rough." Evidently our friends of No. 11 filled the bill, for we read that on their return each evening from the trenches, four weary miles away, they found the old lady had tea ready for them, and, like true British soldiers, " we tried to repay the old lady by making ourselves generally useful." Field kitchens had not yet been received, and rations were, in some cases, sent out cooked from the base in King George Dock, by lorries. According to one writer, " we never had hot dinner, only having tea made," but according to another, " I had my first experience of cooking at Kilnsea, more or less successful. . . . My turn came when it was a rainy week, so at least I had some luck. The worst job was obtaining water, which had to be carried about half a mile. . . . What an anxious time I had the first time I made stew! However, it was a success." Various unusual items appeared in the menu, numerous small birds, local name " stint " (the cook says he did not partake of these), " hedgehogs," which were suspiciously like barn door fowls, and once the Platoon Officer provided rabbits, but there seems to have been some mystery about what became of them, for, though the cook called the resulting dish " rabbit stew," the only sign of rabbit about it was a few hairs.

" Our duties at this period were to spend one night and day on the coast—in the sentry-box and patrolling alternately—one day and night in reserve, one day and night on guard in the village, half a day's rest, and then on the coast again. In the day-time (when on the coast) we dug trenches, that is, when not on sentry go. From 6 a.m. till 8 a.m. each morning everybody had to man the trenches with loaded rifles and fixed bayonets." The defensive system was organized in depth. Each platoon was distributed between a defensive post near the sea-shore, and supports and reserves farther back. There were sixteen posts, surrounded with barbed wire and provided with dug-outs. The intervals between these posts were patrolled constantly. The siting and designing of these posts were excellent, and was mostly the work of Major Auckland Geddes. "When out on night patrolling or on sentry go, we had several alarms. It is very easy to imagine you can see something moving when standing gazing into the night for two hours at a stretch."

No wonder, for remember, only two months ago these lads were placidly carrying on the work of the N.E.R. Suddenly they found themselves turned loose on a wild coast armed with rifles, and warned to look out for spies and Germans, who might land any night. "We were the most green and serious chaps then who ever wore khaki—if a chap did not halt right sharp and give the counter-sign straight out, he ran a big risk of being 'drilled.'" This risk was, however, considerably diminished by the fact that these zealous "serious chaps in khaki" had fired but little with their D.P. rifles, but certainly they did their best, and tradition tells of a certain gallant subaltern who, having lost his way on a very wet, dark night, furtively essayed to find it by use of his flash-light—a proceeding of which the nearest sentry showed his disapproval by firing a few rounds in his direction, fortunately without result, and the gallant officer, who rose to field rank, lives to this day, and will, I hope, smile when he is reminded of the incident.

Tradition also speaks of posts which, to the anxious watchers of the night, seemed certainly to move, and received five rounds. Next morning the firer would walk past it with his eyes half-right turn on it. Some may remember "the battle of Mons," when such a nervous watcher turned out the guard saying there was a man near his post. The guard extended, then everyone seemed to get windy, and first one and then another would shout, "He's here, Corporal! Have I to shoot?" Then some did shoot, and there was hurrying to and fro. "I reported to the officer what was going on. He seemed either vexed or surprised that there was firing going on—I don't know which." Well, it all turned out nothing. One of my kind correspondents admits still feeling quite creepy while he writes me an account of how, on a very dark night, he heard a noise, and saw some big black object coming towards him. It paid no heed to his challenge, and he was on the point of firing "when I noticed it was a big black retriever dog. Well, it did give me a fright, and I nearly shot it in my temper."

Of spy rumours there were many. One was said to wear a swallow-tailed coat and trilby hat. In an attempt to bring

PLATE V.

ARRIVAL OF RATION VAN FROM BASE
Q.M. STORES. EASINGTON.

THE RANGE CONSTRUCTED BY THE 17TH NORTHD FUSRS. PTS.
BARDON MOOR.

THE HORSE LINES AND FORGE.
BARDON MOOR.

THE ALDERSHOT OVENS.
BARDON MOOR.

this suspiciously attired individual to book, a sentry fired one round which went through a barn. In this barn was a farmer milking a cow. Needless to say, the farmer came out and expostulated very strongly. The civilian residents at this time were not allowed out of their houses after dusk. I may add, the people were very good and never showed their noses after dusk. No doubt it was a very trying time for them. Apparently the relations between the residents and the soldiers were of the best, and there was none of the " excitement and disorganization " so vividly described by a local historian of the time, when in 1798 this area was occupied by red-coated soldiers in anticipation of an incursion of the ancestors of those who are now our gallant Allies.

The German bombardment of West Hartlepool, on 16th December, disturbed the even tenor of the battalion's way, supports and reserves being hurried up at 1.30 a.m. to man the trenches. " It was a damp, foggy morning, and away we trudged, grousing like soldiers only can grouse. Naturally, we thought it was only a practice alarm and said our officers might have chosen the day-time for it."

"We spent our first Christmas in the Army at Easington. The section I was in (No. 10), composed of clerks, arranged to combine the contents of our parcels and have a spread on Christmas Eve. The villagers very kindly cooked the puddings and made the sauce, but we added the necessary flavouring to the latter." Unfortunately, the festivities were cut short by the fog coming down, and No. 10 had to turn out to guard the coast.

Boxing Day saw No. 10 Section in quite a different and unexpected rôle, which it, however, filled, naturally, very satisfactorily. A steamer ran aground near Kilnsea in very rough weather; the rocket apparatus was requisitioned, but the weather was so bad that the two horses usually employed were insufficient to drag it, and, no more being available, " C " Company took their place, and " we all had to turn out and run it up to the shore. By the time this was done we were wet through and exhausted, as it is no easy job to drag a rocket apparatus through the sand. . . ." The company was afterwards commended for its promptness on this occasion.

Writing of these times, another correspondent says : " Rough as it was, however, we had many good times, which more than compensated for the hard training we had to endure. One had only to mention the name of Captain ' N ' to raise a smile." This officer seems to have been rather over particular regarding certain matters of military etiquette, and highly critical of the minutiæ of a soldier's duty, so when, one evening as night was falling, he tried to get past

"Big Geordie," who was on sentry at the Beach Huts, without giving the password, that canny warrior felt that the fates had delivered his critic into his hands, and gave his officer a bad few minutes standing with his finger suggestively on the trigger, while Captain " N " shivered and expostulated, " It's me! Can't you see it's me? Don't you know me? " " Whee's me, onyway? " said Geordie, playing with his trigger. " Don't be a silly ass, I've forgotten the password." Finally Big Geordie relented and let him by, only to be severely told off for doing so.

On the 10th December the battalion ceased to be a mere unit and became part of the 114th Brigade, commanded by Brigadier-General Holdsworth, and on the 13th Lieutenant-Colonel Pears took command.[1]

Colonel Preston had done wonders; the 1,100 individuals who, three months previously, had been just 1,100 individuals, each eager to serve his country, but with no very clear notion of how to do so, had been transformed into the 17th Battalion Northumberland Fusiliers, an organized body, with a soul of its own, believing in itself, each member ready to work in his appointed place for the common good, and to sacrifice his own convenience and wishes to attain it. Colonel Preston would have been the last to say that his work was finished, that the battalion was perfect; he was far too old a soldier for that, but he could justly claim that it was a body of men that any soldier might feel proud of commanding, and with which a good Commanding Officer might do great things, and this was proved by the report issued by the Commander-in-Chief, Northern Command, after his inspection of the coast defences on 9th January, 1915, when Major-General Lawson, C.B., wrote, " The General Officer Commanding-in-Chief was much struck with the hard work and excellent defensive arrangements of the 17th Northumberland Fusiliers (N.E.R. Battalion)," adding that other portions of the defences were by no means up to that standard. The General commented on the great difficulties of soil and weather, which the battalion had so completely overcome by hard work skilfully employed.

Among the component parts of a division there had long been a battalion, which was not part of any brigade, but was known as

---

[1] Colonel Pears, who was forty-three years of age, was the eldest son of Mr. M. E. Pears, I.C.S., and grandson of Major-General Sir Thomas Pears. As Lieutenant in the Cameronians, he served in the Tirah Expedition, and was wounded at Dargai. He also served with his regiment through the South African War, and was a Staff Captain for railways at the Army Headquarters.

When war broke out in August, 1914, he was in East Africa, but hastened home, and was immediately gazetted to the N.E.R. Battalion as Adjutant.

the Divisional Battalion, and was directly under the Divisional Commander's orders, available for any special duty, ready at hand to reinforce any weak spot in the line or to be hurled against any point where the enemy seemed wavering. When trench warfare came in, it was determined to convert this Divisional Battalion into a Pioneer Battalion, the rôle of which was defined by the War Office as " to fight as infantry, and in addition to provide organized and intelligent labour for engineering operations." No battalion could have been found more fitted to fill that rôle than that raised by the North-Eastern Railway, which contained an unusually large number of skilled men in its ranks. So that it was not surprising that on the 11th January, 1915, the title of the battalion was altered to " The 17th Northumberland Fusiliers (N.E.R.) (Pioneers)." One not unwelcome result of the change was that the pay of a private was raised twopence per day, and later various other advantages were found to be associated with the title of Pioneers.

In December " A " and " B " Companies returned to Hull to continue their training, but came back to the coast the following month, " C " and " D " going back to civilization. The battalion was finally withdrawn from the coast on 8th February.

Although some portion of a soldier's training had been interfered with by its transfer to the coast, yet the battalion had undoubtedly learned much, and had greatly increased its value as a fighting force. " The town-bred lads had found the life very hard, but it did them good, and I don't think there was a man who didn't put on good weight during that time. It was the sea air. Whatever quarter the wind was in, it came off the sea, and, my word, wasn't it cold! We used to call them ' lazy winds '—too lazy to go round you, always went through you."

The battalion was in Hull till 20th June. On 13th March it took part in a great " Recruiting March " through Hull, in which some ten thousand troops were concerned.

St. George's Day was observed with all due solemnity, as was befitting in a battalion, though a young one, of the Old Fighting Fifth. Red and white roses were worn by all ranks, and a good programme of sports was carried out in the football field.

The usual training consisted of : " Réveillé 5.30 a.m., half-hour's doubling, breakfast, musketry, platoon drill, bayonet fighting, physical exercise, dinner, visual training, section drill, then finish. Sometimes we had lectures at night. The physical training was under an Aldershot instructor, nicknamed the ' India Rubber man,' a regular ' terror.' He certainly did us good, but he made us sweat profusely, and he had a great command of language."

About May, the battalion was put through a course of plate-laying at Hessle, going to and fro in special trains. Some of the lads found plate-laying productive of blisters. Night operations also began about this time, and route marches got longer and longer till twenty-five miles were accomplished. "In those hot days the ash-strewn ground in front of the warehouse, on which parades were carried out, was no heaven, and by the time we had finished our day we were covered with dust and almost choked."

Saturdays were keenly looked forward to, "for we trained till 12 noon, then had dinner, and afterwards marched out about three miles from the docks in jerseys and trousers or running kit if we possessed it. We then had to run back—the sooner we got back the sooner we finished the week's work. The lucky week-end leave men got off at 11 a.m.; for the others there were the pictures or a theatre, and good square meals in Hull. Church parade on Sundays was put early so that many of the lads could eat their dinners and spend the afternoon and evening at home. On June 6th a party of these lucky ones was returning to barracks on the top of the bus, chatting over the pleasant experiences of the afternoon at home when someone spotted what looked like a cigar in the sky. Shortly afterwards the first bomb dropped with an ear-splitting explosion. We all made a very hurried descent from the bus." The Zeppelin, having dropped some thirty bombs, departed, and our friend adds, "I had had enough excitement for one night and I was glad to get to bed." This was the first Zepp raid and was followed by the looting of houses and shops owned by Germans, and the battalion was called upon to supply detachments of guards for such places, a very uncongenial job, but all in the day's work, and "the people living in the street were very good—they brought us tea, etc., at intervals during the night."

On 20th June the battalion packed up and moved by train to Brough Park, Catterick Bridge. Here we were under canvas along with other battalions, Lancashire Fusiliers and Northumberland Fusiliers forming the 96th Brigade. We were at Brough Park five weeks, just doing the usual drills and route marches. On becoming "Pioneers" the battalion had been removed from the 114th Brigade. At Catterick it was attached to, though not an integral part of the 96th Brigade, one of the brigades of the 32nd Division which was now being got ready for foreign service.

On 27th July the battalion moved to Bardon Moor, near Leyburn, Wensleydale. Here we were occupied most of the time in making rifle ranges,[1] living under canvas among the heather.

[1] This mighty practice range among the hills consisted of no fewer than fifty-six duplicate targets, with a trench in front four or five yards wide, and a huge embankment behind, which necessitated the excavation and piling up of

While the battalion was at Bardon Moor, the transport took shape: "a collection of horses and mules arrived, and from a non-transport point of view it was very amusing to see the way these animals took to their new owners, particularly the mules; most people gave them a wide berth."

However, the men worked hard, and within a very short time the battalion had reason to be proud of its transport. One correspondent tells me that "before I joined the transport I had an impression, with many others, that a man on the transport had a cushy job, and that he had nothing to do but ride a horse. I was quickly made to see things differently." That is often the way; t'other fellow's job is always a cushy one till it becomes one's own.

At that time there were sixty men to look after a hundred and four animals, clean all the harness and the wagons in the intervals of making long journeys for rations, etc., so that "really there did not seem enough time in the day to do what you had to do."

It was about this time that Major A. C. Geddes left the battalion to take up a staff appointment which led on from one high post to another till he attained cabinet rank. In the intervals of building the ranges, the battalion took part in manœuvres, and one day a certain Company Commander became aware of the unpleasant fact that he did not know where he was. A Staff Officer arrived opportunely, but he, too, was not quite certain of his whereabouts. After some discussion it was agreed that the company was under the B in Bardon. A listener lying under a furze bush was heard to remark to his pal, "Wal, it seems to me we are under the Y of B——y well lost."

"On 21st August we moved by train to Codford St. Mary on Salisbury Plain, Wiltshire. The camp was wooden huts, more comfortable than tents. The food here, as at Hull, was good and very plentiful. Here also we worked on rifle ranges, afterwards going through our course of firing on them. We used to go out on to the downs for two or three days' manœuvres; the whole of the 32nd Division was here." The division was put through a brief course of intensive training, ending up with a grand attack; "we carried ball ammunition and fired at some dummy men near a big wood." The artillery also used live shell. Evidently its training

---

ten thousand or fifteen thousand tons of earth. The engineering work included the laying of a light tramway, and the transport over rough country of an immense quantity of material, to say nothing of an amount of skilled mechanical work. The rapidity with which this range was completed is said to have constituted a record, and the achievement was decidedly a feather in the battalion's cap—if one may put it that way. Only sixteen working days were occupied, and the range was in use exactly three weeks after the first pick had been struck into the ground.

was nearing completion, and about the middle of November Sir A. K. Butterworth, the General Manager of the railway, came down to say good-bye to the battalion.

Between the 19th and 23rd of that month the whole division was quietly transported to France.

CHAPTER II

EARLY EXPERIENCES IN FRANCE

THE battalion left Codford in several trains on the 20th November, and after a trying wait on the quay and in sheds at Southampton, embarked that evening on the *Empress Queen*.

The passage is variously described as "fine," "somewhat rough," and "somewhat choppy," but otherwise pleasant. Havre was reached about 3.30 a.m. "Having disembarked about daylight we were marched off along what seemed to be endless quays to a rest camp, where we were housed in tents, sixteen men to a tent. This was somewhat crowded, but still it kept us warm." As it snowed, the warmth was welcome.

After a day and night in this so-called rest camp, tents situated in a swamp, which no one was allowed to leave, the battalion went forward in two parties. "The first marched off at 3.45 a.m. to Gare du Magasin station and there entrained at 8 a.m. in cattle trucks (covered), thirty-five per truck. Travelled till 8.30 p.m., when we detrained at another mud-hole, and, after unloading, marched about ten miles to Ailly-le-haut-Clocher, everybody being played out on arrival. Billeted in an out-house (luckily with a bed). Turned in at 2 a.m. Slept till 8 a.m. The second party left Havre at 10 p.m. on 22nd, and reached the mud-hole known as Pont Remy at about 6 a.m. The morning was dark, misty and cold, and we all felt thoroughly miserable."

After a short halt, during which "Tommy's cooker" was found useful to make tea, the march was begun. "My pack felt tremendously heavy, and as we had a stiff hill to climb I was soon very warm." The Transport and Machine-Gun Detachment, which travelled separately from Codford, joined the battalion at Ailly-le-haut-Clocher early on the 24th. The following few entries may serve as reminders of the very welcome halt in that little village :

"After a morning's so-called rest, Platoon Commanders practised route marching independently, 16 Platoon getting lost till 7 p.m. Weather fine but cold." "Billeted in empty houses, etc. Grand orchard behind." "We got plenty of apples here." "Rifle and machine-gun inspection. Easy day. In two or three cafés at night. *Café au lait.*" "Played French billiards with Stan Hood. Easy day." "Drew first pay—five francs. Short route march with limbers for exercise. Lieutenant Ellis thrown from horse. In hospital for a time. (Never came back.)"

Later on Lieutenant Gordon was given charge of the Machine-Gun Detachment, and on the 10th December we read: "Physical drill and rifle exercises under Lieutenant Gordon. Rather against the grain, as there'd been nothing doing since Lieutenant Ellis's departure."

On 27th November the peaceful period ended and "we marched for about twelve miles through lovely country, mostly keeping to the valley of the Somme. We arrived at Belloy-sur-Somme, where we stayed the night." Here my correspondent was billeted in the usual barn, and made the acquaintance of an old couple, with whom he got on very well, " in spite of the difficulties of the language." Does not that bring back memories of many little groups of khaki-clad men, old women, young women, and children, all cheery and laughing, evidently thoroughly enjoying themselves " in spite of the difficulties of the language."

Three of the companies billeted in the centre of the village were treated to *café au Cognac* with such lavish hospitality that the Adjutant had to be summoned. As he entered an estaminet, in which there appeared to be " ructions," Madame, relieved at his arrival, greeted him with " Merci, merci, Monsieur le Capitaine." The Adjutant's reply, " Mercy, madam, mercy! There's no blooming mercy in the British Army," became historic.

"The next day we again set off on the march, doing twelve miles through Flixecourt on to Flesselles.[1] We stayed in the latter place two nights, and were billeted in a loft . . . not very pleasant, as there was a good deal of rain and the roof was not water-tight. It was not possible to stand upright, and there was no floor, but just a thickness of straw laid on the rafters, so in places where the straw was thin one went through."

Billets naturally were of great importance, and the diaries so kindly lent me contain full particulars of most of those occupied by the writers. At Belloy-sur-Somme one party " Stayed the night in a hen-house. Pulled down yard gate and slept on it. Place filthy and awfully cold."

On 30th November " D " Company left the battalion for a time, going to Bouzincourt to be attached to the 51st Division, the rest of the battalion going to Freshencourt, but " C " had to go

---

[1] The writer's memory is at fault. Flixecourt was passed on the previous day, which was the long march.

PLATE VI.

OFFICERS, WARRANT OFFICERS, AND SERGEANTS.
CODFORD CAMP—SALISBURY PLAIN.

THE 17TH NORTHD FUSRS PRS ON THE EVE OF DEPARTURE FROM CODFORD CAMP SALISBURY PLAIN.

a bit farther to Montigny, " a small village set in the heart of the woods and about ten miles from the line. The flashes from the guns could be seen plainly at nights. The day we marched to this place we must have covered fifteen miles, and were all ' dead beat.' . . . I happened to sit on a doorstep, and soon after was very pleased to see a window open and a bottle come in my direction. This contained cider, and after that there was a rush." Later in the evening our friend re-visited the cider-house and was given *café au lait* and bread and jam. " This was the first time I had any *café au lait* in France. It was surprisingly good to eat and drink before a fire after a hard day's tramp."

The last march in to Meaulte was done in heavy rain over chalky roads, so " we arrived in a lovely condition." Meaulte was then about two and a half to three miles from the front line. It was protected by rising ground and could not be seen by the enemy. " We were billeted in a tumble-down house and very crowded; the place too was filthy and swarming with rats. It was very weird in Meaulte at nights. The night might be pitch black, yet all the time in one direction there was a flickering, ghostly sort of light over the whole country, due to the flashes of the guns and the Véry lights.

The battalion, less " D," was now attached to the 18th Division, and worked under the orders and supervision of the Engineers of that formation. The other units of the 32nd Division were similarly at school with other divisions, qualifying for the task of holding the line as a complete division.

On 2nd December, the day after its arrival, the battalion commenced its labours in the trenches, which the War Diary enumerates as " clearing falls, improving and making dug-outs, wiring and draining." The unofficial report says: " Several platoons out at the trenches at various times. Seeing men return from the same is a sight, looking just as if bathed in mud. Trenches up to waist in slush. In addition, to-day rain is falling steadily."

" C " Company's first job was wiring on the night of 3rd December. Any survivors of that party may smile when reminded how " two or three of us stood talking—I remember at the time none of us knew where we were, and of course we did not take it seriously. In fact, an argument was started about some football teams, and so lively did it become that a first West Kent man came creeping up and said, ' You chaps shut up or you'll have us blown to . . . heaven.' Sure enough ' Jerry ' put a machine-gun around them, but without result. I often smile when I think what a green bunch we were in those days."

"5th.—Seven British 'planes up over German lines. Heavily shelled, but none hit. Very exciting. Church service in old barn. Parson had to chase cockbird off with lump of wood during prayer."

"6th.—Managed to have a bath and change of underclothing in afternoon. 'A' Company had first casualty, a man named Robson getting shot in the ankle at Becordel."[1]

On 8th December "A" and "C" moved to Becordel; the companies went in small parties by day, the route being under observation, but the transport moved by night. "The enemy was fond of shelling this road, and it was a very weird sensation going along the road and seeing the flashes of the guns, and not knowing whether a shell would drop on the road." We've all felt like that, haven't we?

Becourt—Becordel was only about a thousand yards from the front line; it was much under observation, and frequently shelled, so that it was no health resort, and, further, the billets were very bad, and the number of rats and mice unduly large; these animals got very familiar and even ate the iron rations, to touch which, without the Colonel's orders, was a high crime and misdemeanour. "One chap felt something moving under his shirt, and on examination he found he had been carrying a mouse about with him." The battalion had brought out "war dogs" to help the sentries. One of these, named "Tango," proved a good ratter, and once slew thirty-six rats in an hour.

Another drawback to Becordel was that the nearest baths were at Ville, about seven miles away, and going and coming you were very apt to be shelled. "The baths were in a house, and were of the 'everything-at-the-double' kind . . . having undressed, all our clothes were hung on a peg. Suddenly a trap door opened in the ceiling, and clothes, peg and all, disappeared. This caused us no little consternation, but it appeared they were only going to be fumigated. We had to run in our birthday suits into a big concrete-floored room, hop into a tub, spend about two minutes in it, out, and into another room to dry ourselves, and then out into the yard and upstairs into a loft, where we found our clothes waiting. The whole business occupied about ten minutes, and it was decidedly funny to see a file of naked men running from one room to another, spurred on by the bath attendant shouting ' 'alf a minute to go,' with a pronounced Cockney accent." The writer, from whose diary the above is an extract, has recorded many methods of bathing, thinking, rightly, that they may be of interest. He mentions "tubs with four inches of water, usually well mixed with disinfectants," and once he struck it lucky finding a tin bath and a wash-house with

---

[1] Actually on Albert road a mile from Becordel.

Early Experiences in France

a boiler and water laid on. " What more could the quality want? " Yet another kind of bath is mentioned—that particularly vexatious kind in which you stand under a meagre spray of water, which may be either icy cold or boiling hot, and has a way of shutting off just when you have soaped yourself.

On 15th December, first party of M.G.S. " went out to Becordel and took turn in emplacements. Six hour shifts. Had a bath (first in France—and landed on 23rd November).''

" D " Company all this time had been working with the 8th Royal Scots in the Aveluy Thiépval sector, and had a pleasant time, for the Royal Scots were hospitable and kindly supplied their pupils in many little comforts not included in the official scale, but calculated to increase the comfort of the troops. Alas! shortly after its return to the battalion, the C.O. ruthlessly overhauled its transport wagons, much to the grief of all ranks, whose " finds " went west.

On 21st December there was a game of post among the companies, " B " going to Bouzincourt when " D " went to Becordel and " C " returned to Meaulte. The following entries refer to this period :

" 23-12-25.—Becordel. Bullet passed through sand-bag of emplacement; just missed Stan Hood. Germans shelled us again. Teddy Marsden ('D' Company) killed. Battalion's first (fatal) casualty. We buried him at Meaulte to-day (24th) at 3.30, Mr. Douglas bringing his section in from Becordel to attend as mourners. Sergeant Swales was slightly wounded at the same time, but was back on duty on 26th.

" 24th, Christmas Eve, recognized as Christmas Day in our division. Holiday for us, no firing. Spent evening in café and had sing-songs to organ. In bed at 8." Another correspondent speaks of finding " a nice spot where we obtained some genuine champagne and had a nice little supper to round off the day," and yet another, " and I had a pleasant hour or two at a café with some good champagne, tinned lobster, crab, etc. The landlady was in good form, her husband, a Sergeant in the French Artillery, and their son also arriving on leave, so we were quite a party."

" Christmas Day.—Removed from stable into barn farther up village. Another sing-song in café. Wound up with Marseillaise and The King."

On 28th December the Headquarters and " A " and " D " joined " B " in Bouzincourt and relieved the 8th Royal Scots, the Pioneer Battalion of the 51st Division, which the 32nd Division was about to relieve. " C " Company records of this day—" Passed through

Albert, arrived at Martinsart 7.15 p.m. Dark and dreary and up to the ankles in mud. Our camp was in a slack just behind the village. We had to cover our tents with tree branches on account of observation from the enemy's aeroplanes. The camping ground became a veritable quagmire, the weather being rather severe at this time of the year. The trouble was to keep the mud out of the tents."

The rest of the battalion in Bouzincourt was better off, for we are told that the billets were fairly good, "but the place has the usual smell of all the places we have found up to now, and that is not a good smell." Still, were they downhearted? Apparently not.

31st December.—"We kept things going until midnight, when we welcomed the New Year by singing 'Auld Lang Syne' in great style. After a speech or two we broke up and retired to our respective bug-walks."

1st January, 1916.—"Up at 6 a.m. Poor ——'s head so bad!!!"

The division's period of instruction was now over, and on 2nd January Major-General Rycroft, G.O.C. 32nd Division, took over the portion of the front known as G Sector and Authuille defences and F Sector and Aveluy defences from Major-General Harper, commanding 51st Division.

The battalion remained at Bouzincourt with "C" at Martinsart till 10th February. During this time the War Diary tells us that the companies were employed as follows:

"A."—Making a new road from Bouzincourt to Martinsart.

"B."—Making dug-outs, Aveluy-Crucifix Corner. Revetting and clearing trenches, building and framing tunnel, sinking new shaft.

"C."—Half company Highland Bridge, Black Horse Road, draining, excavating, and building iron shelters. Half company Bouzincourt-Martinsart road.

"D."—Coniston Street, clearing trench, revetting fire-bays, rebuilding sand-bag walls, and revetting also at Pendle Hill, Weening Street, Mitchell Street. Trench tramway, Martinsart-Johnson Post, tunnelling, laying tramway.

"C" Company's informant tells us the road they worked on with "A" was afterwards called "Pioneer Road," but it is officially referred to as Northumberland Avenue. This road was one of many works undertaken in preparation for the great offensive, which was being planned for the summer.[1]

[1] Pioneer Road, made by 8th Royal Scots, joined Albert-Martinsart road to Aveluy-Hamel road.

"On Wednesday, 26th January, 3.15 p.m., we were leaving work in Gordon Castle Road when the enemy opened fire on us with artillery, one shell dropping into the communication trench and killing five of our chaps."[1]

These were "C" Company's first casualties. Two days later "C" had two more men wounded. Shortly afterwards, Captain H. V. Phillips was invalided home, and Captain G. Stamp Taylor took over command of "C" Company.

The battalion had been working close on two months in the front line or immediately behind it, and its casualties had so far amounted to six killed and nine wounded. Other unofficial entries for this period are:

"2nd January (Sunday).—Played football in afternoon and had physical drill.

"5th January.—In trenches with 'A' Company, under Reg. Sadler, clearing trench bottom. Liquid mud up to knees. Wearing fisherman's waders, Aveluy (Blighty Wood).

"7th January.—Ditto, but well sniped by whizz-bangs. No one hurt. Rain filled the many local pools, creating lovely perfumes all over the village (Bouzincourt)."

Still, life in Bouzincourt had its advantages, for we read of impromptu concerts. The piano borrowed from the parish priest by the R.S.M., who shared the duties of Chairman with Lieutenant-Colonel Cross, Senior Church of England Chaplain (Vicar of St. Mary's, Carlisle), at which excellent turns were given by Sergeants Swales, Iley, Littlefair, Quartermaster-Sergeant Dorward, and Privates Vokes and Wilson, and a few nights later the 15th H.L.I. gave a concert. "A very pleasant hour and a half ensued, after which —— and myself adjourned to our special Café Corner, where we had a good meal of steak and wonderfully cooked chips. Retired about 10 p.m."

But another concert did not go off so happily for the organizer, as one performer "had been got at and well 'oiled,' and sang one of his worst. So my feelings, sitting beside the Padre, whom I had promised that the programme should be all it ought to be for a parson's concert, can well be imagined."

The battalion had visitors from home in January. The Duke of Northumberland looked in on the 17th, and after seeing the new road and some billets, "went off again in his car, taking the Colonel with him (presumably for lunch)." On the 19th "Lord Nunburn-

---

[1] Killed: 1413 Swainson, 1438 Lamming, 1485 Willans, 522 Hodgson, 1467 Reid. Wounded: 163 Thackray, 1255 Robson, 155 Shaw, 216 Hoggard, 648 Lance-Sergeant Freeman. Lance-Sergeant Freeman behaved so well on this occasion that he was granted the M.M.

holme and a party of Staff Officers passed down the trenches and had a chat with Hull men (' D ' Company)."

All the while work was going steadily on. Trenches always needed draining and repairs, being frequently blown in by canister bombs. Much of this work had to be done at nights, and as the weather was bad, the men were very thankful to get their tot of rum when they came in. Of all this work my correspondents say little, it was just the regular routine and not worthy of being recorded. Still it was hard, trying work, generally carried on under shell-fire, and on its execution in a thorough manner the comfort of the troops in the line, and the success of the impending operations, largely depended. About the end of this month thare were rumours of a Boche attack.

" 29th January.—Machine-Gun Section moved up from Bouzincourt to Authuille by night to take over emplacements behind the first line in event of German attack threatening.

" 31st January.—Violent artillery duel at night. All stood to, expecting advance, but nothing happened." However, the enemy got troublesome.

" 5th February.—Corporal Syd Wade killed in village (Authuille) our first M.G.S. casualty. Germans had at least four batteries on the village, and had given everyone a most uncomfortable half-hour.

" 6th February.—Buried Syd Wade in a nice little graveyard behind the line (Authuille).

" 9th February.—Gas attack on Aveluy. Germans captured small advanced trench. Very few badly gassed.

" 10th February.—Four of us nearly knocked out. Four German batteries turned on us, but none hit. Had been making a new emplacement all day, apparently in view of Fritz."

The Divisional War Diary entry on the 9th February reads: " Slight fall of snow, which soon melted. Heavy bombardment of our line, especially the Nab and Authuille Wood. We lost seven killed, twenty-nine wounded, fifteen missing, and one machine-gun. Enemy entered demolished trenches and carried off wounded."

On 11th February the whole battalion was concentrated in Albert, " getting wet through in the process. Into new and better billets by dinner-time. Fine billet in a house vacated by French civilians. Tables, chairs, pictures and everything up-to-date; sink and tap; even curtains across windows, but what a colour! "

The official account of this period is : " Battalion in billets. Work : by pass road north of town, tracks from north of town across Ancre to Crucifix Corner, defences of Aveluy, construction of assembly shelters for two battalions at Crucifix Corner, fire-bays in Coniston Street, in F.Q. Sub-sector."

The unofficial report of " C " is : " This time being occupied in making those famous dug-outs at Crucifix Corner, Aveluy. They were built into a very steep bank, and afterwards proved a great boon to troops on rest out of the trenches. It was impossible for the Boche to hit them with any kind of shell."

Albert, at the time of the battalion's stay, was in good condition as towns went in those days. The ruined cathedral, with its well-known tower, from which the statue of the Virgin holding up her child overhung the street, was the centre of a desolate area in which little remained but heaps of bricks, but elsewhere there were many houses still habitable, and a considerable number of French still clung to their homes, mostly living in the cellars. But even in these parts one came across houses wrecked by shells, and one diarist wisely remarks that " it made one feel glad that England was not a frontier country." There was a beauty spot in Albert which seemed all the more beautiful by contrast with the wreckage round about it. It was the " Grotto," and had evidently been the scene of religious pilgrimages. There was also a canteen in Albert, and civilians hawked eggs, milk, etc., from door to door, so all got fat.

Leave became available, and the lucky ones, in small parties, travelled home in jolting G.S. wagons, slow, cold trains, crowded steamers—an uncomfortable journey—but then the joy of getting home, free of mud and filth, able to go to bed in peace when one felt inclined, and, more important, to stay there as long as one wanted, the warm welcome from friends and loved ones made it well worth while. And then occasionally untoward events such as blizzards or the activity of Boche submarines gave one unexpected but very welcome extensions of a few days, when one stayed at the Union Jack Club and saw the sights of London, and was duly presented with tracts by " some good lady " on the platform at Waterloo before one left.

Most of the houses in Albert had good cellars, very useful to dive into when the Boche started shelling, and sometimes for other reasons. " Two of our men found a barrel of cider down a cellar, and they promptly took cover in the approved manner." The generous liquor so warmed their hearts that they brought some up and pressed it on all the passers-by.

The battalion headquarters remained at Albert till 4th April, when it returned to Bouzincourt. The following notes are supplied by the official diarist :

" 26th February.—Captain H. M. S. Redmond and fifty other

ranks of 15 Platoon to Corbie to work on Daours-Contay railway line; they returned on 1st March.

"6th March.—'D' to Aveluy to work on Coniston Street, etc.

"7th March.—'A' to Vacquement, for railway construction.

"15th March.—17/1125 Private T. Chatt killed and four men wounded. Lieutenant R. de P. Dallin, 28th Reserve Battalion, and Second-Lieutenant R. Fletcher, 18th Northumberland Fusiliers, join and are posted to 'C' and 'B' respectively.

"16th March.—Major P. H. Compton left to rejoin 6th D.G.'s. Major H. C. Oxley temporarily Second-in-Command.

"21st March.—Two men of 'D' wounded.

"24th March.—Second-Lieutenant J. Garvie, 32nd Northumberland Fusiliers, Second-Lieutenant J. Donald, 14th Northumberland Fusiliers, one Corporal and thirty-nine Privates join. Captain A. Mackenzie, back from hospital, takes over 'B' on 25th.

"26th March.—Second-Lieutenant N. Hope, 28th Reserve Battalion Northumberland Fusiliers, joins and is posted to 'D' Company."

Unofficial notes for the period record the arrival of a parcel of cigarettes for the Sergeants from the Sergeants of the Reserve Battalion (32nd Northumberland Fusiliers). Heavy fall of snow. Visits to "our favourite café at dinner-time, one opposite the Sussex Pioneers Headquarters, kept by Madame Brocquart."

Pleasant memories those, but next day—"as the reply shells (to our bombardment) started whistling over our roof, we retired to our cellars." Does this entry awaken any memories? "To hospital at Warloy in motor ambulances suffering from trench fever. In civilized bed for first time since leaving England. Sheets and cleanliness. French Sisters of Mercy, who didn't know English!"

"Went to Amiens by Red Cross motor to have a tooth stopped. A fine town. Spoke to first Englishwoman since coming to France."

An old friend visited the battalion in the person of "our late Major Geddes (Auckland), now a Colonel on the staff, on a visit to-day, stopped his car to shake hands with me and congratulate me on my promotion to Regimental Sergeant-Major."

In the middle of March we read: "The weather in March was very variable. 2nd, mild sunny day. 4th, snowing at intervals. Bitterly cold all day. 5th, beautiful mild day. 13th, summer-like weather, very sultry evening, finishing with thunder and lightning."

The Boche, however, interfered with the enjoyment of these pleasant days, for about this time the entries of bombardments necessitating dives into cellars are frequent. "A heavy shell went

PLATE VIII.

BOUZINCOURT CHURCH.
AND C COYS BILLET.

H.Q. 17TH NTH FRS PRS
BOUZINCOURT.

PIONEER ROAD NEAR AVELUY.
LOOKING TOWARDS MARTINZART FROM PUC'S YARD.

NORTHD AVENUE LOOKING TOWARDS
MARTINZART, AND MARTINZART WOOD.

PHOTOS BY CAPT G.S.S. GORDON. M.C.

PLATE IX

BECOURT CHATEAU, NEAR ALBERT.

OLD BATT^N H.Q. ALBERT. 17TH NTH F^{RS} P^{RS}.

LA BOISELLE MINE CRATER.

THE ANCRE VALLEY, AND MARTINSART WOOD FROM THE CAUSEWAY NEAR AVELUY, SOMME.

BLIGHTY VALLEY, NEAR SOMME
TWO FOOTBALLS IN FOREGROUND

PHOTOS BY CAPT C.S.S. GORDON M.C.

THE RUINS OF MOUQUET FARM SEPT 1916.
I.W.M. PHOTOGRAPH. CROWN COPYRIGHT.

PLATE X.

AVELUY VILLAGE AND THE ANCRE VALLEY.
FROM CRUCIFIX CORNER DUG-OUTS.

LA BOISELLE CRATER ACROSS MASH VALLEY.
FROM OVILLERS.

THE ANCRE VALLEY AND BLACK HORSE DUG-OUTS.
NORTH AUTHUILLE

PHOTOS BY CAPT. C.S.S. CORDON, M.C

BRIDGE ACROSS SWAMP AT AVELUY.
I.W.M. PHOTOGRAPHS CROWN COPYRIGHT

ACHEUX WOOD.
FIRST TANKS ASSEMBLED HERE, SEPT. 1916.

VIEW SHEWING CONEY STREET DUG-OUTS IN DISTANCE.
CONSTRUCTED BY 17TH NTH FUSRS PRS.

THIEPVAL WOOD.
PHOTOGRAPHS BY CAPT. G.S.S. GORDON, M.C.

PLATE XI.

through 'B' Company's billets, but owing to acquired celerity in cellar diving, no one was caught by it. The business here is getting hotter. Sergeant Jubb of 'C' Company wounded slightly in seven places by shrapnel."

"A" Company, at Vecquement, was doing great things.

"3rd April, Monday.—Working on railway from 7 a.m. to 10 p.m. Laid one mile thirty yards broad gauge. 'A' Company, along with section of 110 Company R.E. under Lieutenant Ross and some infantry working parties. This is a record for present campaign.

"9th April, Sunday.—Moved to Contay. Rotten billets."

Here the company remained till the last of the month, doing good work on the railway, which was interspersed with soldiering, in the form of musketry, bayonet fighting, platoon drill, and lectures on field work and morale. Time was also found for relaxation, football matches. "Went to Amiens, had quite a nice time shopping. Decent lunch at Hôtel du Rhin."

"B" worked in Aveluy, Becourt Wood, Maxse Redoubt and then on Northumberland Avenue till 30th, when it went to Meaulte for railway construction. "C" slogged away at those "famous dug-outs" all the month. "D" finished Coniston Street on 4th, then worked on Bridgehead till 10th, and then did eight days' training, after which it joined "B" on Northumberland Avenue. Lieutenant Jellicoe, 18th Northumberland Fusiliers, and Captain S. C. Wells, 28th Northumberland Fusiliers, joined and were both posted to "B." On 26th, the Machine-Gun Section was broken up and divided among the companies, each company receiving two guns and their crew.

St. George's Day was observed in great style. Work for all was over by noon, and then the fun began. First came football. "'A' played 'D' and got the verdict, in the last minute, by a penalty kick," but only after four periods of five minutes each extra play. "B" and "C" were so equal that after several extras had produced no decision they tossed up and "B" won. The struggle between "A" and "B" went on until dark, and was finally abandoned with a score of one all. The result of the bombing contest was: 1, "B"; 2, "D"; 3, "A" and "C" equal.

Wrestling on bare mule back, in which twenty-four men of the transport contested, provided everyone else with much amusement. Several contests ended in both competitors being left festooned from the necks of their mounts until a downward movement of the head and an upward one of the heels deposited them before their astonished chargers. The struggle was so prolonged that the final had to be put off to a later date, and even then, after twenty minutes wrestling, it was only brought to a close by Private J. T. Stephenson retiring in favour of Private J. Mounsey.

Another event which was more amusing for the onlookers than for those engaged was the passage of a barbed wire entanglement 3 feet high and 6 yards deep by teams of eight men from each company, who were allowed to make use of such materials usually to be found in the trenches as they could carry. " D " Company selected ladders and sheets of corrugated iron; " C " pinned its faith on sand-bags and poles, while " B " believed in sheets of expanded metal. The excitement was intense. A giant of " D " bore to the front not only the ladder allotted to him, but also pendant from the other end the comrade who had been told off to assist him. Many a competitor, urged to great efforts by the jeers and cheers of the spectators, learned that, when caught by the breeks in barbed wire, more haste means less speed. " D " romped in an easy winner in one minute thirty-five seconds.

It was a great day, and all enjoyed it. Of course, all who had the honour to belong to the Fighting Fifth wore red and white roses, and felt themselves the salt of the earth. Greetings were received from Sir A. Kaye Butterworth, Lieutenant-Colonel E. C. Geddes, A. D. Munitions, and from other battalions. General Rycroft and many other officers and men came to look on, and for a time all forgot the Boche over the way.

" A " Company, away in Contay, had its own celebrations. " Went to Communion in French Protestant Church at 7 a.m. with K—— and G——. Padre Fawkes took service. Church Parade at 9.30 a.m. Very nice service. Fawkes in top-hole form. Commenced sports at 10.30 a.m. Boxing, wrestling, tug-of-war, footer match, and obstacle race. Last two very funny; all men drenched to the skin at the water jump. Twenty-two a side, two balls, two referees, one whistle—great amusement. Sergeants entertained officers in evening. Wonderfully well done; flowers and other decorations. I sang twice, and no one went out, to my surprise.

" Monday, 24th.—All rather piano after yesterday, and more than one sore head (not mine)."

The following entry will awaken sad memories in some bosoms: " French woman complained about our row in the billet at night time. Very unfortunate, as we had to vacate a nice room for very old hay-store with rats. No bon! . . . cleaning up new billet and clearing away straw from roof. Old Froggie played war. No compris! "

There were no casualties in April, but May began badly. On 7th May, Sergeants Terry, Teasdale and Spencely and one more were sent up to the front line to learn trench routine with the Dorset Regiment. At eleven that night the Boche, after a very heavy bombardment, broke in at three places near Hammer-head Sap, and there was heavy fighting before they were ejected, with the loss of several killed and one taken prisoner. The Dorsets lost heavily, and Terry and Teasdale were wounded, and Spencely reported missing.

Early in May, " A," after doing eight days' training—i.e., square drill, which all hated—joined " D " on Northumberland Avenue till 15th, when it was put on to a job of wiring in No-Man's-Land for several nights. The Boche worried them a good deal, but they only lost No. 1072, Private J. Brown, killed, and a couple wounded. The company was then put on to wiring and digging a reserve line about 80 yards behind the front line northwards from Aintree Street. The wiring was done in one night, and though it was bright moonlight the Boche did not trouble them, but during the digging he paid them a good deal of attention, and they were lucky to get off with one man wounded and several sets of equipment and rifles, which had been laid down while working, sent west by shells. After the second night, as the Boche seemed to have got the range and to dislike the trench, Captain Ker decided to finish it by sapping during the day and night-work between the showers, which was successfully accomplished.

" B " Company was on railway construction the whole of May, being billeted first at Meaulte and then at Morlancourt.

" C " Company moved from Albert to Bouzincourt on 9th May, and finished the famous Coney Street dug-outs on 17th. It then turned its attention to wiring Tobermory Street, Campbell Avenue to Thiépval Avenue, and improving and traversing Campbell Avenue; this was all night work.

" D " Company also moved to Bouzincourt and continued its work on Northumberland Avenue, and to fill up odd moments " screened " at Aveluy, made dug-outs and tramway sidings in " Blighty Valley " and at Authuille. On 16th May, Second-Lieutenants Drury and Germain joined the battalion and were posted to " A " Company, and on the 12th a draft of a Sergeant and nineteen men was received. Though battle casualties had been few, there had been a steady reduction of strength due to sickness, and the battalion was brought up to strength in anticipation of the casualties to be expected in the forthcoming offensive, for which all its efforts were a preparation.

The knowledge of the tough time ahead of him did not prevent the British soldier enjoying himself, and there are many records of football matches. The Pioneers beat the Stretcher-bearers by 4 to 1. C.S.M. Lonsborough of " A " challenged the R.S.M. to find a team of Sergeants which could beat the Sergeants of his company. The match was a good one, ending in the defeat of the challengers, but only by 1 goal to 0. The match between the 16th and 17th Northumberland Fusiliers was a great fight, ending in a draw, each scoring 1 goal. " A " Company's team was a strong one, and defeated the 1st Battalion Dorset Regiment by 2 goals to 1. The 161st Brigade R.F.A. was easily beaten, even though the battalion was deprived of " A " Company's contingent, which was employed wiring out in No-Man's-Land. Encouraged by these successes the battalion team went over to Henencourt to play the Scottish Rifles (Lieutenant-Colonel Pears' old regiment). " C " Company was so keen that it marched over *en bloc* to see the game. Unfortunately, its zeal was not rewarded by witnessing a victory, for " we were well beaten 4 to nil by the finest team I have yet seen out here." Later on there was a return match played on the ground at Bouzincourt, which the visitors again won, this time 6 to nil. On each occasion the two teams had tea together before the match. The visitors won the Divisional Cup, beating the Cyclists by 3 to 1.

On 16th, Lieutenant-Colonel Pears was compelled by ill health to leave the battalion. He was sent to England, and in the War Diary of 28th June we read : " Lieutenant-Colonel Pears struck off strength 26-6. Medical Board, W.O.S.4a." But Lieutenant-Colonel Pears, though sick, was not to be disposed of so easily, and on 30th June the War Diary records : " Lieutenant-Colonel Pears returns and takes command." How he did it is not explained, but those who knew him were not surprised to see him back. It would take more than a Medical Board to keep Lieutenant-Colonel Pears at home when he knew a fight was coming on.

On 3rd June the Colonel was gazetted C.M.G., and on 18th his name appears among those " mentioned in despatches " along with that of Captain and Adjutant G. W. Martin. 648 Lance-Sergeant Freeman received the M.M. at this time.

During June, drafts amounting to one hundred and thirty other ranks were received, and the following officers joined : Second-Lieutenant O. Smurthwaite, Second-Lieutenant F. de Bock Brisley.

Work was carried on with increased energy, even " servants, batmen, etc., set to work in spare time on excavations." There was no time even for football. The only amusement of which there is any record is a Pierrot Show at " The Empire " in Senlis, two hours' excellent entertainment by the Divisional Cyclists Concert Party, aptly entitled " The Peddlers."

During this month there were several raids by troops of the 32nd Division and others, and gas was discharged all along the front, but as this is purely Battalion History, these incidents are not dealt with.

On 21st June " B " arrived in Bouzincourt from Morlencourt, and the remainder of the month was occupied in completing the preparations for the great attack which will be dealt with in the next chapter.

CHAPTER III

THE FIRST BATTLE OF THE SOMME

HITHERTO it has been possible to deal with the doings of the battalion without touching much on those of the other units of the division, because, although an integral part of the division and engaged on work for the benefit of the troops generally, and especially for that of the battalions holding the line, whose comfort and safety depended very largely on the proper maintenance and drainage of the trench system, a Pioneer Battalion was, to a certain extent, a unit apart. It belonged to no brigade and carried out its operations under the direct orders of the C.R.E.; therefore, during normal times, its story can be told without dealing with that of any other unit, but during the period upon which we are now entering this is no longer possible, as in the turmoil of the great offensive a Pioneer Battalion's story becomes merged in that of the division to which it belonged. No attempt, however, is made to give a complete history of the operations, but only a sufficient summary of them to make the story of battalion's doings intelligible.

A reference to the map at the conclusion of the book will show the position of the contending forces and the three objectives of the 32nd Division, which were:

(1) The front line system, including the whole village of Thiépval and the complicated system of trenches to the south of it.

(2) The intermediate system (Blue Line) and Mouquet Switch, including the strongly fortified post of Mouquet Farm.

(3) The German second line system (Green Line)—a continuous trench system, well wired, on the right about 400 yards and on the left about 750 yards in rear of the intermediate line.

On the 30th June, the 96th and 97th Brigades were holding the front line, and to them fell the task of capturing the first two objectives, the 96th on the left being responsible for taking Thiépval, and the 97th on the right, after capturing the three or four lines of the front system, was to take Mouquet Farm. The 14th Brigade was to follow the 97th, and when the latter had taken the second objective, it was to push through, and, breaking in a little north of Mouquet Farm under a smoke barrage, capture the Green Line from the flank and rear.

As each line was captured, strong points were to be organized, and to aid in this a section of the Field Company of R.E. was to be attached to each brigade. The remainder of the Field Companies and the 17th Northumberland Fusiliers were in divisional reserve, to be employed in opening up communications between our lines and the positions won. The division attacked on a front of 1,850 yards from Chowbent Street to Union Street. The frontage of the 97th Brigade was 850 yards and of the 96th 1,000 yards. Each had two battalions in the front line—one in support and one in reserve. The 14th Brigade was in dug-outs behind steep slopes south of Authuille and north of Crucifix Corner, the "famous dug-outs" of which we have already heard.

The division had on its right the 8th Division and on its left the 36th, which were to attack simultaneously. The orders of Lieutenant-Colonel E. P. Brooker, C.R.E., specified the following tasks to be performed by the Pioneers. During the bombardment: Repairs and control of Authuille Wood tramway. Repairs of Dunbarton track bridges. Control of Thiépval Wood line traffic and to take over from the Miners the five saps which had been made from our front line towards that of the enemy.

The duties of the battalion during the assault were:

(1) To open up the five saps and extend them by zigzag trenches to the German front line so as to allow of free communication between our lines and such portions of the enemy's system as might be in our hands. The communication trenches leading to these saps were also to be kept clear. The saps were known as Sanda, Tyndrum, Inverary, Sauchiehall and Arthurlie. This task was allotted to " C " Company.

(2) Repairs, control and extension of Authuille Wood tramway.

(3) Opening up artillery and transport routes.

The second task was allotted to a platoon of " D," two more platoons being told off to the third task, the fourth platoon of that company being in reserve.

These two companies worked directly under Colonel Pears. " A " and " B " were placed at the disposal of the officers commanding 218 and 219 Field Companies respectively, which were attached to the 96th and 97th Infantry Brigades. Their duties were to carry stores for the strong points, and to help in their construction.

The battalion, it will be seen from the above, could not carry out the task allotted to it unless the assaulting columns were successful.

The assault of the German lines was originally fixed for June 29th, but on 28th it was postponed till 7.30 a.m. on 1st July. The preliminary bombardment began on 24th. " It is tremendous, it is awful, but it is glorious, because it is ours. Six months ago, had you told us such a bombardment by the British Army was possible, we would not have believed you; had you told Fritz, he would probably have laughed. We can hear the short, sharp bark of the eighteen-pounders, constant, always, like the roll of a drum, then the deeper boom of the 'hows' but a little behind in the rapidity of their fire, and then, over our heads, the swish of the heavy shells from some great monster, either on the railway or behind in the woods."

30th June.—" All packs handed in to Quartermasters. Troops of 32nd Division pass through Bouzincourt on way to the trenches ready for advance. Very gay, and singing and whistling, " Pack up your troubles in your old kit-bag," " Tipperary," etc. All of us addressed by our own officers and told of to-morrow's events. Pessimistically inclined making wills. There is a strange feeling about the whole night. I cannot explain it. It is not to be explained—only felt. . . . The companies are off, and we find ourselves, we, the Reserves, with empty billets, empty messes—waiting anxiously for to-morrow."

The morrow, the first July, a day none of us will forget, broke fine and in glorious sunshine. At 7.30 a.m., for some twenty-five miles southward of Serre, the British and French troops quitted the trenches in which they had been stationary for so long, and, preceded by a moving curtain of shells of all calibres, which their guns, ever lengthening their range, poured down on the enemy, attempted to capture the defences on which the industrious Huns had been labouring incessantly for the last eighteen months. It appears that in the extreme south the enemy was not expecting and was not prepared for the attack, and on the whole of the French front, about eleven miles, and as far north as Fricourt on the British front, the Allies achieved a great success, but north of Fricourt the successes were only partial, and there were some bad failures. The 21st Division penetrated a considerable depth to the north of Fricourt, the 34th carried on the lodgement as far as La Boisselle, and though it failed to take that village, it established itself to the south of it.

The 8th Division, on the right of the 32nd, suffered so severely in its gallant assault on Ovillers la Boisselle that it had to be immediately relieved by the 12th Division. The 32nd Division achieved a lodgement to the south of Thiépval, viz., Leipzig Redoubt, but failed to take that village, which indeed turned out far more strongly fortified than had been expected and was not taken till 26th September.

On the left of the 32nd the 36th Ulster Division pressed forward and penetrated some distance north of Thiépval, but alas! while Thiépval was still in the enemy's hands, these gains to the north could not be maintained and the Ulster men had to retire, some of their most venturesome parties being cut off. North of the 36th Division the attacks were unsuccessful, though the 4th Division did make some impression north of Beaumont Hamel, but had to withdraw, its flanks being unprotected.

The 32nd Division attack must now be briefly described. The left battalion of the 96th Brigade was the 15th Lancashire Fusiliers. It made good progress, and at 9.10 a.m. its leading troops were seen east of Thiépval. A party of the 16th Lancashire Fusiliers was pushed forward to attempt to reinforce them, but the Hun machine-gunners from Thiépval maintained such an effective fire that the effort failed. The 16th Northumberland Fusiliers, the right battalion of the 96th Brigade, and the left of the 16th Highland Light Infantry, the left battalion of the 97th Brigade, were held up before the enemy's front line at Thiépval by machine-gun fire from nests of guns, which had escaped the bombardment. Efforts made by part of the Lancashire Fusiliers and the 2nd K.O.Y.L.I. to help them forward failed, and they stayed in shell-holes till dark, and were then withdrawn. The right of the 16th H.L.I. managed to get across to No-Man's-Land, and to effect an entry into the German lines, and on its right the 17th Battalion of the regiment established itself in Leipzig Redoubt and in the approaches to Hindenburg Redoubt. It made good progress up till 8.30 a.m., when it was held up by machine-gun fire from Hindenburg, Lemberg and Wundwerk Redoubts. About 9 a.m. it was reinforced by a party of the 2nd K.O.Y.L.I. with four Stokes guns, which enabled the fight to be maintained, but no progress could be made. The 11th Border Regiment, Reserve Battalion of the 97th Brigade, debouched from Authuille Wood at 8.30 a.m., but at once came under such heavy artillery and machine-gun fire from hostile positions to the south of the divisional area that only a few got across into the German lines. Lieutenant-Colonel Mitchell, C.M.G., D.S.O., was killed, and the survivors were collected in our front line. Thus the net result of the day was a lodgement in a small portion of the enemy's position south of Thiépval by the 17th H.L.I. with some of the 16th H.L.I. and 2nd K.O.Y.L.I., whose position was very perilous. They were exposed to attacks from the front and from both flanks, and, as the Border Regiment's advance had shown, to reinforce them was difficult. It was in anticipation of just such a contingency that the five saps had been prepared by the Miners, and therefore it is only natural that we find D.H.Q. at 5 p.m. asking the C.R.E. to request Colonel Pears to hasten on the work of opening out Sanda Sap. Colonel Pears was able to reply that he had received a report timed 4.15 p.m. that Sanda Sap was then being opened out, and in the War Diary of the Divisional General Staff we read that at 4.30 p.m. this work was completed, and the comment is, " This was of inestimable value."

It will be remembered that to " C " Company had been confided the task of prolonging the five saps to the German front line. That Company's correspondent writes: " At 4 a.m. on a lovely fine day we marched out of Bouzincourt along Northumberland Avenue, past Martinsart, along Black Horse Road, through Aveluy Wood to the railway embankment just outside Authuille; we were in battle order—that is to say, no pack, just tin hat, rifle, ammunition, water-bottle, haversack and the barest necessities, including our emergency ration. We stayed in shallow assembly trenches just behind the railway embankment till 7.30 a.m. All this time the artillery had been steadily increasing the rate of fire until when zero was reached the shells were fired as fast as they could be put into the gun. The uproar was terrific. It was impossible to distinguish whether the enemy was replying or not."

The work of opening out Sanda Sap and making a trench from its far end to the enemy's front line had been entrusted to Lieutenant Cole and No. 9 Platoon. Cole found the sap choked with dead and wounded men of the assaulting battalions, who had crawled in there for safety from the incessant machine-gun and whizz-bang fire which swept the whole front. A few men were sent along the sap who, with great difficulty, crawled through among the dead and wounded and broke through at the far end, which had been blown in by a chance shell. Having thus ascertained the point from which the trench was to start, Cole led out the rest of the platoon across the open, going warily from shell-hole to shell-hole under heavy fire, till he had the men distributed in a rough line, four men in each shell-hole from the sap end to the enemy's front line opposite, which was now in our hands. The men worked towards each other, two each way, and thus, with the loss of only two or three men wounded, the trench was completed, but not at 4.30 p.m. as stated in the divisional narrative, though the " break through " was made about that hour.

The work of opening out communication was much interfered with by the constant passage of wounded men back from the front and of carrying parties with bombs and water to the hard-pressed fighters in Leipzig Redoubt. At 7.10 p.m. Lieutenant Cole sent a request to Captain Stamp Taylor for the services of Sergeant Ellis and twenty men of No. 10 Platoon to relieve his men, but he himself remained on the job most of this night.

What the completion of this trench meant to the weary troops in front is shown by the following entry in the diary of the 97th Brigade: "Various bombing attacks took place during the night, which were easily repulsed owing to the fact that communication could be kept up from the Sanda Sap, which proved a godsend."

It may, I think, be fairly claimed that but for the good work done by Cole and the stout lads of 9 and 10 Platoons, there would have been considerable danger of our troops being driven out of the Leipzig Salient during the night, in which case the division would have had nothing to show for its heavy losses. That the work was accomplished with so small a loss shows conclusively that it was carried out by well-trained men scientifically handled. The "green bunch" had come on a good bit since that first wiring "stunt" on the 3rd December.

The other saps entrusted to "C" could not be worked on, for the Boche was still holding his front line opposite them, so the rest of the company spent the day in such shelter as could be obtained in and near our front line, under continuous fire of artillery and machine-guns, witnessing the depressing sight of the constant stream of our wounded passing back, but cheered from time to time by seeing batches of prisoners, the first of whom is described as a typical German, such as the illustrated papers portray, who "greeted us with 'Good morning.'"

"A" Company's record is: "Having had about two hours sleep during the night, had a scrappy meal. Moved to Authuille North half an hour after zero, and got there without any casualties. Met by Ker and rest of the company. Here we waited till the time should come when we were to go forward and consolidate."

This time never came, owing to the failure of the attack at this point, and the only work "A" was called on to perform was at 9.30 p.m., when, with No. 3 and 4 Sections of 218 Field Company, Captain Ker and Lieutenant Plumptre took up Nos. 1 and 2 Platoons, and went up to attempt to repair wire and rebuild our front line.

"B" Company, which worked under orders of the officer commanding 219 Field Company, had a more arduous time. After the Leipzig Salient had been occupied, Lieutenant Mitchell's Platoon No. 5 did valiant work carrying water, bombs, etc., across No-Man's-Land, to the H.L.I. in the Leipzig Redoubt. The whole situation was one of extraordinary confusion as our infantry were momentarily expecting a Boche counter-attack and were very short of bombs, while the Hun was armed with the "egg" bomb, a lighter type than the Mills hand-grenade we were using, and in consequence he was giving our fellows a very bad time. Lieutenant

Mitchell had a very narrow shave, a machine-gun bullet cutting right through his collar.

No. 3 Section of the Field Company was sent forward somewhat later to consolidate the gains in the Boche lines, and Lieutenant Riddel was ordered to take 6 and 7 Platoons to the R.E. Dump at Sandbag City near our old front line, and thence carry material and tools to the head of Campbell Avenue in readiness for a further move forward after dark. Progress up the Avenue was found to be impossible owing to the procession of wounded, some walking, some on stretchers coming down from the salient. The Pioneers tried to struggle forward, some tried to get up Durham Street, but every trench was choked, and in the end, after spending a miserable night, the weary men were told to take the tools back to Sandbag City. Subsequently, however, the company was detailed to dig a trench from our front line to that of the Boche, parallel to Tyndrum Sap, but the War Diary of the Field Company records that, " owing to the enormous squash in the trenches, due to relief, ration parties, ammunition parties, etc. . . . only one Platoon of Pioneers (No. 5) got any digging done before daylight; the remainder got held up in the trenches, and it was too light to dig when they arrived."

On morning of 2nd July, " after reaching Aveluy the Machine-Gun Section, " B " Company, were billeted separate from the rest of the company, being placed in a very rickety old building which was exposed to shell-fire, near the church. Shortly after our arrival the Boche commenced shelling us, and one of his shells came right through the doorway and alighted in the midst of a crowd of the Machine-Gunners, who were playing cards, etc. Sergeant Syd Morris, one of the whitest men we had in the battalion, and Private Val. Gent, another fine lad, were instantly killed, and other twenty-six were wounded."

Of " D " doings on " Der Tag," an account reads : " The work allotted to Lieutenant Douglas with 13 Platoon, and Lieutenant Lakeman with 14 Platoon, in bridging trenches for artillery to advance, was completely held up (Douglas's famous bill hook went west) and Lieutenant Robertson with 16 Platoon, who had been detailed for the extension of Authuille Wood tramway and upkeep of artillery tracks, had finally to report late in the afternoon that the work was completely held up owing to heavy lachrymatory shelling, and were then ordered to stand by, spending a very unpleasant night attending to the burying of the infantry. The following early morning was a complete contrast—everyone worn out—almost complete silence in the woods except the whistling of the birds ! "

With headquarters in Bouzincourt, a certain number of all ranks of each company had been detained to fill the gaps which it was expected would be made in the battalion. Some notes from one of these are of interest. "1st July, 5.30 a.m. We are on the hill looking away to Thiépval, Ovillers, and farther back behind Pozières, a sheet of flame, from north to south as far as the eye can see." Later, after the attack had been launched, come many entries full of anxious doubts and longings for news, allusions to the fierce, constant rattle of the machine-guns. Then the sight of the first batch of prisoners gives rise to hopes that all has gone well, but these hopes are dashed to the ground by the sight of the stream of wounded and the tales they tell of the hell they have been through. Anxious inquiries are made as to the Pioneers; news, very conflicting, trickles in; all spend an anxious day. By midnight the truth is approximately known and the result is summed up. "Still, with all its failures, all its sorrows, all its pain and suffering, it's been a great day for us; it has proved that Tommy is better than Fritz, that the New Army can attack and win through even in the face of the greatest odds."

The night brought no change in the situation. On the 2nd July, the 14th Brigade relieved the 97th in the Authuille Sector, the 15th H.L.I. relieving the 2nd Manchester Regiment in the Leipzig Salient. The 75th Brigade of the 25th Division was lent to General Rycroft, and the day was occupied in arrangements for attacking the enemy's position south of Thiépval, in conjunction with the 12th Division attack on Ovillers. These attacks took place on the 3rd at 6.15 a.m. The 15th H.L.I. enlarged our holding in the Leipzig Salient, but the other operations failed, and during the night of 3rd/4th the 32nd Division was relieved by the 25th, and withdrew to the Senlis-Warloy-Contay area, the artillery remaining in action. The casualties suffered by the division in the three days' fighting amounted to 214 officers and 4,462 other ranks.

The 2nd July was spent by " C " in improving and increasing the communications between our old front line and a portion of the Hun lines which was in our possession; this work continued all the next day. The fire of the enemy was still so severe that working on top was impossible, and a message from Lieutenant Cole to Captain Stamp Taylor, timed 2.45 p.m., says that all is going well so far, and he is sapping from our old line while Sergeant Smith, with four men and two of the South Wales Borderers, is working towards him.

17/52 Sergeant W. Smith is spoken of as having done great work, and shown coolness and bravery throughout these three trying days.

" C " Headquarters were moved to Sandbag City No. 2 on 3rd. This city was on the hill-side just below the cemetery of Authuille village, in which the men killed during these days were buried. The Boche shelled the place constantly, but that did not prevent "many men indulging in bathing in the Ancre." "A" remained at Authuille North, waiting for orders till the evening of the 2nd, and then moved to Authuille South, where orders for the next night's work were received. Lieutenant Sadler made a reconnaissance of the ground at 5 a.m. on the 3rd, and that night the company, after a trying march through trenches thronged with troops, owing to the relief of the division being in progress, reached the site of the trench which it had to dig, which had been taped earlier in the night by Captain Ker and Lieutenant Sadler; the trench was some distance north of Sanda Sap and crossed the German front line. The enemy, who was very close at hand, resented the encroachment on his territory, and, while the work was in progress, made a bombing attack on the left of the line, which was beaten off by the Pioneers, who showed they were as handy with bombs and bayonets as with picks and shovels. Sergeant Oliver received the Military Medal for his gallant leading on this occasion. The trench was dug to a depth of four feet before the company was relieved by a company of the 6th South Wales Borderers, the Pioneers of the 25th Division, at 3.30 a.m. on 4th July. In this operation the company only had two or three minor casualties, but the troops which relieved them were not so lucky, for, in marching up, they lost eighty men, one company losing all its officers. It seems that the 17th was a lucky battalion, for "A" had hardly left Authuille North before the Boche shelled it so severely that sixty casualties occurred in less than fifteen minutes, and the headquarters of "C" had just moved forward to Sandbag City No. 2 when the spot it had vacated was hit by a shell which caused many casualties. Scientists laugh at luck—well, let them laugh. Soldiers and sailors know there are lucky regiments and lucky ships as well as unlucky ones.

The battalion collected in Bouzincourt. The casualties had not been heavy, only two officers and fifty-eight other ranks, but the men had had a hard time during the three days of the attack under heavy fire all the time, getting very little sleep and living on bully and biscuit.

"B" was not to have any rest; it was left in Aveluy to work for the 25th Division, and suffered severely during the next few days. Jake Caminada says:

"We stayed at Aveluy until the morning of the 3rd July, when we marched up past Crucifix Corner, and entering the 'La Boisselle' road, we went into some trenches at a place called 'Scott's Redoubt' or 'Scott's Farm,' and making that place our temporary headquarters, we started off up the ' La Boisselle ' road again until we reached our old front line trenches, and on this job I think we were engaged two or three nights making our way back to our temporary headquarters at daybreak. During the time we were staying at this Scott's Farm we had a great many casualties with the gas ' Jerry ' was sending over in shells, and seeing that it was our first experience of gas shells, I think the majority of them (casualties) was owing to the fact that everybody thought these gas shells were ' dud ' high explosive or shrapnel shells. I know, personally, I sat and counted thirty-three of these shells before I ever thought of putting my helmet on. I think we left this place on 6th July, and after spending another night at Aveluy, we joined the rest of the battalion and marched off to Loos."

The headquarters, with " A " and " C," marched to Contay in heavy rain on the afternoon of the 4th. " D " only went as far as Senlis and remained there to work for the 10th Corps, on repairing roads, for easier passage of Red Cross motors carrying wounded. " D " had an easy day on 6th, but on 7th, after being flooded out of its tents by heavy rain, it went back into the fight, moving to Crucifix Corner. The party in Contay found the billets " rotten lousy," being a mild term, but Contay is a well-situated village in the heart of a fine wooded country, and some fine views were to be obtained from the surrounding hills. " What a change from what we have just left! From blood, death, and all the other accompaniments of war, to almost perfect peace."

" A " Company had less than twenty-four hours in which to enjoy the change, for at 3 p.m. on 5th it started back for Aveluy, to be attached to the 12th Division. As far as possible, those who had been in the first scrap stayed behind, their places being taken by those who had been in reserve. After a night spent in its old camp in Aveluy Château grounds, sadly altered for the worse by the last few days of war, the company found " more peaceful quarters " behind a hedge about six hundred yards from Brookers Pass.

Then followed some strenuous days, when life seemed a nightmare; a series of moves and counter-moves in trenches thronged with troops, infantry collecting to attack, wounded struggling back, carrying parties patiently plodding forward amid frequent showers of shrapnel and the never-ceasing whine of the machine-gun bullets. So completely had the bombardments of the last few days obliterated all landmarks that it was almost impossible to identify the spot on which one was to begin work, and, so rapidly did the situation change, that not infrequently after a night's hard digging, often in ground full of dead Germans, " staff arrive and kindly tell us that work we are doing and have done is useless and not required. We go home, arriving about 7 a.m. ' I am ready for bed! ' "

" B " all this time was working in conjunction with 218 " E " Company R.E. attached to the 12th Division which was engaged in the attack on Ovillers la Boisselle and the area between that village and La Boisselle. The assault was to be delivered early on the 7th. The duty of the R.E.'s and Pioneers was to consolidate strong points at previously selected spots as soon as the infantry assault had progressed sufficiently. Half a Field Company, a platoon of " B," and a carrying party of a hundred infantry formed a unit for each strong point. The parties assembled at Gardiner's post at 9 p.m. on 6th in heavy rain which lasted all night. No move could be made till 10.35 a.m., and " owing to condition of trenches and congestion, etc., parties did not reach destination till about 5 p.m., and most of carrying parties had been lost en route, heavily shelled, very exhausted, only able to work for one hour and then withdraw to bivouac. Exhaustion largely due to night in the rain in the open at Gardiner's post." After this unsatisfactory day " B " returned to Bouzincourt, and on the next day, 8th, at 7 p.m., moved to Senlis. During these operations Lieutenant Riddel and twenty-four other ranks were wounded and one man was killed.

Colonel E. P. Brooker, C.M.G., who had been C.R.E. of the 32nd Division since its birth, and who had been a good friend to the battalion, was promoted to be Chief Engineer of the 13th Corps on 6th July, and Major Cruikshank, R.E., succeeded him. Pending the new C.R.E.'s arrival, Colonel Pears acted as C.R.E. for a few days, Major Oxley taking command of the battalion, with advanced headquarters at Crucifix Corner.

While the Gunners, Pioneers and Field Companies had been working hard for other divisions, the infantry of the 32nd Division had been resting and refitting. On the night of 8th/9th the division returned to the fray and relieved the 12th Division in western portion of Ovillers la Boisselle and thence to Mersey Street, north of the Nab. The 14th Brigade held Ovillers portion, the 97th occupying our old front line from Rivington to Mersey Street.

The stay of the division in the front line lasted till 15th July. Throughout this period there was constant fighting at close quarters, resulting in certain gains to us, but no great change was effected in the situation. The casualties suffered during the second period were: 46 officers and 809 other ranks. Our battalion's losses were 36. The total losses of the 32nd Division during the first fifteen days of July were: Killed, 6 officers and 661 other ranks; wounded, 160 officers and 3,382 other ranks; missing, 24 officers and 1,202 other ranks; making a grand total of 190 officers and 5,245 other ranks.

The battalion's doings during this week must now be related. Headquarters and " C " Company moved from Contay to Senlis on 7th, and on 9th " B " and " C " relieved the North Hants Pioneers on the hill crest above Aveluy. They were relieved by the 6th Royal Sussex Pioneers a week later. " During this week we had it fairly rough, having two or three bad gas attacks. We had a few casualties with gas, and one morning about fifty-six reported sick. Our job was putting a communication trench between our old front line and the front line of the enemy, of which we now held part. On the night of Tuesday, 11th, about 4 p.m., as the company was returning from work, a chum of mine, young Tommy Bradley, saw an arm waving a dixie lid. He and another man named Dick Potter went over and brought the man in. He was a 9th Royal Fusilier and had lain there badly wounded since the 7th."

Another account of this gas reads : " It was a new kind, which did not take effect till six hours had elapsed, so the doctors could find nothing wrong with the men who did not get their helmets on in time, and sent them back again. In six hours many of them were dead. We were very glad to leave this place. . . . Ever after I always had a profound respect for my gas helmet."

" A " Company rejoined the battalion from the 12th Division on 9th July and occupied " those famous dug-outs " made by " C," but " D " did not return from the 10th Corps till 12th July, when it also went to the " famous dug-outs," which certainly seem to have proved very useful. The first work of " A " was that sad and necessary but very disagreeable task of burying the dead. " It is the most awful job we have had, and yet we feel it is a work of love." The work was often stopped by Fritz shelling the area.

From the end of Rivington Street a tunnel had been dug, by some previous occupants of these trenches, towards the enemy's front line. It was the job of " A," assisted by some of " C," to prolong this and join up with the opposite line as soon as that was cleared of the Huns, who were still holding on stubbornly, although the trenches on the right were in our possession. The ground was very hard and flinty, and the enemy kept up a heavy fire on the place, so that progress was necessarily slow.

Lieutenant Glendinning and Second-Lieutenant Germaine started the work with their platoons on the night of 9th/10th July. Captain Kitching and Second-Lieutenant Drury, with the remainder of these men, carried on during the next day, and the other two platoons continued during the next night, and news having been received that the line opposite was in our hands, Germaine got out of the sap and went towards the German line to make sure of the direction. He was never seen again.

The Manchesters were across in what had been hostile territory, but it was not clear whether they or the Boche were opposite the tunnel, and there was considerable danger—if "A" pushed on too energetically, they might let the Boche through into our trenches, which were very lightly held.

During the night of 13th/14th the Brigadier and C.R.E. visited the spot, and, after examining the sap and comparing maps, directed Drury to "Keep the sap closed and your eyes open." Later a Machine-gun Company was sent up to reinforce the Pioneers and make the line safe till the Boche opposite could be ejected, but this took time, so that "A" departed on the relief of the division without the pleasure of completing the connection. "D," after its return to the fold, worked on a tramway track from Ovillers Post to Crucifix Corner.

All through these days of war the transport had been working unceasingly, frequently in very hot corners, and my correspondent writes: "I remember one of our drivers, Simpson, went to Campbell Avenue, a trench in Authuille, near Thiépval, to bring out the Machine-Gun Section, and the place was so hot that this section could not come out. This man stood there with his horses about three hours. I am sure it would take a man with a good sense of duty to behave as he did."

On 16th, at 6.30 p.m., the 5th Royal Sussex Pioneers of 48th Division relieved the battalion, which next day started on a tour through France which ended on 27th at Loos.

The battalion's casualties during the sixteen days of the Somme battle were ten other ranks killed, three officers wounded and one missing, and eighty-three other ranks wounded. A remarkably small number considering that for nearly the whole of the time it had been in the battle area, under artillery and machine-gun fire. Besides those already mentioned, I have only records of the deaths of Billy Crisp, on 8th; Frank Bayes, "C" runner, either on 1st or 2nd; and of the following being wounded: 2nd, Second-Lieutenant Mucklow; 7th, Lieutenant Riddel; 12th, Lance-Corporal Bell; 13th, Private Wilson, 1036.

Though few casualties had occurred, the battalion had had a very trying time, and the men were "just about knocked up." Some had been eight days in the trenches without even taking their boots off, living much of the time on bully and water, and getting little sleep; the effects of this were felt during the succeeding days.

CHAPTER IV

OUR FIRST MOVE NORTH

THE battalion left Bouzincourt, which it had come to look upon almost as home, at 8.30 a.m. on 17th July. "It was raining as usual."

Then followed five days of marching through pleasant country, bearing no marks of war. The nights were spent at Authuille, Ivergny, Ecoivres, Fleury, and on 21st Bailleul-les-Pernes was reached. "All these villages were small and off the main routes, and we stayed in the usual kind of old barns." At Ivergny, in the interests of mobility there was dirty work in the transport lines, the thought of which will still bring a tear to the eyes of many an officer. On 19th "Continued trek at 4.30 a.m. Passed through Frevent (a fair sized town). People turned out to see us pass through. Whole battalion gay enough, but dead beat. Finished up at Ecoivres about dropping." Except on the first day, everyone was carrying his full pack, and it is clear that, after the rough times they had been through, the constant marching tried the men very much, especially as on the last three days the sun shone all day with full July power. However, on the first day "General Rycroft watched the battalion march past, and complimented the C.O. on the condition of the men after their arduous time," and that evening they were not too done to enjoy a good rag concert. The country is described as "ripping." Many seem to have slept for choice out in the open and found it "fairly comfortable, but bulls rather annoying." Naturally, after being so long dependent on rations, and these often scanty, everyone sought eagerly for a more varied diet, but eggs seem to have been all that could be got, so that one diary reads: "More eggs!! I shall begin to lay them if we do not stop soon."

On 22nd, "Church Parade under our C.O. at 11 a.m. Quite refreshing. C.O. addressed the battalion after service and said G.O.C. was very, very pleased indeed with our work from 1st July onwards." At Bailleul-les-Pernes the battalion stayed till 25th July, re-fitting and resting. "This village was small and situated in a hollow. It looked exceptionally pretty as we saw it." "People here very hospitable. . . . Beer down to a penny a glass." No wonder all were sorry that their stay was so short.

"C" Company's recorder says: "On 25th we marched through Pernes and Bruay to Houchin, where we spent one night under canvas. . . . Next day we marched through Nœux-les-Mines, a fairly large mining town, which was often shelled, to Petit Sains, a small mining village about five miles from the line. The rest of the battalion left us here and went on to Loos, where they stayed five weeks as garrison of that place, never coming out of the trenches the whole of the time. We thanked our stars that this was not our lot."

"C" stayed in Petit Sains till 5th September, "during which we rested, did some work on dug-outs near line, and drilled and played cricket." No wonder "C" felt "cushy." The rest of the battalion slept the night of 26th/27th at Les-Brebis. "A few shells over in afternoon. Billets good, mostly upper rooms in working men's houses." The next day "we marched off in sections at three hundred yards interval, and after doing about a mile and a half, we entered a communication trench, after which it took us three hours to paddle along duck walks into Loos, our destination. What a place! Snipers' bullets, machine-gun fire, etc., to risk on leaving cellars and dug-outs (the only billets). . . . Loos, a terrible wreck of a town, every building in it partially or totally destroyed. Enemy's lines on three sides of us, and it is here we are to take up garrison duty, Colonel Pears as Commandant Loos. All living in cellars, and all through communication by trenches or tunnels. The trenches smothered with cornflowers and poppies. . . . Oh! a delightful summer residence that will grow on one daily."

The battalion relieved the 11th Hampshire Regiment Pioneers on 27th July. Lieutenant-Colonel Pears was not able to enjoy the honour of his Commandantship very long, for on the 4th he was compelled to go to hospital and Major Oxley took over the command with Major King, who had been commanding "D," as Second-in-Command. "C.O. leaves us. He said good-bye to all the officers about 2.30 p.m., and seemed very much cut up at having to go, as he was almost certain his health would not permit of him ever returning. Personally, I feel sure that we shall miss him and regret his departure. *He was a soldier.*"

Lieutenant-Colonel Pears knew, and had known for long, that he was suffering from cancer. It was this disease which had caused him to be sent to England in May. Most men would have accepted the verdict of the doctors and stayed quietly at home; not so Pears. There is no record of how he got over the Medical Boards order striking him off the Active List, but out he came and carried on all through the period of fighting; but even his tough nature could not hold out indefinitely, and, the battalion being apparently likely to be out of the hurly-burly for some time, Pears went home, but it was only to die on 20th October the same year.

While in Loos, the battalion was detached from the 32nd Division and placed under the orders of the G.O.C. 16th (Irish) Division, which was holding the line in front.

The battalion stayed in this uncomfortable locality till the end of August. It was an uneventful but extremely uncomfortable time, especially for the transport, who made their nightly visits to Loos along machine-gun-swept roads, there being little or no cover, and, although the wheels of the wagons were muffled, the Boche seemed to have uncanny knowledge as to when they were moving up and back. Transport Sergeant Calvert was shot through the knee on one occasion. One correspondent sums it up thus: "Routine trench work and gun duty. Sector very quiet owing to the big Somme battle proceeding farther south. Baths in brewery at Mazingarbe, about three miles through communication trenches called ' Northern Up ' and ' Piccadilly.' Bath earned."

Though quiet compared with the Somme, there were frequent doses of shells, and machine-guns played overhead regularly, so that it was unwise to come to the surface. The rats were a terrible plague, " they insisted on playing games on the bed and the table." "They climb like cats, and run all over everything."

The battalion was distributed in several posts termed " keeps," which were connected by various trenches about seven feet deep, which " twist and twine all over the place." The Lewis Gunners garrisoned emplacements which they also had to build and keep in repair. Whenever the wind was in a dangerous quarter for gas, all troops had to stand to from 4 to 5 a.m. As working parties frequently did not get back till 2 or 3 a.m., the direction of the wind was anxiously studied. The weather on the whole was remarkably fine all the month.

One of the minor events which occurred was the arrival of " transfer badges for steel helmets," which seem to have been rather tasty, for a few days after their arrival a wearer of one was stopped by two Generals who wished to examine the work of art.

On 10th August " D " was put on to repair the front line, which it did so efficiently that the officers commanding the battalions holding it, brought the matter to the notice of the G.O.C., who wrote a most complimentary letter thanking the battalion for the " invaluable assistance in rebuilding a great part of the front line." This may explain why a bottle of rum was issued to the Sergeants of " D " Company in lieu of a bottle of lime juice on that day.

In odd moments the Pioneers dug cable trenches for signals,

and supplied guards day and night, so they may be said to have earned their pay.

On 16th August Major Oxley went on special duty to Divisional Headquarters, and Major King took over temporary command. "C" Company's holiday at Petit Sains finished on 5th September, when the company moved to Annequin, where it was engaged in tunnelling under No-Man's-Land on the 32nd Division front. Captain Cole was sent ahead to get the hang of the job. He found that the Tunnelling Company officers thought that, being Pioneers, "C" Company would be fully competent to take over the work and carry on, without more than an occasional visit from them.

Now Captain Cole's railway career gave him no previous experience of tunnelling, and in fact Captain Stamp Taylor and the whole company were equally ignorant. However, nothing daunted, Captain Cole set to work to master the extremely complicated lay-out of the galleries and the purpose of the various saps. After twelve hours of asking questions from patiently helpful R.E. officers, Cole felt prepared to put his Company Commander wise of all that had to be done, including the best method of employing infantry working-parties and of frustrating the efforts of the Boche to blow in the shafts by day or night raids.

Captain Cole was told that the enemy had succeeded shortly before in dropping 50 lb. bombs down the shafts, causing much damage. To prevent him doing this again, "C" Company's Lewis Gunners were placed in posts at the shaft heads, and a little later Lance-Corporal Lockwood and a party of No. 12 Platoon beat off such an attempt.

The work was carried on thus: "Two platoons working day-shift and two working night-shift, not very nice work down in those saps, working twelve hours in candle light. . . . Besides our mining work we made trench-mortar emplacements and repaired trenches, etc."

Captain Cole had but little chance of using his extensive, if hastily acquired, knowledge as he was shortly afterwards sent to the 2nd Army School to absorb the varied knowledge thought necessary for a Company Commander. Lieutenant Robertson and a party from "D" joined the moles.[1]

While the battalion was in Loos, the transport was first at Petit Sains and then at Nœux-les-Mines.

During this period there were not many casualties. On 1st August, No. 1519 Private G. Bruce of "A" was killed by a

---

[1] "C" Company's labours earned the approbation of the Corps Commander, which was communicated on 25th September, 1916.

dud anti-aircraft shell, and two men attached to Divisional Headquarters in Bethune were killed there on 7th, when the enemy shelled that town heavily. 1223 Private Dawson and 353 Private Richardson were wounded, and on the march to Annequin on 30th August Captain Ker's groom, Private A. Scott, lost an arm, a shell bursting in front of his horse.

Battalion Headquarters with "B" Company moved to Le Preol on 30th August, and "A" and "D" joined "C" in Annequin. The transport remained in Nœux-les-Mines.

The battalion was once again with the 32nd Division. Major Oxley returned to the battalion for a short time, but soon left again to take command of another unit, and Major King was gazetted to the command of the battalion 1st September. This involved the following promotions: Captain Stamp Taylor to Second-in-Command, Captain Cole to command of "C," and Captain Kitching to command of "D." On 2nd, the Lewis Gunners, who had been left behind in Loos, rejoined the battalion.

Annequin was about the average village of those parts, and is described as partially destroyed, but very scattered. The billets are described as comfortable; one company "managed to bag a good place for our mess. The two girls at the café, where it is, are quite nice, and, I think, quite virtuous, and one, who is a schoolmistress, speaks English passably. She says my French pronunciation is quite good."

The village was frequently shelled. "However, we found out later that all the shells usually dropped short or went over the house, so we did not get worried."

As the Boche's balloons commanded a good view of the village, walking in the middle of the road and collecting in groups was prohibited, as it always brought on a shell shower. As in most places near the line, the French civilians clung to their homes with wonderful tenacity. "Quite a large family occupied our billet. The grandmother had been twice wounded, but she would not leave the place. . . . They were very good and seemed as though they would do anything for us."

In front of this billet was a fosse, to which Fritz gave much attention, as from it one could observe his line for a long way. "A" was employed on cable trenches, digging a new evacuation trench, repairing and draining Wilson's Way communication trench. We read: "Shelled just before we came away, but no one hurt. Out at 4 a.m. Boche quiet until about 9 a.m.; he got several 5·9's very near No. 4 Platoon." "D" Company was on several jobs—a light railway, a broad-gauge line, and rebuilding front line trenches alongside La Bassée Canal. Eerie spot, "making sniper's post overlooking brickfields in No-Man's-Land." "Wiring in Death's Valley and No-Man's-Land."

"B" Company during this time remained at Le Preol and was responsible for the lowering of the water in the La Bassée Canal, by means of special pumping barges used to counteract the Boche flooding the trenches.

In addition, the company drained two long communication trenches called Wilson's Way and Maison Rouge Alley, from the ruined house of that name, just in front of Cambrin village as far as the support line. It was a long trek from the billets to the trenches, part of it through the much damaged village, and as the weather was warm a little old lady who kept an apple stall "at the end of the communication trench by the church, did a roaring trade. I wonder how long she remained there."

What a number of similar conundrums the war has left. Who was Wilson, after whom the above Way was named? What Dawson gave his name to the unhealthy Corner, near which the advance ration dump was placed near Brieleu in August, 1917? What careless carter dropped the "dirty bucket" at another corner in the same neighbourhood? Had these places no names? or did the first-comers of the Contemptibles not trouble to inquire?

About the middle of September a case of typhoid occurred in the battalion, which led to everyone being inoculated.

On 17th September the whole battalion, with the 1st Dorsetshire Regiment and 206th Field Company, suddenly moved to Acq and Ecoivres in the 17th Corps area. The weather was bad the whole time, and the troops suffered a great deal. The march to Acq was about fifteen miles, but, to everyone's joy, the packs went in lorries. The Lewis Gunners had to push "new gun carts like fish-hawkers. Stayed night under hedges." Others were more fortunate as regards billets, some being in French barrack huts, others in an empty château.

At noon on 18th, carrying their packs, alas! the battalion "moved off to trenches behind Vimy Ridge and near Neuville St. Vaast and Mont St. Eloi, just north of Arras. Trenches in terrible state due to torrential rain. . . . Got wet through from head to foot. Dug-out flooded with water and thick with rats (big ones)." Strange to say, though, the deeper the water got in the trench, the higher everybody's spirits seemed to get. The duck-boards were wobbly and provided much amusement in trying to negotiate them. The rations and blankets did not turn up till about 10 p.m., and then had to be carried from Neuville St. Vaast. "This was no light job as it was a very dark night, and the distance was about half a mile through a winding trench littered with bricks

PLATE XII.

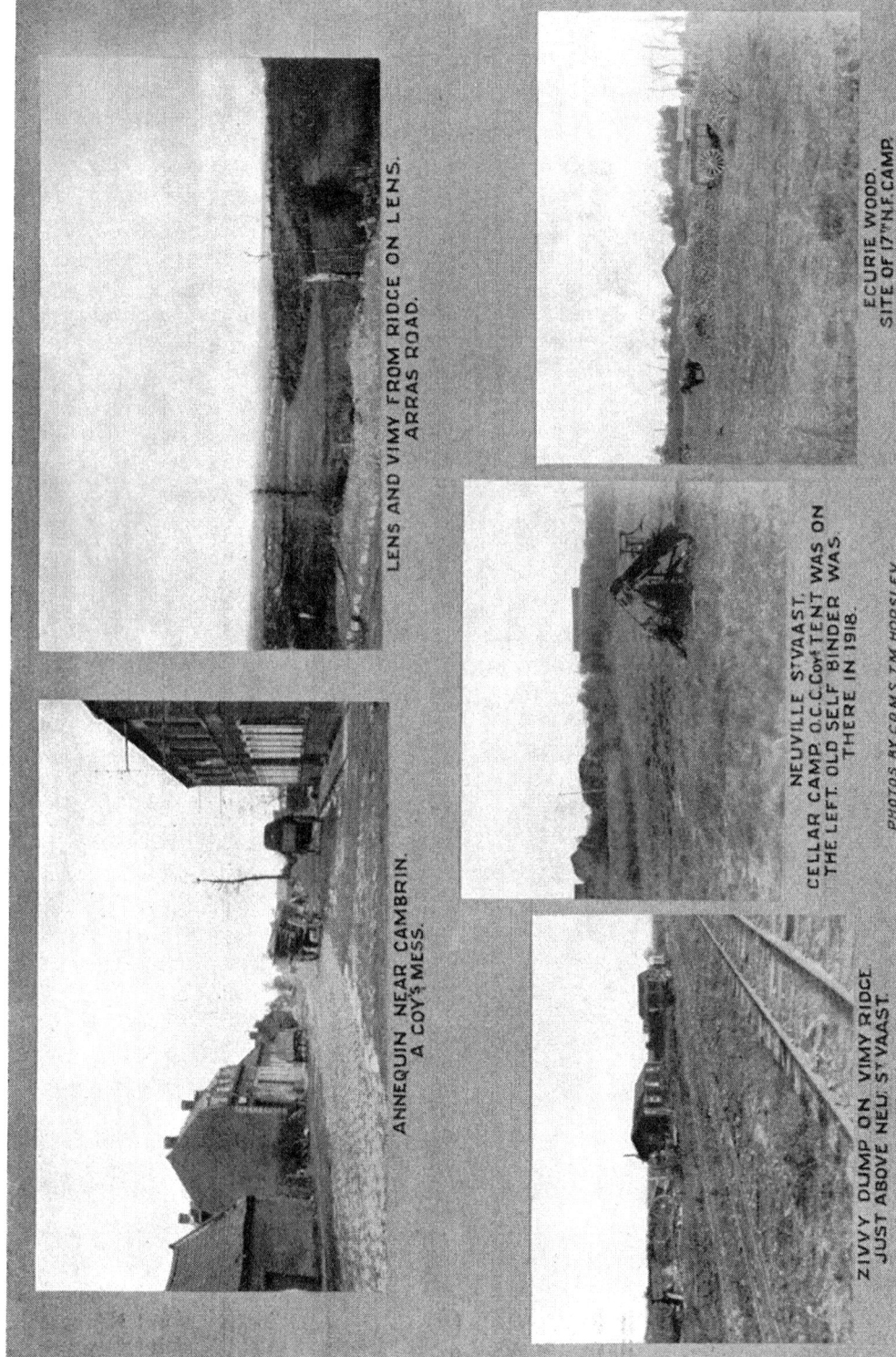

and unstable duck-boards. Every man had to do the best he could as regards cooking them (rations). I believe they did very well. The officers of ' C,' seeking warmth and comfort, joyously seized on a dug-out labelled Cavalry Club. Alas! it smelt, it leaked, and the floor was moist and muddy, but a brazier was got going and garments were dried, their owners the while shivering in their birthday suits."

The next day, " Working with R.E.'s in second line. Received orders to return to Annequin. Waded once more in the dark, with water up to the knees and trousers rolled up. Met some Jocks minus kilts! Trekked once more to Acq. Fed up!"

A further account gives a story that an officer, in directing a fellow-officer (a dour Scot) how to avoid the sump-holes, measured his length (some length) in one of the said sump-holes, which caused the dour Scot to laugh uproariously for a quarter of an hour, and rendered him incapable of giving assistance—he not having dropped a " saxpence."

" 20th September.—Left Acq and marched the fifteen miles over again through heavy downpour of rain. Wet through and beaten to a man." Another version is : " 20th.—Up at 5.30 a.m. Left Acq at 8.40 a.m. for Annequin. Arrived 4 p.m. Eighteen kilos. Glad to get back. Biggest mystery was—Why did we go? " The solution of the mystery was, that information had been received which pointed to the Boche being about to attack, to meet which this force from the 32nd Division was hastily moved up to the threatened point, and, as the attack did not come off, as hastily moved back again. It was hard on all concerned, but these things do happen in war.

During September, the following officers joined the battalion: Captain T. B. Craggs, Lieutenants Hutson and Watson from 28th Northumberland Fusiliers, and Second-Lieutenants E. W. Smith and G. R. Neville from 32nd Northumberland Fusiliers. Captain Craggs left again almost at once to join the 19th Battalion of the regiment.

The battalion was not to stay long in Le Preol and Annequin, for the progress of the battle of the Somme rendered it necessary to increase the railway facilities for bringing up supplies and reinforcements, and among the measures taken for this purpose was the conversion of the 17th Northumberland Fusiliers into a Railway Battalion to work under the Director of Railways. No better selection could have been made, for no battalion of the British Army contained more railway experts.

On the 27th September, " Left Annequin for Bethune, from whence proceeded by rail to Acheux (Somme). Travelled in trucks and got frozen through. Slept all night in a wood, and raining fast. No blankets." Another version: "Early brekker. Left Annequin at 8.30 a.m. to entrain at Bethune. Left B. at noon and arrived at Acheux just after dark. Bivouacked in wood for night. Very pretty sight—men's fires, etc., amongst trees." Another version: "On arrival at Acheux in the darkness, and amid great confusion, much amusement was caused by an officer calling out in peeved tones, 'Where are the officers' chargers?'" The Canadian Y.M.C.A. was patronized by all those who were fortunate enough to find it.

There was a scene of joyous recognition when "B" Company marched on to Bethune platform, for Hero, the company war dog, who had disappeared at Preol, greeted the leading fours with ecstatic barks. He could not tell how he had got lost nor where he'd been, but that he was glad to be back again was very evident, and he took care never to get lost again, but my informant, alas, cannot say what was the old dog's fate after the company was demobbed.

The next day "D" Company records: "28th September.—Marched to Martinsart Wood, where we slept in the open once more. Still raining." "A's" report is: "Moved to Mailly-Maillet at 1 p.m. into huts in wood. Officers in tents. Bombardment simply terrific and practically continuous day and night. Country round about quite interesting."

Headquarters, with "B" and "C" Companies, remained in Acheux Wood, and "We were told to make bivouacs in the wood. Three of us laced our waterproof sheets together and stretched them across uprights, thus forming the roof of our bivouac. The sides were composed of branches interlaced. . . . After four days like this, we were moved into huts in the wood—these had some lively inhabitants who would not be shaken off."

The first experience of the battalion of being "Army Troops" cannot be said to have been very pleasant, but a unit leaving its division was "Nobody's Child" till it got under the sheltering wing of its new parent.

CHAPTER V

RAILWAY WORK ON THE SOMME AND AT BERGUETTE

THE battalion now found itself a unit in Group Five of the Railway Construction Engineers, under command of Colonel C. W. P. Ramsay, C.M.G., working in the Reserve Army area. The other members of the group were the 119th and 227th Railway Companies R.E., with the latter of which the battalion was more closely associated.

The battle of the Somme was in full progress, and the railway system, which had sufficed hitherto, was found to be inadequate for the transport of the large numbers of men and the huge quantities of material now required, and had to be altered and extended. The battalion's share in this work was the conversion of the Beausart-Aveluy line from metre to standard gauge, and later, in November, the extension of the line to Mouquet Farm.

Battalion Headquarters and transport remained at Acheux the whole of October, but the companies were located as near as possible to the scene of their labours, shifting their camps from time to time. " A " started the month in Mailly-Maillet Wood, " a narrow belt of trees three hundred yards wide, which sloped down towards the road. Our quarters were huts, wood-framed and canvas-covered, very old, very dirty, and much out of repair. It rained heavily at night." So " A " was uncomfortable till they had made necessary improvements, in which work Pioneers were especially proficient.

" B " stayed a week in Acheux working with " C " and then marched via Forceville, Hedauville and Northumberland Avenue, which they had helped to make, to Martinsart Wood, where " D " had already made itself comfortable, and the officers of the two companies spent a pleasant evening in " D's " mess. " One has no pleasant memories of the camp at Martinsart Wood. It soon became quagmire, and was noisy, with a brace of six-inch long guns just below and ' Pooping Percy ' at intervals, and as we had nothing but tents and as no fuel could be begged or ' scrounged,' it was very cold."

" We worked on the construction of the line between Mesnil station and the cross-roads near Aveluy. We made great friends with some of the Gunners whose batteries we passed, particularly with one eight-inch How. Battery, in a bank near Mesnil. After this section was finished we went forward and worked between Black Horse Bridge, where the line crossed the Ancre and the Moquet Farm terminus, the line passing through Blighty Wood. Great work there! Some good souvenirs scrounging in old Boche dug-outs. We then had a short spell on the light railway line from Blighty Valley to Ovillers la Boisselle."

"C's" report reads:

"Acheux, Sunday, 1st October.—Put up tents.

"Monday, 2nd.—'C' Company loading railway material 3.30 p.m. to 8 p.m., and each day up to Saturday, 7th, we were engaged loading and unloading railway material in Acheux Yard and at Mailly-Maillet.

"Saturday, 7th.—Up at 6 a.m. Bath 6.15. Moved off to Engelbelmer, five kilometres away, 4.30 p.m. Arrived at 6.30 p.m. Small village and empty of civies."

"D" left Acheux on 28th September for Martinsart Wood, in which it bivouacked to the tune of "a tremendous bombardment of Thiépval."[1]

The next day more permanent quarters were found, 13 Platoon sand-bagging themselves in on Hillside, the other three platoons being in dug-outs. "Bombardment continued, streams of troops, wounded and otherwise, with German helmets, caps, etc., passing by, all in the best of spirits." The Boche did not take this punishment lying down, and I read of "heavy Boche shelling in the wood at 11 p.m. and again at 4 a.m., but few casualties, none among our men." The line, too, was frequently broken by his shells, and one of the battalion's duties was to repair such damage, a not very pleasant task, as the enemy often "dropped his gas shells around." Another far from cushy job was going up with the material train at night from Acheux to Mesnil. The sound of the train was easily audible to the Boche, and he showed that he had heard it in a manner which was most disagreeable to those on the trucks.

The mention of Mesnil will recall some exciting moments to many of the battalion, among whom it earned the name of "Hell with the lid off." Sometimes the battalion had the assistance of infantry carrying-parties. "Great work. In these three days we have laid one and a half miles of track. The infantry are splendid. They tumbled to the job fine, and had sleepers, spikes, etc., all placed in required numbers ready ahead for laying." Much

---

[1] Thiépval was captured on 26th September by 18th Division of 5th Army, and Stuff Redoubt and part of Schwaben Redoubt captured on 27th September by 11th and 18th Divisions.

of the work had to be done by night, for obvious reasons, but the progress was well up to schedule, and on 13th October I read, " Worked till 11 p.m. in order to close gap. Material, etc., just worked out correctly in spite of being Friday and the 13th. Had only to cut one rail to make closure at Auchenvillers." Although all were working at high pressure, one or two got days off occasionally. " Rode to Albert, which place was full of troops. Visited our old favourite café, and strange to say found the owner, Madame Brocquart, in for the day from Amiens, examining the effects of shell-fire in her domain, from which she was driven out three months ago. She asked us to call again after she'd got things in order."

On the 20th October " A " Company reports: " Rudely awakened at 5.30 a.m. by Boche shelling our camp; one dud practically under my tent. Boche hit two huts, causing twenty-three casualties in our company, and almost as many among Royal Scots. Eleven of ours were slight, and two killed. Plumptre was wounded slightly in the arm. Shelling continuous for a quarter of an hour." From another source I learn that one of those killed was a lad named Little, who had given up his leave that week to a man whose wife was seriously ill. Little was the third of three brothers to be killed within two weeks.[1] What made the affair especially vexatious was that the company would in the ordinary course of events have been out at work at that time, but having done a particularly good day's work the day before had been given a day off by a " brass hat from Railway Headquarters," who had come to see the progress of the work.

Captain Ker decided to move the camp " about three-quarters of a mile behind this place, across the valley on the reverse side of the rise amongst some bushes and undergrowth," so that when the Boche repeated his performance the next morning " A " could afford to treat it with contempt. Captain Ker left that day on leave and never returned to the battalion, as a Medical Board, before which he was sent, refused to pass him as fit for general service.

This was a serious loss to the battalion, but, of course, his company felt it most, for they best knew the value of their Commander. Lieutenant Plumptre, who was back at duty the next day, took command of " A " until Captain Glendinning's return from the 32nd Divisional School, early in November. On the 25th of that month Captain Kitching handed over the command of " D " to Lieutenant Douglas, and went to G.H.Q. in Railway Transportation

---

[1] Other names given are: A. R. Smith, Corporal Dunn, killed; Atkinson, Sergeant Smith, Sergeant Morris, Corporal Ridley, wounded.

Department. Battalion Headquarters moved to No. 2 Quarry, North Avenue, where it remained till 23rd January.

My friend in the transport says: "I often remember an incident that occurred when the transport was stationed in Acheux. One of our G.S. wagons went down to Martinsart Wood with rations, etc., and I waited till they came back. This wagon had a team of four animals, ride and drive, riding the near side animal and leading the off side one. When they came back, one called Peck said 'We did come along, Sergeant,' and on looking round the wagon we found that the two rear wheels were missing, and when daylight came we found the wheels a good two and a half miles back, so they must have been in a hurry."

There were many rumours going round as to exactly what was going to happen to the battalion. Some said it was about to become a Labour Battalion, pure and simple. All doubts were solved on 14th November, when orders were received to convert it into a Railway Pioneer Battalion. The various jobs on which the battalion worked during the period after the completion of the Aveluy-Mouquet Farm line were: Maintenance of that line from Beausart to Aveluy; making railway from Courcelles Loop on above line to Hebuterne; maintenance of Valheureux siding, Candas, Candas-Acheux line to mile seven and from Varennes East to Euston Dump, Colin Camps; completion of transhipping siding north of Mesnil; completion of Mailly-Maillet gun siding and relaying Beausart; Aveluy metre gauge track.

The battalion worked mainly with the 277th Railway Company, but "A" worked from 26th October to 11th November on a sixty centimetre track from Aveluy to Pozières with 119th Company, working parties being provided by the Life Guards.

The job took them over historic ground, and the changes that had occurred in the last few months were startling. The officer in charge of the advance party thought he knew of a nice quiet spot on which the company might camp, but on arrival found it "covered with railway sidings, store-houses, work-shops, huge piles of materials—a humming hive of industry." The old bivouac ground in the grounds of Aveluy Château was found occupied by the R.O.D. hut alongside a broad gauge siding. Blighty Valley no longer caused any tremors as they laid their line across it. A station was made in the middle of what had been Ovillers la Boisselle, the taking of which stronghold cost us so many lives, and on 7th November Pozières was reached. The Boche resented their operations and greeted them with a salvo as they entered the ruins, causing two casualties. My informant sagely remarks in his diary, "I feel truly thankful I have not been offered the job of station-master."

The next few days were occupied in completing the station and yard, the work being frequently interfered with by shell showers, the last of which caught Lieutenant Neville's party, who were finishing the ballasting, on the 11th, and caused twelve casualties, of which two were fatal.

The following entries are interesting :

" 12th November.—The bombardment, which had been going on for several days, now seems to intensify gradually. I am thinking of the poor fellows who are to attack at dawn to-morrow.

" 13th November.—Attack began about 5.45 a.m. Roused by terrific noise of bombardment—worst I've yet heard. The Boche must have got pretty big hell. This continued very heavy all the morning, and not quite so bad in the afternoon. About 8 a.m. large batches of prisoners began to pass our camp, and a considerable number of our own wounded, though not so many as we had expected. The prisoners are not at all a bad-looking set of men, though a few are very young, whilst others are quite the reverse. During the day about forty officers passed, amongst whom was one of evidently high rank. The officers looked a pretty good type on the whole, but naturally rather dejected. Total prisoners passed our camp, about 1,200. One of our men, T——y W——d, in search of souvenirs, approached the aforementioned officer of high rank and pow-wowed with him in broken French, only to be told, in perfect English, to ' Go to h——! ' The bombardment continued throughout the night, rather desultorily, and commenced with renewed violence about 6 a.m. More wounded and a few prisoners pass down the road during the morning.

" 14th.—Heavy bombardment during the afternoon. Understand each gun fired twenty-five gas shells, followed immediately by twenty-five shrapnel. Rumours are that Beaumont Hamel, Beaucourt and St. Pierre Divion all in our hands. 39th Division seem to have done awfully well. We have about one gun to every eleven yards of enemy trench. Capture of Beaumont Hamel and Beaucourt confirmed in Corps Intelligence. North of this nothing seems to have been captured on account of bad state of ground. Fighting still goes on.[1]

" 15th November.—Heard that an Army Chaplain and six Irish-

---

[1] On 13th November, 19th Division cleared trenches north of Schwaben and Stuff Redoubts, 39th Division took its farthest objective at St. Pierre Divion, 63rd Division advanced to Beaucourt, 51st Division after heavy fighting took Beaumont Hamel, north of which 2nd Division was partially successful. Heavy ground prevented the capture of Serre, but on 14th Beaucourt was taken and secured by 51st and 2nd Divisions, pushing along spur north-east of Beaumont Hamel. Over seven thousand prisoners were taken in the operations.

men captured four hundred prisoners in dug-out at Beaumont Hamel—good effort. The attack seems to have been a great surprise to the enemy."

After Beaumont Hamel had been captured by the gallant 51st Division the tide of war rolled eastwards, and the battalion only got a little desultory shelling.

"B" Company's scribe continues: "On 6th December 'B' and 'D' Companies moved northwards over our own line by train via Mesnil. 'D' went to a spot just north of Beaussart. 'B' built itself a camp between Beaussart and Mailly-Maillet. We had Nissen huts instead of tents, and were thankful for the warmer quarters. Our work now was maintenance and construction of the Mailly-Maillet gun siding. 'B' Company's officers at this time were Captains Mackenzie and Lakeman, Lieutenant Mitchell, Second-Lieutenants Jellico and Smith."

A "D" Company diary reads:

"30th September.—Company commenced making broad gauge line Aveluy to Acheux.

"To 22nd October ditto. Big bombardment at night near Bapaume. Hundreds of prisoners.[1]

"To 6th December.—Working on railway between Charing Cross (Pioneer Road) and Blighty Wood (old No-Man's-Land). Packing sleepers, etc., and digging chalk out of quarry near Tramway Corner for ballast.

"7th December.—'B' and 'D' Companies moved to temporary camp near Mailly-Maillet (Colin Camps) to lay gun sidings. Billeted in Nissen (Bow) huts. Not bad.

"17th December.—Jobs finished and moved farther behind line to Raincheval in huts. Typical infantry 'rest,' navvying in general.

"25th December.—Christmas Day. Sports and day off. In village at night.

"31st December.—New Year's Eve. No lights out. Grand time in village and camp. *Bonne année* with civies."

Another account—all joined in concert in the village. No piano, but very jolly time. The Sergeants and men afterwards serenaded the Officers' Mess with carols. The Canteen Funds had provided the men an excellent dinner, not forgetting the turkeys.

I won't say whence I have culled the following: "Went to canteen meeting at night, where nearly everyone talked rot."

---

[1] Regina trench, west of Courcelette-Pys road, stormed by 15th, 18th, 19th and 4th Canadian Division on 21st October.

I find constant reference to work at the quarry—I presume the one above referred to, which gave the battalion much employment—from 21st November onwards. Sport was not altogether neglected.

"20th December.—Company holiday. Hutson and I played footer, 1 and 2 *v.* 3 and 4 in the afternoon.

"21st December.—Very stiff from yesterday. Out with Hutson all day at quarry.

"24th December.—Out at quarry with Hutson. Sergeants from company serenaded us after dinner with Christmas Carols.

"25th December.—Played Sergeants and Officers of 'A' against 'C' in morning. 'A' won 3—0. Watched company team in afternoon. We won again 4—2. 'C' Company officers dined with us. Had a jolly good dinner. Joint smoker, 'A' and 'C' Officers and Sergeants—not very exciting."

About 16th January, 1917, Second-Lieutenant Jellicoe, with seventy men of "B," left the battalion temporarily for work with the Railway Operating Department, and another party of similar strength, under command of Second-Lieutenant Smith, went to assist in working the light railways of the 1st Army behind Vimy Ridge. This job turned out interesting; the billets were good and "we were well looked after," so that in spite of the long hard frost of that spring, which most of us remember, they enjoyed their time, although for some reason known only to the Powers that were, the detachment was sent from Acheux to Bethune via Abbeville, Etaples, Calais, and St. Omer, which took them thirty-six hours, whereas in the previous September the same journey, only in the opposite direction, had occupied seven or eight hours. Both these detachments remained away some three weeks and rejoined the battalion after it had moved to Isbergues.

The following account of the move of "A" to Candas cannot be improved: "6th January.—About 7.30 p.m. we moved off, but on the Mesnil Valley the old engine refused to go farther up the big gradient there till she got her wind. This was the third stop for steam. Whilst standing, Brother Boche became unpleasant, and shelled Mesnil Valley with Pooping Percy (high velocity 5·9 gun) No shells very near train fortunately. Old Hutson (Moonface) was going on leave next day so hadn't much to say. We, Drury and I, sang (?) to cheer him up. Here the guard discovered that his assistant had left three wagon brakes on, and the language flowed. After this we got right away to Beaussart, where we discovered there was no engine to take us on, and after parleying with R.T.O. (who had not been advised of a move by headquarters and did not like us going into his office *en masse*, three of us anyway) we were pushed into a R.E. dump siding. (Our reputation for acquiring material hadn't reached this R.T.O. evidently.) It was putting temptation in our way, as we had no roof to our mess; we have now a beautiful mess roofed with new corrugated iron. Having thoroughly awakened everyone to the fact that a company of the great 17th Northumberland Fusiliers was stranded we retired to our box wagon, where we had our beds bunked and a nice little table and stove. The servants were very active and gave us a splendid meal. Two hours later the R.T.O. (somewhat chastened) informed us an engine had arrived." The rest of the journey was performed without adventure, and " Monday, 8th, 2 a.m., Hutson went on leave."

" 21st January.—Hutson arrived at 2.30 a.m. and woke me up; he's full of his happy experience."

The company's stay at Candas appears to have been very pleasant. I read: " This is a cushy job and nobody seems to be in a hurry." The work was railway construction in conjunction with 277th Railway Company. The only incidents of importance recorded are the burning down of the C.S.M.'s hut on 8th February—" Thank goodness the company papers were not in it "—and a prolonged stoppage of the mails, for which no cause is given. This naturally caused some caustic remarks in the letters which the Platoon Commanders had to censor, but the camp was all smiles when, on 11th February, sixteen bags of mails arrived. " I got twenty-two letters and four parcels, being second to ——, who got twenty-eight letters and three parcels, and then the blighter groused because he expected more." " Needless to say he has a girl."

The company remained on its " cushy job " till 16th February, on which day entrained for Berguette, arriving there at 4 a.m., but did not wake until 7, when it marched to billets at Houleron. The rest of the battalion was found to be close by, having arrived at the end of January. The headquarters were in Isbergues, " B " at La Lacque, " C " at Houleron, and " D " at La Roupie. " C " Company were particularly fortunate in their billets, especially those billeted in the farm of Monsieur Vasseur Delplace, where the officers had their mess, Monsieur and Madame, not to mention the two Mademoiselles, were kindness itself.

The work on which the battalion was employed for over two months was the construction of light railway workshops. Just before, on 30th December, Captain Glendinning had been sent with Lieutenant Garvie and twenty-eight other ranks, specially selected according to trades, to do the preliminary work. After the usual journey round France, in a slow train, and a night in the waiting-room of the station at Thiennes, the party got busy. The first work to be done was putting up a hut for keeping tools, and use as an office, etc. The site of the shops was between the railway line and one of the main canals. To this site a broad gauge had to be laid from Isbergues station, with numerous sidings for both broad and narrow gauge track. Except for two bridges over a public road, and the canal, which were erected by a railway construction company, the whole of the work, from the setting out and levelling to the driving of the last spike of this line, was done by the battalion. The preliminary operations were completed about 20th January, and the battalion then arrived.

The shops covered an area of about 75,000 sq. ft.; they were under one roof of five spans supported by columns on concrete foundations. Plans of the shops and of the various machines were provided, and the work had to be carried out with great care, according to the plan, as the whole of the sections, columns, etc., were sent out from England in barges which were towed across the Channel and brought right up to the site by canal, all pieces being carefully numbered so as to assist in the erection. The concrete foundations had to be very accurately set out, and holding-down-bolts fixed in them ready for the columns, roof trusses, etc. At each end of the shops were large doors, and broad and narrow gauge tracks were laid right into them. Heavy concrete foundations had to be put in for the lathes, drilling machines, etc., which were to occupy one side. In addition to the shops, many other works had to be carried out, such as huts for workmen, roads, drains, and a water supply system. The job was completed by the last day of March, and handed over to a Mechanical Company, R.E., which was to put up the machines and run them. A gang of Hun prisoners worked well all the time.

So much for work. As regards play I find: " Visited Aire, six kilometres distant, once or twice. Discovered pastry shop in Molingham, resulting in nightly visits with —— and little —— for sing-songs. Hostesses, Joanne, Marthe, Simone, Maria, etc. Bon. Helped pit girls push tubs dinner-times. Novel experience."
" 2nd April.—Spent last night in the pastry shop. Said au revoir to the girls in the Boulangerie." " We suffered a little with the severe weather; our bread and butter, and jam, froze quickly, and what an awful job it was to shave. Despite these little drawbacks, I think we all enjoyed our stay at Houleron, and most of the boys will always remember this place, as the civilians were so good to us, and gave us as good a time as possible under the circumstances." Apparently the gay lads of the north country did their share towards cementing the *entente cordiale*, for when the sad day for parting came " most of the civilians got up to see us leave (at 4 a.m.), and how the Mademoiselles did cry."

Extracts from War Diary for this Period

5.11.16. Lieutenant Blair to Flying Corps.
24.11.16. Lieutenant P. Dalbin rejoined from C.R.E., 32nd Division.
9.11.16. Private A Taplin 17/871 killed by shell-fire at Pozières.
13.11.16. 17/1095 Private J. Johnson wounded by shell, Bouzincourt.
18.12.16. Draft of 150 arrives.
21.12.16. Draft of 75 arrives.
22.12.16. Captain and Adjutant G. W. Martin to G.H.Q. for temporary duty with D.G.T.
13.1.17. 17/1095 Private J. Johnson, " B " Company, died. See above, 13th November.
30.3.17. Captain and Adjutant G. W. Martin rejoins from G.H.Q.

CHAPTER VI

FIVE MONTHS IN THE SALIENT

THE march from billets to Berguette station, where the companies entrained, was performed in a blinding snowstorm, which, however, was over before the Battalion Headquarters left by road.

After a three hours halt in Hazebrouck, where the fortunate ones had a " ripping lunch," the journey was resumed, and Poperinghe was reached about 3 p.m. One informant notes that the journey was made in carriages, not our old friends " 8 chevaux 40 hommes," so in spite of the sad parting and the uncomfortable start, everyone arrived in a happy state of mind. " Pop," in those days, was by no means a bad spot in which to spend a day or two, so no one was sorry to hear that " orders have been changed and we are not going on to the job we expected, and nobody seems to know what we are going to do; meantime we are to stay in Pop. Not so bad." It was true that, on examination, " we find many of the buildings knocked about by shell-fire, but they are scattered in many places, which cheers us." For officers there is a club, which, if not quite up to Pall Mall form, is, " to us from the Somme, something new," and during the next few months there are many entries such as " jolly good dinner at the Officers' Club "; " dined at Cyril—decent dinner."

Here, too, was Talbot House, that peaceful oasis in which weary, war-worn men could always find rest and comfort, and, for a time at least, forget the beastliness of war. " Easter Day. Went to Communion at Talbot House at 8.15 a.m. Ripping little church—beautiful service. It was a gorgeous morning and the birds were singing gaily."

The 55th Division Concert Party had a revue running, to which some went. " We find we have picked the right night, for the building is a blaze of red tabs and gilt, from the humble brigade caps to Lieutenant-Generals. S. and I, however, pass in unnoticed. A very good show. The British soldier is a wonder; here, about ten miles behind the line, and the worst point of the whole front, we see a show that beats many I have seen at home."

Whatever would we have done without lorries? " Free day, so slipped off to Abeele (5 ks. 5); jumped a lorry, to see Mamma A.

and family; met Alice and Marie Louise. Eggs for tea, and returned to Pop." And I bet he felt all the better for the trip and the little spell of peaceful comfort by Mamma A.'s hospitable fireside, even if jumping lorries was strictly forbidden.

The battalion's holiday only lasted one day—having arrived on 3rd April, it started work on the Great Midland Railway on the 5th. This was to be a broad gauge line, extending from near Peselhoek, about two miles north of Poperinghe, eastwards to the Yser Canal, a distance of about ten thousand yards, beyond which its destination depended on the success of operations to be undertaken at some future date, of which the battalion knew nothing at the time, but to the success of which this line was essential. The battalion was now a unit of Railway Construction Engineers, Group II, working under the orders of the Chief Engineer's 8th Corps.

The officers commanding the four companies of the 17th Northumberland Fusiliers were each made responsible, by Lieutenant-Colonel King, for the construction of a certain length of line, the skilled work being carried out by their men, while, for unskilled labour, to each company there was attached one or more companies of Infantry or Labour Battalions.

The work occupied the battalion until the middle of June. During this time the headquarters and " A " and " B " Companies were in " P " Camp, " a wooden-built hutment off the Pop-Western Road, in a wood. The quarters and general accommodation we find to be first class." " C " Company was also in a wood in " D " Camp, farther east; and " D " Company was still farther east, in " Les Trois Tours," about two miles out of Ypres and a half mile from Brielen, billeted in an old farm-house. Many pleasant hours, however, were spent playing water-polo in the moat of the Trois Tours Château in spite of sometimes having to leave the water very hurriedly through the attention paid them by the old Boche. The whole of the area was subject to shell showers, but, naturally, " C " and " D," working near the front, got more than the rest of the battalion. " C " Company reports that they were several times shelled off the job, and the following extracts from " D " Company's correspondent show that they were not allowed to forget that there was a war on.

" 24th April.—Billets and batteries round heavily shelled by 5·9's. Four of our lot wounded.

" 1st May.—Great aerial battle above us—two Germans down and one of ours. Fine sight. Commenced night work near Ypres.

" 3rd May.—Gas attack by Jerry. Had to walk two miles in dark with gas mask on! Gas blew over towards Nieuport.

" 4th May.—Another gas alarm, but nothing doing.

"5th May.—Germans set neighbouring farm-house on fire—big blaze.

"14th May.—German 'plane set fire to Belgian balloon near Dixmude. 'Plane returned over our billet about three hundred feet up. Six-inch guns turned on him, and our rifles. Brought him down in No-Man's-Land."

"20th May.—Bank Holiday (in England)! Gas alarm at 2 a.m. Had box respirators on in bed. Up at 3.30 a.m. and back to the canal bank.

"1st June.—Gas alarm 2 a.m. in bed. Lachrymatory shells round billet and batteries. Captain Lakeman and two or three men slightly gassed.

"11th June.—Fritz bombarded batteries near billet. Several of our " B " Company men,[1] attached to " D," badly wounded, and one trench-mortar man killed."

The country was fairly level, but there were many ditches, small streams, and fences. The two main obstacles were, however, the Poperinghe and Yser Canals. The former, which was in " A " Company's section, lay in a wide depression, the water level being 22 feet below rail level. A timber pile bridge with a span of 120 feet was erected, the construction gang being under the immediate charge of Sergeant Oliver. The filling on each side took a great deal of earth. On 30th April, " we have put in 60,000 cubic feet to-day, but it seems to go nowhere." However, the earthwork was finished in fourteen days, and on 21st May the bridge was crossed by the first train, and reported quite satisfactory.

" A " had also to construct a very considerable station at Peselhoek, with several sidings. During this period, one warm evening, the officers—luxurious fellows—were taking their after-dinner coffee under some trees, soothed by a tune on the gramophone, when " three nasty bangs, and bits fly round. Then the sound of an aeroplane, as Fritz starts up and goes home. He must have planed down with his engine off, guided by our lamp." When the excitement was over, it was noticed that though some " great brain had turned off the gramophone, no one had turned out the lamp." That was their night out, for at " 1.30 a.m. we were roused by a tremendous din—Gas! We sit, the whole company, out on the duck-boards, clad in various degrees of undress, from pyjamas with orange spots on, to an army blanket."

" B " about this time moved up to " D " camp, and one night " gas alarm disturbed our rest." Lieutenant Marple kept us all cheerful with Geo. Formby's " I've got a sore chest to-night, boys."

The Yser Canal was broad and deep, and the spoil of the

[1] No. 6 Platoon.

original construction had been piled up high on either bank. These two mounds, some 30 feet high, had to be cut through, and an embankment thrown across the canal, which was nearly dry. The German front line was only about 1,800 yards distant, and the canal banks were under observation from High Redoubt and other points, so that it was not unreasonable to expect that the operations of cutting through the mounds and filling in the canal, which must involve collecting a large number of men in a very small area, would attract unfavourable attention from the Boche gunners, but, by a skilful and extensive use of camouflage, " D " Company managed the job without any casualties.

" 6th-13th May.—Filling in Yser Canal for railway and tanks. Task work—one hundred and fifty barrows per day per man. A big job. Working three shifts—4 a.m., 10.30 p.m. Signs of an advance on our part brewing."

On 23rd May Second-Lieutenants Jellicoe and Brisley left to join the Indian Army. They were treated to a farewell dinner to which ten sat down, and a correspondent describes the evening as " tall." Brielen was not a place to which one resorted for pleasure in those days, for the Boche gunners disliked it, but Lieutenant Douglas, having occasion to pass through the village one morning, was rewarded by meeting the Prince of Wales, whose duties had also brought him to that unhealthy locality.

By 12th June the Great Midland Railway was completed, and the battalion was put on to light railways, working under the Assistant Director Light Railways (V). I have mentioned that the battalion had been assisted by various other units of Infantry and Labour Battalions. It is pleasing to remember the co-operation was of a most friendly nature. Such references to the work of these units as the following are frequent: " Queen's Labour Company commenced work with us. . . . Very good workers." " The officers of the Cambridge Regiment, which has been our working-party on the job, dined with us. . . . They are a fine lot, and their men have worked with us splendidly."

The light railway system in this area was well developed, and in view of the forthcoming offensive, arrangements were made on a large scale for its extension, as rapidly as, it was hoped, our assaulting troops would drive back the Boche, but at the time that the Great Midland was completed, " Z " day was still unknown to us—maybe it had not even been fixed. In the meantime, the responsible powers found employment for the battalion on various useful tasks. " D " Company, which had been in the forward area during the last two and a half months, was employed in the safe regions north of " P " Camp. " B " and " C " were at " D "

PLATE XIII.

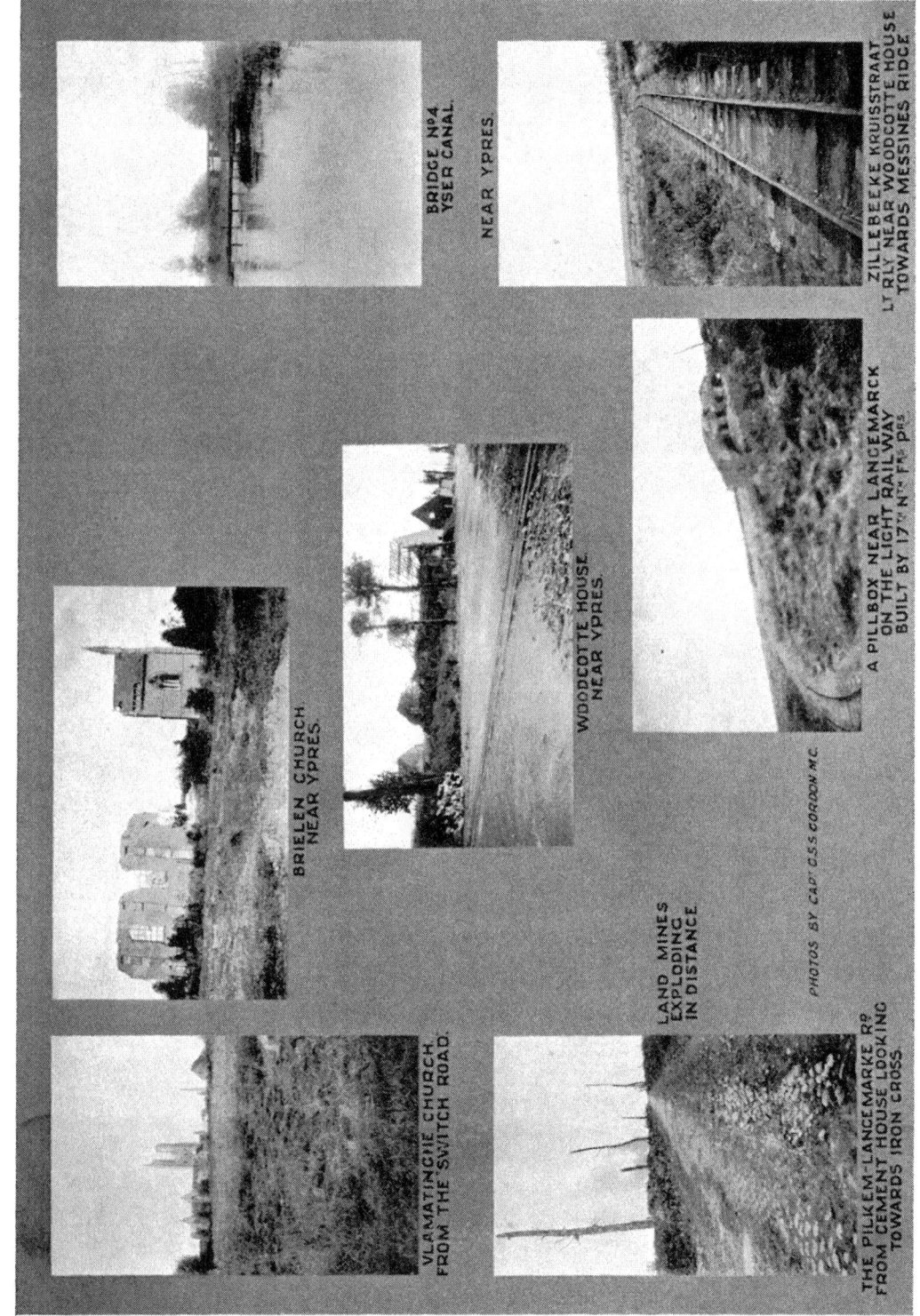

PLATE XIV.

Camp, while "A," which had the safe spot on the Great Midland, was sent forward, and the entry, " Glen thinks our new job is a very rough one," records the result of the preliminary inspection by O.C. "A."

"D" Company, however, was not entirely neglected by the Boche, and the term "safe," applied above to the scene of its labours, must not be taken too literally.

"19th June.—At Church Army Hut Cinema. Germans dropped shells around during show, so returned to camp.

"24th June.—Germans shelled us out of the huts in the rain.

"27th June.—German 'plane dropped three bombs near our camp at daybreak, also shelled horse-lines near us and killed seventeen horses.

"4th July.—Two men killed and six wounded in our camp, through shell hitting hut.

"7th July.—Jack King and Tommy North badly wounded by 5·9, near International Corner. Jack King to Blighty with shattered leg."

However, the diary contains pleasanter entries, such as "Slipped off to Abeele to see the Famille A." "Visited Abeele with Tommy Howard to see the A——s." "To Pop for baths. Visited Tivoli. Good show, including Du Collion, the ladder tongue-twister."

"B" and "C" were doing "a lot of Decauville work in various areas between Poperinghe and Ypres and Elverdinghe. Working at all hours." "A's" job turned as rough as expected. For a day or two the company journeyed to and from the work in buses, but this took too much time, so on 14th June it moved to a camp near the job, which does not seem to have been a very pleasant spot on which to live under canvas. "An open area behind which runs a belt of thick hedge, and in the belt are a nice collection, 9·2 howitzers and sixty-pounders. We get all the noise and all the short ones. The first night we suffer from noise, though one big one from Fritz lands in our horse-lines, and the battalion now requires four new heavy draught."

On the way up to this pleasant resting-place 1 and 2 Platoons got caught in a shell shower, and lost four wounded, of whom one—Langhorne—subsequently died. The job consisted of extending the light railway from Dickebusch towards our newly advanced positions near Battle Wood. For obvious reasons, work had to be carried out at night. The following may be taken as typical of the way "A" spent its time: "Left camp at 1 a.m. to commence formation beyond road at Woodcote House. Boche sent over gas shells as we went up. Rather a job finding pegs and setting out in

E

dark. Boche balloons up at dawn, overlooking us. He sent a good many H.E. shells over between 6.30 and 7.15, and we had to clear out—one man slightly wounded. Spent rest of day in pyjamas, sleeping out on the grass." It was not always possible to sleep. " Up nearly all night, as the Boche scattered stuff very close to our camp. One man of ours hit, but several casualties to men and horses in the immediate vicinity. Drury walks into the pond." There are many allusions to the destruction of our " sausages " by the enemy's airman, which calls forth the remark, " The Boche is too cocky these days."

" C " Company was called on to assist in the good work " to lay the track to road at Woodcote House," which work " brought us into warm quarters." On 22nd June the company moved back to " D " Camp.

" B " Company left " D " Camp on 23rd for work farther north, and " spent a few days in the woods north of Woesten on the Z system of light railways. Very quiet in day-time. Terribly rackety nights. Making new lines apparently to help feed the French troops on our immediate left." " C " followed a few days later, " to a field about five kilometres from Poperinghe. Here we did Decauville work around Woesten. In the same field there was a battalion of Maori troops—Pioneers—and fine fellows they were. Every spare minute they had they seemed to be playing Rugby." The variety of peoples collected around here was wonderful. " Plenty of Aussies about, also Chinks and Nigger B.W.I.'s."

The time had now come for making final preparations for the battalion's share in the big push, arranged to commence on 31st July. A training camp for units concerned in the construction of the projected light railways had been established near Watou, and to this detachments were sent in rotation. Here all sorts of tips for the rapid laying of light lines were shown, and different units demonstrated their special schemes. It was a very pleasant interlude. Well out of reach of shells, and not often visited by these pests of the night—the bomb-dropping aeroplanes—all were able to enjoy life and meeting men of other regiments. The instruction was not too strenuous, and some apparently thought they had little to learn. " Went to demonstration in the afternoon, but H. and I got bored, so we cleared out and got a lift to Pop. Very merry evening, too. I am enjoying our half training, half rest, as the C.O. calls it, and we have quite a nice camp."

Lieutenant-Colonel King was appointed to command the 18th Corps Light Railways Advance. The troops under his command were: 17th Northumberland Fusiliers, 18th Northumberland Fusiliers, " A " Company 1/8th Royal Scots, " A " Company

6th East Yorks, " B " Company 13th Gloucesters, " B " Company 5th Royal Sussex, and the 172nd, 49th and 148th Labour Companies, totalling 3,913 all ranks.

The 18th Northumberland Fusiliers arrived in the first week in July, and camped in Crombeke Wood. Colonel King decided that the best method of organizing the force at his disposal was to amalgamate the 17th and 18th for working purposes, and divide them into two shifts, each of which would work eight hours on the job. Each shift was organized into the following gangs: Survey, Demolition and Bridging, Formation, Plate-laying, Ballasters, Crossing Loops, Police, Maintenance New Lines, Maintenance Old Lines and Traffic. During July the two battalions worked together, and the 18th men and officers did their best to imbibe as much of the art of railway making as possible from their opposite numbers. The greatest good-will existed between the battalions throughout the time they worked together. The other units of Colonel King's command arrived later, and were divided between the two shifts as was found necessary. Captains Glendinning and Cole were in charge of the work of the shifts, while Major Sweet and Captain Dodsworth, of the 18th, looked to the " Q " duties. The rations for the Pioneer units were drawn in bulk by Lieutenant and Quartermaster A. G. Tindill, and sent forward by lorries to the forward ration dump, which was under charge of Lieutenant and Quartermaster A. R. O. Draper, 18th Northumberland Fusiliers,[1] who issued the rations to shifts and any detached parties. Each shift had its own body of cooks, and each gang bivouacked and messed together. Although the system involved the breaking up, temporarily, of platoons and companies, yet it worked well. The gang became, for the time being, the unit intsead of the platoon.

The work allotted to Colonel King's column was to carry forward the light railway, which had been completed as far as the Yser Canal, which it reached at the same point as the Great Midland Railway, as fast as the progress of the attack permitted. The alignment had been approximately decided as far as our front line, and beyond that the maps supplied us were marked with a blue line, showing the anticipated course of the line to St. Julien, and on to the edge of the map.

Every contingency that could be foreseen was provided for, and the orders were full and explicit, and amended not infrequently, as was usual in such cases.

Just before " Z " day there was a mishap. The Ballasters of

---

[1] Lieutenant Draper was killed in Bailleul on 13th April, 1918.

No. 1 shift went up on the morning of 29th July, and as they were returning they were caught by a shell at Mission Junction, and there were forty-seven casualties, several of them fatal.

Zero was 6 a.m. on 31st July, and so certain were the Little Tin Gods that all would go well, that the column was ordered to advance from " P " Camp at 6.15, so as to be ready to begin work without any delay.

At five minutes to six the guns all speak together " as though each battery—light, medium, heavy—were connected to one button." No. 1 shift moves forward at 6.15, as far as Mission Junction, and as the news is good, goes on to the canal. " No shells coming over; Fritz must be busy moving his guns. So we get the shovels going. By 8 a.m. have some three hundred men working—well spread out—and also a party working on the fill at canal, also at gap through the canal bank (made by ' D ' Company); this, of course, has to be widened to take the extra light railway. This always was a danger spot, and it is here that we expected a very nasty time. But not a sound. All round us is a busy scene; troops, guns and ammunition moving forward—splendid. 10 a.m., news from wounded. We have taken St. Julien, so we get all men out ahead. A lot of Huns, guarded by two Jocks, just passed. 10.35 a.m. We have now got a length of rail across the fill, and several tip wagons running, bringing earth from borrow pits, so at last the fill shows signs of growing. The immediate jump off through the gap is an awful mess of shell-holes and water, but we drain off and fill sand-bags and build them in solid, which gives us a good foundation quickly. 12 o'clock already! No. 2 shift arrives and we hand over and get back to bivies, which have been moved forward to about half a mile behind the canal. Very tired."

The advanced ration dump was established near Dawson's Corner early in the day, and the shift's bivies were round Agadir. The second shift had the same luck, and got through the day without any heavy casualties.

The attack had gone well on our front, but not so well on our right. St. Julien, the first objective of our little railway, was said to have been occupied. So all went to bed hoping great things, which, alas, were not to come to pass.

" 1st August, 3.30 a.m.—Very dark, and worse, a fine rain falling. Just our luck—and just Fritz's luck. Rain. Just what Fritz has been praying for." Though the rain stopped about 10 a.m. and the sun came out strongly for a short time, it was slow work; the earth was too wet to " throw," and much draining was needed. Still, when relieved at 12.30 by the second shift, No. 1 had " some five hundred yards of formation finished, and another three hundred yards finishing touches only. Another three hundred yards is showing signs. The fill (across the canal) is a good four feet wider."

A second attack was launched at 6 a.m. on this day. "I talk with a Jock. Not going so well to-day. The ground is awful; all shell-holes, mud, and water. Fritz seems to have machine-guns everywhere—and yon Steenbeek is rising fast."

No. 2 shift lost about forty men from a single shell falling among the men working in the cutting. The battalion was lucky, the losses being chiefly among the Gloucester Pioneers. This incident showed how difficult the Boche might have made our job had he kept even one gun firing on this point. It is hard to understand why he did not, for the broad gauge and light railway lines had been laid up the canal, and the embankment to carry them across it made a fortnight or more before the " push " started, and anyone with a little imagination might have foreseen that no time would be lost in carrying the lines forward, as soon as the attack was launched.

Partly to avoid the working-parties having to go through this dangerous defile twice a day, and partly to save time, the Shifts' Camps were moved forward across the canal, to a spot a short way south-east of Burnt Farm, on 3rd August, but they were brought back on 5th, as the men got no rest, the camp being very near several of our batteries, which fired all night, and on the night of 4th/5th there were some twenty-two casualties in the two shifts, from hostile fire, probably meant for our guns.

No. 1 shift moved back to " P " Camp, No. 2 going near Agadir. The battalion worked on this light railway till the end of August. In addition to the main line, which was pushed forward as far as the tactical situation allowed, numerous spurs were made, to allow of ammunition being brought close up to the various batteries, which sprang up in every direction. The work at this period reached a high state of efficiency—one line to a battery being laid at the rate of one Decauville section per minute on a nine hundred yard stretch by No. 1 shift—much to the astonishment of our gunners, who were delighted to receive the same evening ample supplies of six-inch H.E. shells by train. All this work was carried on more or less under fire, and the line was constantly broken by shells. Repair gangs were ready day and night, to move immediately on receipt of news of a break. Space will not allow of going in great detail, but from the following extracts some idea may be gained of what the battalion went through.

" 7th August.—Strafed out of ' P ' Camp by high velocity gun. Two horses killed, two men wounded."

"10th August.—Sergeant Teesdale killed in bivouac."[1]

"18th August.—German 'planes again over camp. Two brought down by machine-gun and rifle fire. Great sport. Using tracer bullets for machine-gun for first time." There are many records of these nightly visits of bombing 'planes.

"26th August.—Germans shelled our bivies at night, in pouring rain, but none of our lot hit. What a night!"

"We are now in the valley beyond Foch Farm—practically a swamp; it's a case of filling sand-bags for our foundation." "Fritz takes a hand. Puts down a perfect barrage—nine casualties." "Just as quiet a day as it was nasty yesterday, so good progress is made; shell-holes are levelled up, and here and there finished formation stands out like islands in a sea." "About 10 o'clock, without any preliminary warning, Fritz put down an area barrage—everything from light to heavy shells. We spent a miserable hour in any cover we could find, whilst it rained shell. We had three killed and thirty-two wounded, but all slightly."

The battalion's casualties, as given in the War Diary for the period dealt with in this chapter, were seven killed and sixty-two wounded. The only name mentioned is that of Sergeant H. Welsh, wounded on 5th July. Other entries of interest are: 19th April, Second-Lieutenant Marple rejoined from attachment to R.F.C. 10th May, Second-Lieutenant J. F. W. Blaikloch joins battalion. 23rd, Second-Lieutenants Jellicoe and F. de Bock Brisley to England to join Indian Army Reserve of Officers. 1st June, Second-Lieutenant Marple to England for Indian Army. 2nd, Second-Lieutenant Neville to be Transport Officer from 6.4.17. 13th, Second-Lieutenant Smurthwaite leaves to join 18th Northumberland Fusiliers on posting.[2] 30th July, Captain and Acting Major G. Stamp Taylor awarded M.C. by Commander-in-Chief. 7th August, Lieutenant J. O. Riddel joined from 31st I.B.D. 15th, Lieutenant Riddel to School of Military Engineering, Chatham.

About 26th August, I am told, Captain Mackenzie handed over command of "B" Company to Lieutenant R. de P. Dallin, and was invalided to England. He joined the 1st Battalion of the regiment in the summer of 1918, and was killed during the advance in August.

On 31st August the battalion was concentrated in "P" Camp, prior to joining its old division and resuming its rôle of Pioneers.

---

[1] Another correspondent thinks Sergeant Teesdale was among the casualties on the night of 4th/5th.

[2] Smurthwaite was killed with the 18th on 17th April, 1918, behind Bailleul, during the great German offensive.

The light railway track at this time was completed to Admiral's Farm in the old Boche line.

"30th August.—Handed over to 7th Canadian Railway Troops and returned to 'P' Camp. Dined in Pop with Plum and Drury (Skindles).

"31st.—Slacked all day. Plum, J. B. Locock, Hut and I dined at La Poupee. Jolly evening."

CHAPTER VII

THE MOVE TO NIEUPORT

THE battalion left "P" Camp on 2nd September. "Moved from 'P' Camp in about forty London buses to Ghyvelde, near Belgian-French frontier. Grand ride in hot weather—twenty miles. Billeted in tents.

"3rd.—Infantry drill in the morning. Afternoon, marched to Bray Dunes, our first sight of the sea in France. Bathed 'à l'Adam.' Had Blighty feeling, but Germans spoiled it by dropping shrapnel about. Could be seen from Zeebrugge and Ostend."

Thus the battalion returned to its old job, and everyone set to work to furbish up his drill and polish his buttons. "Company training in morning and sea-bathing in afternoon—ripping."

On 7th the Divisional General inspected the battalion. I reproduce the following—accepting no responsibility for its accuracy. "The Divisional General has been, seen, spoken, praised and departed, and we are bucked, and—yet? This is what he said: 'I have heard much of the 17th Northumberland Fusiliers and their good work when in the division, and now I have seen you all, I can well believe all that has been said. For I can tell you honestly that I have never seen a finer collection of men in France. (Shouts of "What are you drinking?") But important as your work is, I feel it is a pity that such a fine battalion should be on Pioneer work, and therefore lost as a fighting unit.' Help! Steady, General! (Sounds like 'Over the bags.')"

The next day the battalion moved to Brisbane Camp, which had lately been vacated by some French troops. It was situated between Coxyde and Oost Dunkerke. "Quite a good camp and decent quarters." "C" Company had preceded the battalion on the 4th, and had taken over from the 9th Seaforth Highlanders. The headquarters were in Oost Dunkerke. On the 9th September work was commenced under the C.R.E. 32nd Division on the Nieuport defences.

The number of officers on the establishment of a Pioneer Battalion was greater than on the establishment of a Railway

PLATE XV.

A STREET IN NIEUPORT.

NIEUPORT. CONCRETE PILL BOX BUILT BY C.COY.
17TH NTH FUSRS PBS. NEAR BRIDGE OF SIGHS

BRIDGE OF SIGHS.
NIEUPORT.

PHOTOS BY CAPT. G.S.S. GORDON. M.C.

Construction Battalion, therefore several new postings took place about this time.[1]

The battalion also received one hundred and fifty other ranks from England, who up till now had been employed on various defensive works. The battalion also provided a draft which went to the 6th Battalion and was mainly composed of men who came from the Cyclist Corps in December, 1916. Captain Glendinning left the battalion for duty under the Railway Construction Department, and Plumptre took over command of " A " Company. Captain Dawson rejoined 6th Northumberland Fusiliers about this time as Adjutant. The battalion, especially " B " Company, was very sorry to lose Lieutenant Mitchell, who was selected for service in Egypt, where before the war both he and Lieutenant Plumptre had been in the Civil Service.

Some idea of work and play during this period may be gathered from the following extracts:

" 10th September.—Marched to Nieuport. Our party repairing trenches in Schipstraat. Town heavily shelled. Trenches covered in as protection from falling debris.

" 11th September.—Nieuport. Went with some pals to Coxyde Bains to see ' Bombs ' Concert Party in Church Army Hut. Full house, but saw show through improvised chimney." (Wonder what he means! Some Pioneer dodge.)

" 21st to 25th September.—Filling in lock at Nieuport with sand-bags of cement. Whizz-bangs and 5·9's galore. Belgian troops assisting. Germans regularly destroyed work each night, thus flooding trenches."

" 1st to 6th October.—At Nieuport damming canal." (I wonder if that's spelt right.) " There were enemies who were active at night, and difficult to circumvent owing to their numbers and small size. No, not Huns. Far worse. Sand fleas. It's awful. Not a wink last night. I caught fifteen."

" A " Company began with a job of trench-making and screening, which was not so bad, though the following may be meant satirically : " Hutson has some jolly evenings on his screens."

[1] Lieutenants A. E. Phelan, F. Dawson, T. W. Gregory, A. K. Wardroper, F. T. Basey, G. W. Tindall, B. Gaffney, E. R. Wilkinson, Second-Lieutenants J. Potts, W. Cameron, G. McKay, W. D. Maughan, C. B. Marshall, W. E. Calvert, W. E. Harris, J. G. Pickering, Rutledge, and Piper, joined during September. Lieutenant Phelan was transferred to the 1st Battalion on 22nd, and Second-Lieutenant Gregory to 16th Battalion on 30th. Lieutenant R. de P. Dallin was attached to 19th Field Company R.E. on the 3rd. Lieutenant A. G. Mitchell took command of " B " Company after Lieutenant Dallin left. During September Lieutenant Mitchell went to Egypt, and Lieutenant Douglas took over " B " Company.

On 20th September a portion of the battalion shifted across the road, out of the flea-walk into a " real garden city," in which the officers' quarters were papered with figure subjects from " La Vie Parisienne," and supplied with various articles of furniture. " Our job is changed; we are in covered ways, really covered trenches, which run through Nieuport—in fact, they are the tuppenny tube of Nieuport." Some of these galleries were at a considerable depth, others only just below the surface. " We had several exciting journeys down home, Fritz sending over some very heavy stuff here from his naval guns round about Ostend."

The Belgian area close by appears to have been treated kindly by the Huns, for I read, " A stroke of luck one day. Having made a detour owing to Fritz, I discovered an absolutely untouched spot in Belgian area, the village of Woulperne (Wulpen?), where peaches could be purchased cheap. Bon for the troops."

About this time Captain Plumptre and several of " A " Company were wounded during night-work, a 5·9 falling in a house whence they were obtaining material. Plumtre was badly damaged, and had to go home and never rejoined battalion, Gordon being transferred from " C " Company to take command. When it was known that Plumtre was not to return there was universal grief, for all ranks loved and admired " Plum."

Part of " B " worked on fortifications round the flooded area at Ramscapelle.

The Garden City was treated one night to a spell of frightfulness, after which the battalion was re-united in the flea-infested camp in the sand-dunes which had escaped.

As a Railway Unit our Lewis Gunners had ceased to function, so they were now collected and instructed by Lieutenant Sadler, and lest he should have forgotten too much, he was shortly despatched to school, whence he was able to visit Dunkerque, where he met an old friend, Captain Ker, who, though unfit for General Service, had managed to get sent out to an appointment in the Docks.

" C " had been occupied building two concrete pill-boxes on either side of the Bridge of Sighs and sundry dug-outs. For each pill-box some one hundred and fifty tons of sand, shingle, cement and iron had to be humped on the backs of " C's " lads through lengthy trenches. The building had to be cunningly done, for the Boche was near. The work was started inside a ruined house, the walls of which were gradually raised at night till the box was completed, when they were thrown inwards over it as if demolished by some shell. After the first few days the work could be carried on without much interference.

On 7th October the battalion marched to Adinkerke, where

"umpteen barges were boarded. Teeming rain, and all wet through. Spent night in barge like sardines, and next morning arrived at Coudekerke. Billeted in new barn." Another version of this move is: "Battalion had a rotten move, and didn't get in till 11 p.m., and minus one and a half companies, which did not arrive till next day owing to barges being blocked." At Coudekerke the battalion "in rest" for a fortnight. "Out at rest. Spit and polish." The rest was not one which recalls many pleasant memories. The inhabitants in this neighbourhood were anything but hospitable. A physical jerk instructor appeared on the scene in a striped jersey, and new games were introduced which added greatly to our fatigue. The metal work on the transport wagons, etc., was duly burnished with the assistance of men from all companies, and then, to their great chagrin, they received orders to paint over all burnished parts—a way they have in the army!! The Lewis Gunners were given the full benefit of Lieutenant Sadler's new-found knowledge, and everyone tried hard to forget the war and learn to be soldiers. There were, however, distractions. "Tripped to Dunkerque in French lorry with Jack Hill. Had a fine time." "Dunkerque again for good feed." "Dodged inoculation, and off again to Dunkerque."

"18-19th October.—Resting on account of inoculation."

On 21st October, "Sunday, moved from Coudekerke with full pack to Zemerzeele (sixteen miles). Men dropped out like flies." (Due to inoculation.)

22nd October.—"Resting all day. D—— M—— and self went shopping to Cassel, nice little typically French town. Made a fine tea off meringues."

Tuesday, 23rd October.—"Moved very early by train from Arneke to Brielen. Went into bivouac near Burnt Farm. Nissen hut for mess and for officers' quarters—'A' and 'D' joint."

So here the battalion is back again in the mud, filth and desolation of "The Salient," which it had left less than two months before, and it seemed a bit odd to be travelling in French carriages over the line they had made in early part of the year. After crossing Bridge Four and traversing a mud track, the battalion was halted near St. Jean Station and told it might camp on either side of the road, in the mud, while the rain poured down steadily. The battalion showed itself equal to the occasion, and shelters swiftly sprang up all round. Of course the proximity of a R.E. dump had nothing to do with this rapid solution of the housing problem. An old friend, Captain N. Hope, was found snugly housed in a railway wagon, acting as R.T.O.

In the meantime, the little railway on which it had worked had been pushed forward by the Canadians and 18th Northumberland

Fusiliers up St. Julien and extended in many directions. The 18th were still labouring on the line, but left a few days after the arrival of the 17th, and I can find no mention of the two battalions having met.

The battalion was now taken away from its division, and handed over to the Chief Engineer 18th Corps for work on roads. The companies were in " awful dug-outs. Small and smelly."

The job was " discovering and recovering the St. Julien-Poelcapelle road, and from what I have seen of the job, it's more a case for the Navy than the Army." This was a bad time; the work was dirty and nasty and unsatisfactory, the Boche was troublesome with shells by day and with bombs by night. An account reads: " The camp was situated alongside the St. Jean rail-head. It was a terrible spot. There was no cover—water level was only a few inches below ground. It was here the battalion had its first real experience of aeroplane bombing. Night by night, and at midday too, the Hun 'planes came over. There was a considerable amount of long-range shelling also. Among those killed here were Corporal Barker, and by one bomb dropping on a dug-out three batmen of ' B ' Company—Privates Addison, Grey and Ritchie—and Lieutenants Harris, Gaffney and Smith were wounded at the same time." Lieutenant Robertson had a remarkable escape, being buried, but unharmed. At the same time Jerry showed his accurate markmanship (!) on two successive nights by scoring two direct hits on " C " Company's tool store. Unfortunately, on one of these nights several casualties occurred, including Craggs, " C " Company's cook, a popular fellow with all ranks. " At this time the fighting around Passchendaele Ridge was very heavy, and of course we came in for some hot times during our working hours at Poelcapelle, Langemarck and St. Julien. It was at St. Julien where I myself got lifted one day with a 5·9, two chaps being killed and some wounded, too."

" B " was working out Wietlje way and " C " was slabbing a road on the left of Kitchener Wood, running past Regina Cross, a most unhealthy spot, much hated also by the drivers of the R.F.A. ammunition mules, who often got caught there by dawn breaking. A typewriter was acquired here, being dug up together with the corpse of the poor runner who had been carrying it when knocked over. The machine did many days good work after being cleaned up.

" The scene around St. Julien is one that will be long remembered. Even now, if I shut my eyes, I can see the streams of traffic, mules, limbers, ambulances, men of all branches of the Army, the main road from Ypres over the bridge of the Steenbeek in the village, always fairly crowded, the more or less persistent shelling, men scattered by a bursting 5·9, horses and mules lying dead by the road-side, derelict tanks, a dozen or more within sight, field-guns dotted about the slope in front, the gunners sticking to their guns through everything, hardly a foot of ground between one shell-hole and the next and most of them half-full of brown or yellow water, and yet the front line outposts had to live in them, and all around, mud, mud, mud, as far as one can see. A frequent occurrence was to be caught in an area barrage when it seemed that every Boche gun in France was concentrated on the bit of ground we were on. Thanks to German pill-boxes, the only things which could withstand the rain of shells, numerous shell-holes and the soft ground we escaped with few casualties."

The training of Lewis Gunners was resumed in order to complete the full quota required for a Pioneer Battalion. Classes were formed at the Transport Camp at Westonhoek, and no doubt were not unpopular. "Pop" was within reach, but even so far back the Boche bombers continued their unwelcome attentions. The first effort at firing was not a success "on account of an irate farmer working near," who ordered them off. Fancy! What would have happened to a farmer who objected to a party of Germans shooting over his farm? However, another range was found "at Big Fill Pop Canal" (that made by "A" Company) and several successive classes were trained. Then suddenly the Little Tin Gods saw fit to re-transform the battalion into a Railway Construction Unit, which did not need Lewis Gunners. Thus the connection between the battalion and the 32nd Division was finally closed on 15th November, 1917.

CHAPTER VIII

MORE "SALIENT," THEN EXPERIENCES WITH AUSSIES

ALTHOUGH the battalion became railway troops on 15th November, it did not leave its uncomfortable quarters. It simply worked on light railways instead of roads, and the following extracts show that it had no pleasanter a time.

"Flitted to Foch Farm, near by, as being safer. Only half wall left. Some of 'C' killed, wounded, and gassed at Poelcapelle. Jack Coupland killed without a scratch.

"19th November.—Lieutenant Maughan killed and couple of men wounded at Langemarck." "Maughan killed on work near Langemarck. He was a jolly nice chap. Everyone was sorry to lose him."

"21st November.—Langemarck. Very heavily shelled. Took refuge in old Jerry block-house. Oh! the bodies!

"23rd.—Our camp shelled at night. Driven out for some time."

"29th.—Arthur Akeed killed near Kitchener Wood, St. Julien, by a splinter."

"30th.—Two more of 'C' killed."

The battalion was now working with 7th Battalion Canadian Railway Troops, "each Company working with its opposite number in Canadians, thus 'A' Company Northumberland Fusiliers and 'A' Company Canacks are for a month on the forward section. Next month we shall move back to next section round canal bank, and so on till we get right back to our old section near 'P' Camp; thus each company gets a turn of front and back area work."

The battalion carried on in this way till the last great offensive of the Boche in April, 1918, caused its services to be required elsewhere. The Canadians soon realized that the battalion did not need much instruction or supervision. "As day follows day, we see fewer Canadians. We are now laying the steel, and at last, except for the occasional visit of the Canadian officer in charge of the particular company we are working with, we are in charge of the job."

About the end of the third week in November, part of the battalion moved into company camps scattered about on Pilkem Ridge and its lower slopes. Lieutenant-Colonel King went on leave on 20th, Acting Major G. Stamp Taylor acting for him till his return. The same day Lieutenant Robertson left to take up the appointment of A.D.G.T. Stores.

The casualties for the month are stated to have been one officer and twenty-two other ranks killed, and three officers and fifty other ranks wounded.

" ' C ' Company on 10th November moved to ' Burnt Farm ' and made small dug-outs. . . . As we were in this camp from 10th November to 28th February, we had ample time to make ourselves comfortable in our bivies." "We made stoves from petrol tins, pinched the R.E.'s wood and sand-bags from their dump at St. Jean, and made doors and floors to our bivies. There was a dump not far from our camp, where a train brought up ballast for the railway. Amongst this ballast was always a lot of coal, and it was a sight to see a whole crowd of us ' scrounging ' for coal for our fires. (We were always real good scroungers.)" Two of these " scroungers " one day climbed on to the tender of an engine; before they could get off, the engine started and carried them nearly to Poperinghe before it stopped. It was a weary and dejected pair that crept back to camp about midnight.

The following shows some of the inconveniences of life in those parts: " Friday, 30th November.—Padre Fawkes came to lunch, and while he was there the Boche blew in my dug-out and buried my kit. We were in the mess about fifteen yards away. It was an eleven-inch shell." Next day the officers' quarters were moved to the other end of the camp. An awful catastrophe happened near by. A Boche shell exploded a huge ammunition dump, killing over a hundred and fifty of the Labour Company men who were working there. Such of our men as were working near did all they could to help, Lieutenant McKay and his platoon earning especial praise.

December was spent in the same way, but the casualties were only one officer, Captain Lakeman, and three other ranks wounded. Of Christmas I have accounts from three companies. Choose which you like. It seems to have been a merry day.

" Christmas Day.—' Micky ' Ellis made Regimental Sergeant-Major for the day. All ranks topsy-turvy. Football sports."

" Christmas Day.—Breakfast. Then watched ' A ' Company play R.F.C. at Soccer. We won 4—0. Lunched off pork pie, chicken and tongue, plus some more. Our men had meat pies, plum pudding, also two pints of beer and a hundred and fifty cigarettes as presents. N.E.R. gave them a hundred each, and we gave them fifty. Should have had sports in afternoon, but no one was keen after lunch, so we've postponed them for New Year.

Some of us slept. No tea. Dinner 5.30 p.m. Turkey and about six other courses. Champagne, port and cherry-brandy. Men's concert at 7.30. More port and cigars. Men more beer. Not bad, piano flat. Choruses noisy. Sergeants came on to our mess for snack and more drinks and cigars. Very cheery. Retired about midnight feeling tired but still cheerful.

"Boxing Day.—Got up about 10 a.m. and looked after interior economy whilst company out at work. Hm!"

"'B' Company was at Lancashire Farm. We tried to celebrate the day as it should be celebrated. There was a football match in the morning with the Kite Balloon Section, R.A.F., close by. Then Christmas dinner. I seem to remember turkeys and Yorkshire puddings. The cooking of the latter could not have been altogether satisfactory, for one of the lads was heard to remark: 'The less said about them the better.' In the afternoon we chartered a Y.M.C.A. hut behind the canal bank and gave ourselves an entertainment. There were songs, recitations, and a humorous sketch perpetrated by the officers. In the evening we seem to recollect there was a friendly gathering of Officers' and Sergeants' Messes."

The war had died down about this time, and leisure was found for attending to one's own needs. "In camp all day. We have at last built an open fireplace in the mess, but chimney is wrong, and it smokes. I will have it altered." Four days later we read: "Fireplace altered and cemented; it's fine now, doesn't smoke."

The year closed peaceably and cheerfully.

"31st December.—Sentries acting as 'lucky birds' to dug-outs, and inmates celebrated the occasion in fitting manner."

"Monday, 31st December.—Out on work in the morning. Had a magnificent dinner, and afterwards four of us went 'first-footing' and collected Jock and one or two others. Finished up at 'B.' Returned to our mess, and finally turned in at 2 a.m."

"Tuesday, 1st January, 1918.—Not feeling quite IT. I had a walk to the work and back in the morning. After dinner we went round to the Sergeant's Mess, where we spent quite a pleasant and sober evening. All except——" (erased by Censor.)

For the next three and a half months the battalion remained in this horrible area, working on the network of railways which extended from comparatively safe areas north of Poperinghe almost up to the front line in the neighbourhood of Passchendaele. The headquarters remained at a camp (28.A.23.c.2.3) about a couple of miles out of Poperinghe all the time. The companies rang the changes on various camps, among which were Nuneaton, Byfleet, Toronto, Agadir, Reigersberg, St. Sixte, International Corner,

PLATE XVI.

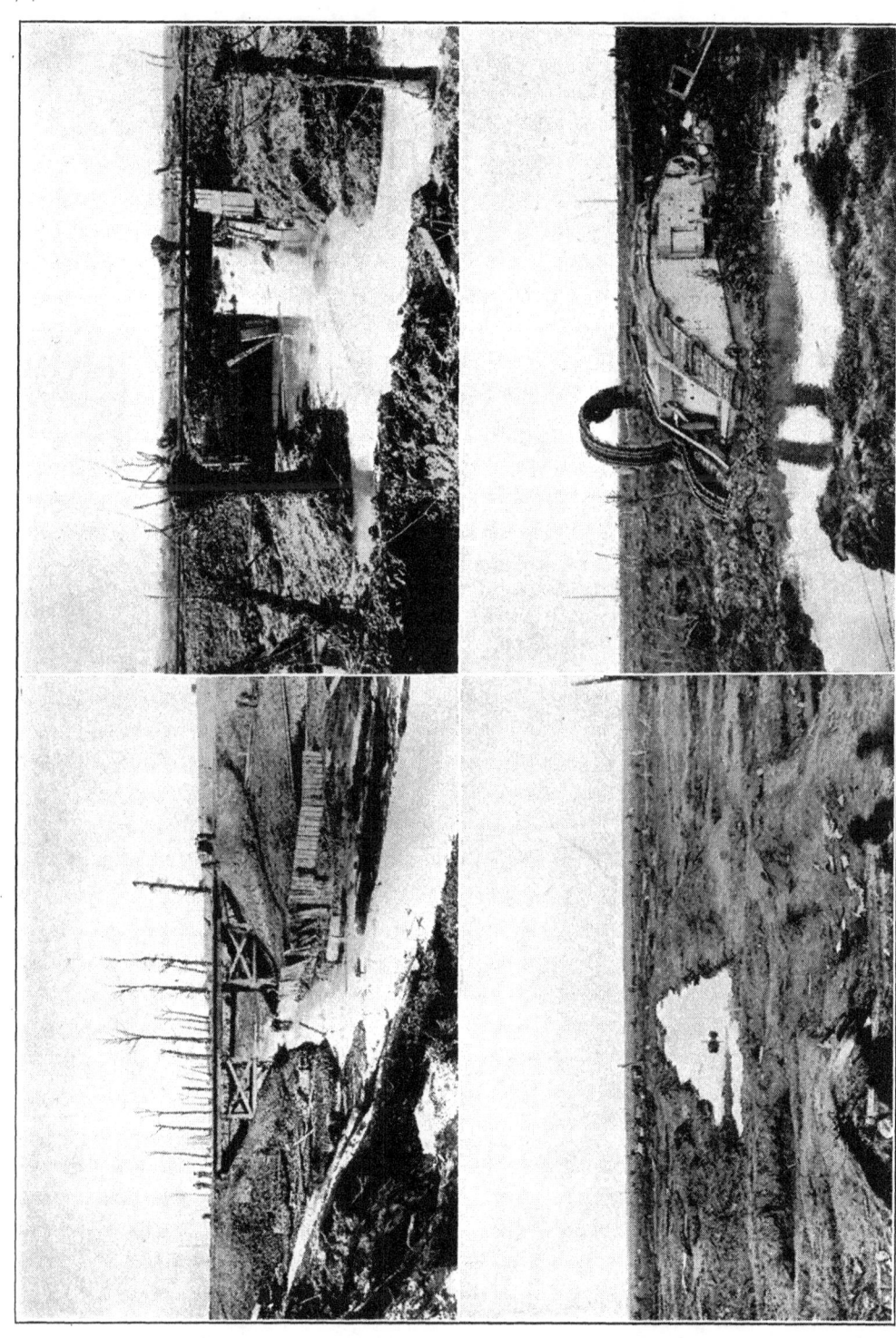

1.—Railway Bridge over the Yser Canal. Remains of "Fill" constructed by "D" Company can still be seen.
2.—Light Railway Bridge over Steenbeek.
3.—Battle Field looking towards St. Julien, showing ground over which 17th Northumberland Fusiliers Pioneers constructed Light Railway.
4.—British Tank out of action and bogged near St. Julien.

PLATE XVII.

PRISONERS WORKING ON PILKEM–LANGEMARKE ROAD.
THE MENIN GATE AND RAMPARTS.
BORDER HOUSE, ST JULIEN, FROM STEENBECK BRIDGE.
THE POPERINCHE–YPRES ROAD.
POPERINCHE SQUARE.
THE CLOTH HALL–YPRES.

PHOTOS BY CAPT G.S.S.CORDON.MC

Pretoria Yard and Swiss Cottage. I give them as I found them, and no doubt they will bring back many, but, I fear, not very pleasant, recollections. "The Salient" even in so-called quiet times was a depressing place. Its waterlogged, shell-pitted wastes of mud, across which you picked your way on groggy duck-board tracks, seemed more haunted by the ghosts of those who had fallen in the long weary years of the war than any other part of the line. Still, as the following entries show, the battalion kept going strong.

"'A' and 'B' soccer in afternoon, but Brother Fritz stopped the match by putting a shell on the touch line." Most unsporting! "Round the work on the 'Man Power Bogie' or 'Harry Tate's Express.'" "Round Langemarck line on motor tractor. Lunched with 'C' Company. Went to Pop shopping for mess. Lunched at Skindles. Saw Corps finals for boxing test in afternoon." "Moved back to 'Foch' Farm in dug-outs. Up to eyes in mud and water. Rotten weather."

"3rd January.—On tramways to batteries. Wilf. Holmes killed in camp by high velocity shell." "Work very dreary, only wish they'd find something real for us to do, but suppose we are fitting into the general scheme of things. Sometimes even cushy jobs grow stale." "Commodious quarters on the Pop canal, right back away in the country. This sector is what may be termed the rest sector, for there is little real work, and for the most part we keep track clear of weeds, and gently, with some artistic touches, rake the sand back to the track again after it has been blown away by the passage of a train." "We sleep, we Pop, and generally enjoy life." "In the evening went to Pop in car to see the Jesmond Jesters. A really good show; female impersonators very good and voice marvellous."

On 10th February two casualties occurred: Private W. Blackburn was killed, and Private T. Richardson was wounded. "Rather a warm time on the work, but no one hit. Four breaks on my sector." "Same job. Boche breaks line occasionally, but on the whole not so bad as it might be." "Boche broke the line in four spots, but we got them all mended by noon, although he was very busy with 5·9's." "The Boche has shelled Pop lately. He's very hot on all back areas just now." "Went out with Gordon to lay out triangle at Tamworth. Boche very lively, and we had to clear three times during the day. Got the job done, though. No. 1 had three casualties, two bad, one light."

"Our camp life is very trying, as Fritz has marked this confined area, and when he does not shell, he bombs. Shells are nasty, very nasty, but whilst not loving them, one has got, in a certain measure, acclimatized. But bombs! Bombs are damnable!" And so say all of us.

In March, signs of the expected trouble were noticed by those whose work lay in the forward areas. "We notice several changes; guns in new positions—this time, alas! they are back, some back even to their original positions of July last, behind the canal bank. Our new line, running practically through what was in old days No-Man's-Land, is nearing completion. . . . A splendid piece of work running right across the whole Salient." Rumours very rife. There was a vague feeling of uncertainty, even of doubt, very different to that of the earlier part of the year. Then the uncertainty was exactly when the attack would begin, and how far forward we should go. In March there was also uncertainty as to when the attack would begin, but it would not be our attack, everyone knew we were not going forward, and many doubted whether we should be able to hold our own, many even spoke of being driven back. I think the doubts increased as the distance increased from the front line. Partly because those in high places behind knew more of what the Boche was getting ready to do, and partly because the precautions which that knowledge rendered expedient were more apparent to those behind than to the garrisons of the forward trenches, who, noticing no change in Huns in front of them, were rather inclined to laugh at the fears of those behind. The work of the battalion went on much as usual; the Boche kept on breaking the line, the maintenance gangs kept on repairing it, getting shelled more or less most days, but by this time the ways of the Boche, which changed very little, were well known, and the gangs knew how to get the work done with the minimum of casualties. About the middle of March, the bridges over the Steenbeek and St. Julien and north of the Langemarck began to sink, which took some days to put right. The Boche got very active "scattering blessings generally, in heavy goods and large numbers."

"20th March.—What a day! Fritz in all his glory; we had two casualties and had to clear out several times. He plastered the place up all right, not only here but all over. . . . However, we got the job finished. The night continued as the day, very lively."

21st March, which cost other battalions of the regiment so dearly, passed quietly in our battalion's area. Some rumours of the Huns having advanced on the Somme reached some of the camps, and the seriousness of the situation was indicated by the receipt of orders to wire Bridge Four, the re-levelling of which had just been completed, in readiness for demolition; to stop work on lines east of the Ypres canal, and to dismantle various sidings, yards, dumps, etc., in that area, and salve all the material possible.

On the 24th, "We got newspapers containing news of the Hun push. We are quite confident." So little was anyone disturbed by the Huns' doings elsewhere, and so confident was everyone that all would end happily, that a meeting was held in "C" Company's mess to arrange about the St. George's Day sports. This confidence was not rewarded, as we shall see, but the whole tenor of the diaries of this period is good. The writers allow themselves to question many things that have been and are being done, but no one doubts our ultimate success, and no one allows the hardships that his fellows in other parts of the line are undergoing to interfere with his sleep or his meals or his visits to "Pop." This is the true soldier spirit, which makes an army invincible. You are sorry for your pals, but you know your worrying won't help them. Your job is to worry as little as possible, keep smiling, keep fit in body and mind, so that when your time of trial comes, you may be able to acquit yourself as well as you know they are doing now.

Just about this time the Steenbeek bridge collapsed while a train was crossing. "The Steenbeek was about twice its normal width, and had washed away some of the bank under the bridge. A repair gang of No. 7 Platoon, under Lieutenant A. K. Wardroper, together with some Canadian railway troops, were proceeding by train to beyond St. Julian for the day's work. The bridge collapsed and the engine and the first wagon fell into the Steenbeek. There were two men on the engine and fifteen in the wagon. They found themselves floundering in deep water, hampered by tools, arms, and equipment. Lieutenant Wardroper and Corporal Barker were conspicuous in assisting the men at once, showing great presence of mind, going to the water, and between them they rescued all the men in the wagon. The driver and fireman, who were pinned under the locomotive, were drowned." Lieutenant Wardroper and 17/601 Corporal E. Barker received the M.B.E. and the M.S.M. respectively.

The battalion carried on though signs were not wanting that the war was extending northwards, and "by the night of the 9th April gun flashes came from almost behind us." On 13th came urgent orders to concentrate at Battalion Headquarters. "All parties returned to camp after lunch, moved to headquarters at 5." "Marched to Pop, and left there about 9.30 p.m. for new zone. Arrived during the night, marched to rendezvous, where we bivouacked for the night. Pretty cold in the open." Another version: "We entrain at Pop, and have a noisy send-off from some Boche 'planes, and arrived about midnight at Steenbeek. Everything perfectly quiet, not even a rifle-shot. News that Fritz is held. . . . We march about a mile on the Hazebrouck road, turn into a field, and get as much sleep as the cold and damp will permit."

The cause of this sudden move and of the battalion being suddenly called back to " soldiering " from the peaceful (?) rôle of G.H.Q railway troops, was the German attack on the Portuguese Corps about Laventie early in the morning of the 9th April. The Portuguese were as good as annihilated, and the victorious enemy pushing through the gap rolled up the 40th British Division, which was on the left of the Portuguese, and by that evening the Germans were across the Lys by Bac St. Maur, and on the 10th a fresh attack delivered by the German 4th Army reached Ploegsteert and the 34th Division was with difficulty withdrawn from between these two hostile forces.

" 14th April.—We are very glad when the morning comes, and still happier when we are told that tea is ready (kindly provided from the field-kitchens of some artillery). Tea, bully and biscuits, and a wash make us more ready to face the day."

By the morning of the 14th, when the 17th Northumberland Fusiliers reached its damp resting-place near Hazebrouck, the first fury of the rush was over, though it was some days yet before the Huns were brought to a standstill.

The battalion was now attached to the 1st Australian Division in the 15th Corps, and was employed on the preparation of defensive lines. A line of strong posts was made round La Motte, and thence to Petit sec Bois, some four thousand yards in all. This work occupied a week, during which time many of the battalion who had joined recently were initiated into the delights of " standing to " from 4.30 to 5.30 every morning, and as the weather was bitterly cold, with frequent sleet storms, it is highly probable that they did not appreciate them.

The companies were given a battalion front to fortify. " A " Company was billeted in a little farm just on the edge of the forest of Nieppe, and within view of the church of Vieux Berquin. News was scarce, but " round about us there is perfect stillness, which, in this pretty country-side, makes one almost forget war." However, the writer soon got reminded of it, for, " on the way out, we heard and saw the first Boche shell since arriving," which dropped bang in the middle of the road, about two hundred yards ahead, and the arrival of several seventeen-inch shells the same morning confirmed the impression that peace had not come yet, although his work did lie " at the farther end of a village, a beautiful place . . . one or two houses still smouldered, but otherwise practically intact—two days later there was not a house left." Cattle and poultry were still wandering about, deserted by their owners.

The diaries speak of certain improvements in the daily fare about this period. There were other dangers to be faced, even worse than German shells. "W—— falls into the well of liquid manure, and the smell is terrific. He dresses in ladies' underwear, etc., while his batman washes and dries his clothes, as all our kits are at the transport lines, and we have only what we stand up in." The next entry reads: "The smell in W——'s billet is still rather odious, but it is clearing." Much of the work here had to be done at night. "Stood to after a strenuous night, and then turned in until tea-time."

A correspondent in " D " Company states: " The night before we moved a shell unfortunately hit a billet and caused several casualties, among the killed being Sergeant Jeffreys, and Sergeant Dunn wounded.

"On Sunday, 21st April, up at 5.15 a.m. Left billets 7 a.m. for farm near Pradelles, arriving 9.15 a.m., ten kilometres. Here we commenced to make trenches near Pradelles and Strazeele on the Hazebrouck-Strazeele road." While No. 6 Platoon was on its way to its work near Pradelles one morning Stretcher-bearer G. McCall was killed by a chance shell.

At this time the Boche got a direct hit on a clump of fifteen-inch shells behind one of " D " Company's billets, which caused a good deal of excitement. The three platoons on this spot turned out to help to extinguish the fire.

" 23rd April, St. George's Day.—Company at work on new line as yesterday. We wore red and white roses, but, of course, could not celebrate the event in any way." But the entry goes on, " L—— and I went to St. Omer shopping for the mess. Had a ripping motor ride and a very enjoyable day." So no doubt there was a certain amount of celebration. " A good deal of bombing all night."

The line on which it now worked was a continuation in a north-easterly direction of that on which the battalion had just been employed, and was intended to stop any advance from the direction of Meteren, which had fallen into German hands a few days earlier. The Hun bolt had, however, been shot. Heavy losses, coupled with the difficulty of getting up supplies, brought him to a standstill, and although in the last fortnight he had taken " twenty-two thousand prisoners, four hundred guns, thousands of machine-guns and a mountain of stores " he found himself still faced by an unbroken line of Allied troops, and though on 25th April he took Mount Kemmel, in the area in which the battalion found itself, there were no more Hun activities to be frustrated.

The last entry redolent of "war" is "4th May, Saturday, 4 p.m.—Billet shelled. Eight wounded, including doctor (Singalese). Fifth day off for company—got a fresh doctor—Australian." The official diary says: "Casualties during May: Captain A. V. Galt, R.A.M.C., and Second-Lieutenant J. Potts wounded; other ranks, one killed and nine wounded. Seven at duty." Captain Galt, R.A.M.C., although wounded himself, went to the assistance of wounded artillerymen beside our own wounded, behaving in an extremely plucky manner.

The Lewis Gunners were got together again under Reginald Sadler, who, a few days later, became a Captain, and worked hard on their share of the system of defence. On 10th May the battalion came under the orders of the C.R.E. 15th Corps was employed on the defences of Hazebrouck. This necessitated another move.

"10th May, Friday.—Up 7 a.m. Moved off 12.15 p.m. to field south-west Hazebrouck, and 2 p.m. in bivouacs. Making trenches four miles from camp near Souverain, and also making trenches near Morbecque."

Another version of the move reads: "Moved to new billeting area. We live in tents and bivouacs in a very pleasant spot. Our old wooden post office provided quite a quantity of timber for bivies, but this later led to trouble, as the absence of the post office was noticed by the authorities. The New Zealand Artillery were lying in a small wood nearby and persisted in letting off their six-inch Mark VII, of which they were very proud, causing us much loss of sleep. Every night we watched our searchlights locating Boche aeroplanes which flew over to bomb the big centres behind us, and we saw some shot down. One saved himself by planing right down the beams of the searchlight firing his machine-gun. Officers' Mess is a very dirty old cottage. This place promises to be very nice if only the weather continues fine."

In the intervals of trench-digging and spells of drilling, one company found time to beat the 12th Labour Company 3—1, and R.G.A. 5—1 at Soccer, and there are records of visits to St. Omer, and altogether this seems to have been a very pleasant time. Unfortunately, it did not last long, for on 29th May the battalion was transferred to 18th Corps for temporary attachment to 52nd Division as Pioneer Battalion.

CASUALTIES	OFFICERS	OTHER RANKS
January, 1918	—	10 killed 5 wounded.
February	—	1 ,, 2 ,,
March	—	1 ,, 12 ,,
April	—	6 ,, 15 ,,
May	2 wounded	1 ,, 9 ,,

CHAPTER IX

NEUVILLE ST. VAAST AND THE FINAL ADVANCE

OF the move southwards to join its new division, the official scribe gives little more than the places at which the battalion halted each night, and two other sources do not provide me with much information, so I presume the march was uneventful. The first day brought the battalion to Aire, where " we had good quarters for officers and men. Officers slept at the convent. A very cheery time on the whole." No doubt! Colonel King suggested a combined mess of all officers for that night. The number totalled twenty-six, and it was discovered in the middle of mess that we formed two tables of thirteen each. Later events, however, disproved truth of the superstition.

" 30th May.—Marched to Divion. A very tiring trip of about fifteen miles. Rather tired." But then they had not " slept in the convent."

" Friday, 31st May.—Marched to Camblaine l'Abbe, about nine miles good road, and company marched awfully well. We have a Battalion Mess in Officers' Club, and a good sing-song after dinner." " One or two songs sung in Tyneside dialect were not understood by some officers from other battalions, who seemed to think it was some foreign language of which they had not heard. A sporting Padre played the piano. Some evening!"

On 1st June Major Martin handed over the Adjutancy to Captain Gordon, and took command of " A " Company, which went to Villers-aux-Bois, about two and a half miles distant, where " we have a ripping camp on a hill with a lovely view all round." Here the company worked on huts for D.H.Q. till 18th June, but two platoons were moved to Neuville St. Vaast, to which place the Battalion Headquarters and the other companies had gone on 1st June. The companies at Neuville St. Vaast were in huts. " Here we commenced to work in the trenches over Vimy Ridge—six miles away—going to work at nights, generally about 8 p.m. Travelled some way by Decaville train, then a long way to walk up communication trenches to Brown Line, reveting trenches and duck-boarding."

The Brown Line was the main line of resistance, in front of which was the post line. Behind the " Brown " at 1,200 to 1,500 yards ran the " Green Line," in the centre of which was the position assigned to the battalion in case of an attack, with one company pushed to the front covering the Bois de Bonval re-entrant. Neuville St. Vaast was about 8,000 yards from the front line, and nearly in the centre of the divisional area. The 52nd Division was the Lowland Division, with a fine record; it was now holding the right sector of the 18th Corps front. On its right was the 4th Division of the Canadian Corps, and on its left the 20th Division of the 18th Corps.[1] The battalion remained in this position till 23rd July, working on pipe-laying, telephone cable trenches, shelters, and front-line defences.

" D " Company for a time lived in dug-outs in the Willerval sector, and was relieved there by " C." " Night work, repairing front line, etc." The laying of the pipe line was vexatious work, for the Boche had a most annoying habit of shelling it, and it was riling when turning out at night to find most of your last night's work blown out. Nor did the enemy limit his activities to destroying the work done. He sometimes tried to stop any being done.

" Friday, 14th June.—Whole company on pipe line. Could not get on to work for a time on account of shelling, but found an alternative route and arrived only half an hour late. Lance-Corporal Smith, of " D " Company, came back to warn us about the shelling at Mersey Tunnel, on his own initiative, and he has since been awarded the Military Medal."

During June there was an outbreak of that mysterious disease termed P.U.O.[2] In the battalion there were five hundred and fourteen cases, and there were three hundred down at one time. There were no deaths, however, a feather in the cap of our Medical Officer, Captain Evans. In addition to the toils already mentioned, there was added about the middle of June the construction of a tramway. There appeared to have been few easy spells during this period; the only ones of which records are found are in occasional shopping trips to St. Pol in the box car.

The 30th June, " War Loan day, we collected £1,970, which was more than any single unit in France in a week." On the same

[1] On 2nd July the Corps were renumbered the 8th.

[2] At this time " D " Company were located in the reserve trench called the " Brown Line," each company being expected to take a tour of duty in the trenches for the period of one week. " D " Company only managed to hold out for their allotted span by the skin of their teeth, the Company Commander, Captain Lakeman, with the larger proportion of the Company, having gone down the line. (Captain Lakeman was evacuated to England never to return.) " D " Company was relieved by " C " Company, who suffered even worse, as Captain Cole was the only officer, with one Sergeant Easby (who returned to company when in trenches, having gone down earlier with P.U.O.), plus about twenty-six other ranks. Their tour of duty lasted three days.

day, orders were received that the battalion was to be again converted into a Pioneer Battalion, which meant an increase in the number of officers, which was pleasant, but it also entailed loss of our motor transport. ("Rotten.") No more shopping trips, alas! Early in July another consequence of the reversion from railway to pioneer establishment occurred, which was the loss of one company. "D" Company was the victim, being broken up, and its members distributed among the other three companies. "Dined at 'D' mess. Farewell dinner. Very happy evening for most people, but we were sorry to see one company broken up. Still, we do our best in the other companies to make them feel at home." There are two records during July of victories at "soccer" over the Royal Scots Fusiliers, otherwise it seems to have been all work and no play. "All manner of courses of instruction being carried out by various people with our N.C.O.'s."

"Lieutenant E. W. Smith and Second-Lieutenant Piper were detailed for one of those delightful holiday affairs known as Corps Infantry Schools. Although there was plenty of work to be done there, the rest among civilized surroundings was appreciated, and much useful up-to-date knowledge of warfare was obtained."

The casualties recorded during this period were: two died of wounds, two of sickness, and eleven wounded.

On 23rd July, "Moved to Tangry, 7.30 a.m., by train. Very wet day, but arrived at destination quite cheerful. Good billets and mess. Nice little girl (Nellie) at mess." "There had been no English troops billeted in this village since 1915, and it was amusing to hear French wagons bring in extra supplies of beer at night. This beer was 6d. a litre in English money, and the cry was always ' Haf you one penny, please?' "

From another source we learn: "Tuesday, 23rd July. Up at 5 a.m., moved off at 7 a.m. Whole battalion entrained at 10 a.m. at Acq to Pernes, arriving 1 p.m. Marched to Tangry, arrived 3 p.m., billeted in village. Stayed in this village until 3rd August for ' rest.' Meant up every morning at 6 a.m. and parade at 8, drilling of all kinds until 3.30 p.m. every day." Rest? However, in spite of the parades and range practice, time was found to beat the R.A.F. team at " soccer," and the officers, in a most sporting manner, accepted a challenge from the officers of 148th Squadron R.F.A. to play them at baseball; it is sad, but hardly unexpected, to read, "We lost, as it was our first attempt." However, the next day when they played their opponents at " soccer," they turned the tables on them to the tune of 8—0. The R.A.F. officers were good sports and gave most of our officers their first experience of flying.

Having during its rest been smartened up and taught many useful accomplishments, the battalion, together with the rest of the 52nd Division, returned to the line on 3rd August. Half the battalion moved off at 8 in lorries, arriving at its destination, Ecurie, at 11 a.m. "A very successful move, and we have a very fine camp." It is hardly necessary to add that that version is from one of the lorry party. The other version is: "Up at 5.45 a.m., parade at 7.20 a.m., left Tangry 8.15 a.m., entrained Pernes 10.30 a.m., St. Pol 12.30 p.m., left 3 p.m., arrived at Acq 4.45 p.m., marched to Flanders camp near Roclincourt, arriving 7 p.m. in huts." Did they also call it a successful move?

The 52nd Division was now holding the left sector of 17th Corps front, protecting south-eastern portion of Vimy Ridge, with 57th Division of 17th Corps on right, and 8th Division 8th Corps on left. All three brigades were in line. The sector was immediately on the right of that held when last in the line. The battalion and one company of the Machine-Gun Battalion were the only reserves. In case of an attack, the battalion was told off to occupy the Pont du Jour—Thelus line. The tour of duty, however, was very uneventful. "Here the battalion commenced work of repairs in the trenches around the 'Brown' and 'Green' Lines. All night work, and sometimes the Boches got 'funny,' causing us to stop work and stand by in case he tried any tricks on."

On 16th August the division was relieved by the 8th and 51st Divisions, and withdrawn into G.H.Q. reserve, under the usual "hate" with which the Boche greeted the return to the line of the famous 51st. The battalion did not move until the next day, when it marched to Estree Cauchie, eleven miles, arriving there at 10.30 a.m. Three days of real army "rest," "parades 9 a.m. to 12, and 2 to 3 p.m." Then suddenly off again at 10.40 p.m. on 20th, marching through the warm night to Tilloy, a small village a couple of miles west of Hermaville, which was reached at about 1.30 a.m. on 21st. The whole division was concentrated in the neighbourhood, and it was evident that something more than the ordinary relief of another division in the line was impending.

The tide had in fact turned. The German offensive of the spring, which had been so successful up to a certain point, had been followed up by attacks in various parts of the Allied front, on 27th May, on the Chemin de Dames, and on 15th July across the Marne east of Château Thierry, between the Marne and Rheims, and between Rheims and the Argonne. The first was brought to a standstill by the middle of June, although it began most successfully. The second ended on the 17th July, and on the following day Marshal Foch launched a flank attack with French and American troops, which was so successful that in a couple of days the German communications in the Marne Salient were cut, and thereby its evacuation made necessary. From then on, the Allies called the tune and the Germans did the dancing. On the 8th August, Canadian and Australian troops, with many tanks, attacked the German Salient facing Amiens, and virtually annihilated the divisions opposed to them as organized units, although these were composed of first-class troops. Certainly 8th August, 1918, was "Der Tag," but not that to which swaggering Germans used to drain bumpers, for Ludendorff has described it as the "Black Day" of the German Army. The French attacked between the Oise and the Aisne on 20th August, and on the next day the British Third Army attacked in the direction of Bapaume and Péronne.

The 52nd Division was, on the 21st August, allotted to the 6th Corps of the Third Army. This Corps also included 2nd Guards, 56th and 3rd Divisions, and was under command of Lieutenant-General J. A. Haldane. The preliminary operations on 21st were successful, and the counter-attacks made by the Huns on 22nd achieved but little. The main attack was delivered on 23rd, and in this the 52nd Division took part. The warning order was only received at D.H.Q. at twenty minutes past midnight 21st/22nd, so that in order to reach the starting point in time, a hurried move had to take place by some units moving in lorries and some on their own feet.

The Pioneers are not on in the first act of a set piece, so the battalion marched. "Moved off 1.30 a.m. 23rd August, for Bretencourt. Arrived at 7 a.m."

By that time the 156th Brigade, which had toed the tape up to time at 4.45 a.m. and gone over on the heel of the barrage at 5.7 a.m. preceded by nine Mark V tanks of the 9th Tank Battalion, had taken all its objectives and captured three officers and sixty-seven other ranks.

On that day the 52nd Division was the left division of the 6th Corps, which was the left Corps of the Army. The front attacked by the Army extended from Albert to Cojeul River, some sixteen miles. The 6th Corps objective was Gommiécourt northwards, that of the 52nd Division was the northern extremity of the line north of Cojeul River. The day was successful all along the line. To the 6th Corps fell Ervillers, Hamelincourt, Boyelles and Boiry Becquerelle, with some five thousand prisoners and many guns.

The battalion, according to the War Diary, had one company engaged on cutting an assembly trench in No-Man's-Land, and two on improving artillery tracks for advance. The headquarters were at Blaireville Quarries.

On the 24th, attack was renewed, and was again successful. The Huns were ejected from Thiépval, that hard nut which took so much cracking in 1916, Grandcourt, Miraumont, Pys, and in the 6th Corps area from St. Leger and Henin, but managed to hold out in Croisilles and St. Martin-sur-Cojeul. The 156th and 157th Brigades of the 52nd Division at 6.45 p.m. 24th August were established five hundred yards west of the Hindenburg line on Henin Hill.

The battalion continued working on the jobs of yesterday. At 7.30 p.m. Captain Cole reported to Battalion Headquarters that the working parties were still out, and that a further move forward was difficult as our field guns were in action immediately in front of the scene of his labours. At 9 p.m. the same day he reports that all the work assigned to the company had been completed, ending his message " men very tired."

In the evening of this day, 24th August, the G.O.C. 52nd Division, Major-General John Hill, issued a very spirited appeal to all officers to act with dash and vigour, pointing out that this was a time for taking risks, and that it was no time for encumbering themselves with prisoners.

The attack was continued until the night of the 27th, by which time the Hindenburg line had been cleared, and Fontaine-les-Croisilles mopped up by 155th Brigade, the process yielding five hundred unwounded prisoners, some field and many machine-guns.

The battalion's contribution to these successes was the repairing of the roads, without which the rapid advance would have been impossible, and various other useful jobs, such as constructing dressing-stations and shelters for the staff. The advance headquarters and companies were by this time bivouacked in trenches between Mercatel and Henin.

" On entering Croisilles we discovered a nasty mess right across the main road. It had been a German ammunition cart, which apparently had had a direct hit from one of our guns some days (or weeks) before. The remains of the cart, the exploded ammunition and the two mules were very much in the way and had to be removed and the mules buried. The platoon turned out with gas masks for the job, there being certain signs of decay about, and performed one of the quickest bits of work ever done by the battalion. They were duly rewarded with an extra ration of rum each, and this certainly was very much needed—phew ! "

The division was relieved by the 57th Division during the night of 27th/28th, and went into bivouacs near Mercatel. I find in an old A.B. 153 which has been lent me, copies of some orders and reports, which help to give me some idea of what was going on then. "Road was badly blown up at T.2.B.4.9, and one platoon has spent the whole day filling in there. Work two-thirds completed." "One man wounded, 17/12/17 L. E. Baker, one man wounded at duty, 17/408 W. H. Bor (?)." "Have chosen camping ground T.4.D. Central, as at 2 p.m. the road beyond T.5.C.2.8 was under machine-gun fire. Men have been going since 5 a.m. (time 3.30 p.m.). Have put in condition an extra track to-day. . . . Also assisted Battery 527 R.F.A. to dig rough emplacements." "T.34 road made temporarily satisfactory. Stream has been dammed by felled trees to make rapid crossing, as road completely destroyed." A plaintive request for clean socks following a statement that the men have returned tired and wet through, brings back vividly the memory of the unpleasant life lived in those times.

The division came back into the line on the night of 30th/31st, and relieved the 56th Division before dawn, which was checked before Bullecourt, which place the 155th Brigade mopped up by noon.

"'C' Company was in at the death at Bullecourt, which contained innumerable machine-gun posts very skilfully concealed, and immediately set about making a road from the top of the hill leading up to Bullecourt straight across No-Man's-Land to the German front line towards Quéant. Another company the next day were doing similar work from German trench towards hill-top overlooking Quéant. The ground was about the roughest ever experienced by us, having been fought over dozens of times. The removal of relays of rusted and tangled barbed wire was not an easy task, and all sorts of obstacles were encountered in cutting a formation for the road. The men worked like heroes, and although not even fresh when they started the job they stuck to it for some thirteen or fourteen hours. A senior officer on the brigade staff did wonders in the way of encouraging the men, and when food was mentioned to him he quickly took the necessary steps, and within a couple of hours the sacred field-kitchens, complete with the equally sacred N.E.R. horses, arrived from their quarters at Blairville Quarry with dixies of steaming-hot stew and tea. The transport received a great welcome, and so did the stew, but the drivers were rather sad when the said Staff Officer told them to get back to Blairville and return with another meal within the next four hours. However, he'd apparently put the breeze up somebody, for a second meal duly arrived, and thus encouraged the men worked on and succeeded in getting the road through by nightfall.

Fortunately the weather remained fine, and the formation being of solid clay we were able to get traffic through straight away, and we actually had ration and water-carts up to our front line that night over the new road.

"It was an inspiring sight the following morning to see our heavy guns lumbering along where twenty-four hours before there had been nothing but desolation—shell-holes, wire, gun emplacements and corpses. The most cheering part of the job was that all the time we were busy the old Hun was plastering the only road from Bullecourt to Quéant—a couple of hundred yards away—with every known form of explosive he could spare. We spent most of the next day collecting and burying our dead, of whom there were all too many, and amongst them we discovered a battalion postman with the mail, which we collected and sent down to headquarters in the hope that it would eventually be delivered. Amongst the prisoners taken at this time was a German officer, who was recognized by one of our men as having been a barber in Hartlepool just before the war broke out."

The attack went on gaily. The 2nd September saw the Hindenburg line mopped up, and on the 3rd Quéant and Pronville were cleared. By 5.30 p.m. on 3rd the tale of prisoners taken since 21st August amounted to 1,132, and in the previous twenty-four hours ten field-guns had been taken.

The Commander-in-Chief called at D.H.Q. on that evening to congratulate the troops on their successes, and thanked them for all they had done.

During the night the division concentrated in Corps support near Quéant, and moved on 7th to bivouacs east and south of St. Leger, where it rested and refitted till 15th. Rest and refitting were never required by Pioneers, so that battalion plugged away. Its casualties in August had been light, only one killed, one died of wounds and eighteen wounded. The battalion was billeted in excellent trenches considerately vacated by their previous occupants and builders, the Boche. The work was most important. At this stage of the war the enemy was more easily moved than in the earlier days, and was relying largely on the destruction of roads, bridges, etc., to delay our advance, so that our rate of progress was largely dependent on the work of the constructional troops, Royal Engineers, Pioneers, and Labour Companies. While the fighting troops of the division were resting, the Pioneers were putting the roads in order to facilitate the moving forward of the artillery and the bringing up of supplies.

The battalion transport, under Lieutenant Blair, was some way back in the valley, and suffered a good many casualties in men and horses, as the Boche airmen bombed the areas immediately behind the fighting line very persistently. Here some of the remaining N.E.R. horses, which had been admired and coveted everywhere we went, got knocked over, to our great regret.

The following is " C " Company's account of its doings during this time, which may be taken as a fair example of a Pioneer's life in these busy days:

" Saturday, 7th.—Up at 6 a.m. Moved off at 7.30. Arrived fresh camp (bivies in trench), near St. Leger, 6 p.m. Made trench midway on road up.

" Sunday, 8th.—Rested.

" Monday, 9th.—Up at 6 a.m. Out at 7 a.m. to work on roads in Croisilles.

" Wednesday.—Up at 6.30 a.m. 7.30 went to Boiry for a bath." And so on.

" Monday, 16th.—Up at 7.30 a.m. Moved off at 1.30 p.m. to trench near Quéant. Arrived at 4.30 p.m.

" 17th/18th.—On road work near Quéant."

The following account has been received just in time to be included. " B " Company's doings during the advance: " First two nights, cable trench immediately behind the advancing line near Henin-sur-Cojeul. Bivouac for night in railway cutting. Advance through Heninel, working on approaches for artillery, transport, etc. Night work near Mercatel. Day work near Bullecourt. Forward again to a bivouac overlooking Quéant— through this area we have seen the wonderful way in which the Hindenburg line has been constructed, with its deep-timbered dug-outs and threefold belts of the cruellest-looking barbed wire. Boche aeroplanes are very busy now bombing by night and balloon-strafing by day. Eventually we find ourselves a little farther forward, living in dug-outs on the Hindenburg support line, working on Divisional Headquarters across the valley. We have been steadily moving forward, and are now in sight of Bourlon Wood, of which we have heard so much. A few days later we move into trench south-east of Pronville village."

The 17th September was a bad day for the battalion. Major Martin and Lieutenant McKay had gone up towards Pronville to inspect their next job. At the cross-roads a German shell got them, poor old Martin being killed and McKay badly wounded. Major Martin, as has already been recorded, was an old soldier when the war began, and had done his full time, yet he insisted on leaving his snug post at York to go again on active service. First as Sergeant-Major, then as Quartermaster and as Adjutant, he served the battalion well with all his heart and soul, and if, as many think, there was no battalion that could hold a candle to the 17th Northumberland Fusiliers, the credit was largely Martin's due. During the short time he had held the command of " A " Company, he had shown himself as good out on work as in the orderly-room. " Martin was buried in a field cemetery between Quéant and Bullecourt, the funeral being attended by as many officers and men of the battalion as could be spared from the various jobs."

The division went into the line again on 15th/16th September, the 155th Brigade taking over the Moevres sector from 170th Brigade of the 57th Division, and the next night the 157th Brigade took over the Inchy sector on its left. " A " and " B " Companies were continually working in the trenches, which were very lightly held, and they, amongst other tasks, strengthened the front line and helped the infantry to man it, in effect acting as moral support to the infantry. The enemy occupied a post line along the western bank of the Canal du Nord. Our hold on Moevres was not very secure, and there was much fighting in this neighbourhood, which I should much like to describe, but as the 17th Northumberland Fusiliers had no share in it, I must forbear, though I cannot resist just mentioning the very gallant defence of a pill-box at Moevres by one N.C.O.[1] and six men of the 5th H.L.I., who, being surrounded during one of the temporary successes of the Huns, held out without food or water for seventy-two hours till relieved by the 155th Brigade, who re-took Moevres on 18th. The fighting continued till the 24th, a strong post known as E.14 Central changing hands six times, the last capture being made by the 4th Royal Scots Fusiliers on 24th September. Throughout this period the battalion was working hard and skilfully on the roads, on the repair of which the success of all forward movements depended.

" ' A ' and ' B ' Companies had some sticky work during the period 16th to 23rd September. They were sent forward to consolidate in the front line near Moevres. No one knew at night just where the front line was, or Moevres, or the Boche, but we just went forward to a destination known as Swan Alley. On arrival we found it unrecognizable as a trench, but we made it just holdable, and when we came under machine-gun fire, withdrew. On another night we were going up again, and as we approached Tadpole copse in the Hindenburg line, we saw in front ' two greens and a red '—S.O.S. Immediately hell was let loose on both sides and we took refuge in the fine deep dug-outs." (And for once blessed the Boche, I bet.) " On the following night we ran into gas shells, and a number of us lost our voices in consequence for some days afterwards. After this we returned to road and track

[1] Corporal David Hunter, H.L.I. He received the V.C.

PLATE XVIII.

1.—Neuville St. Vaast looking North.
2.—Neuville St. Vaast site of "B" Company's Headquarter Hut on Right.
3.—Neuville St. Vaast "C" Company's Headquarter Hut on Right—Remains of Margin Road in Centre.
4.—Quéant, taken from the Lagnicourt Road.
5.—Nine Elms, St. Leger. (Note the ladders in trees).
6.—Sergeant's Mess at Masney St. Jean.

QUEANT VILLAGE
POINT WHERE HINDENBURG LINE WAS BROKEN

HORSE AMBULANCE AND TANK
AT CROSS ROADS IN CROISELLES
I.W.M. PHOTOS CROWN COPYRIGHT

RUINED VILLAGE OF PRONVILLE

TRANSPORT ADVANCING ON ARTILLERY TRACK
CONSTRUCTED BY THE C COY 17TH NTH FRS PRS
OVER THE CANAL DU NORD

PLATE XIX.

PLATE XX.

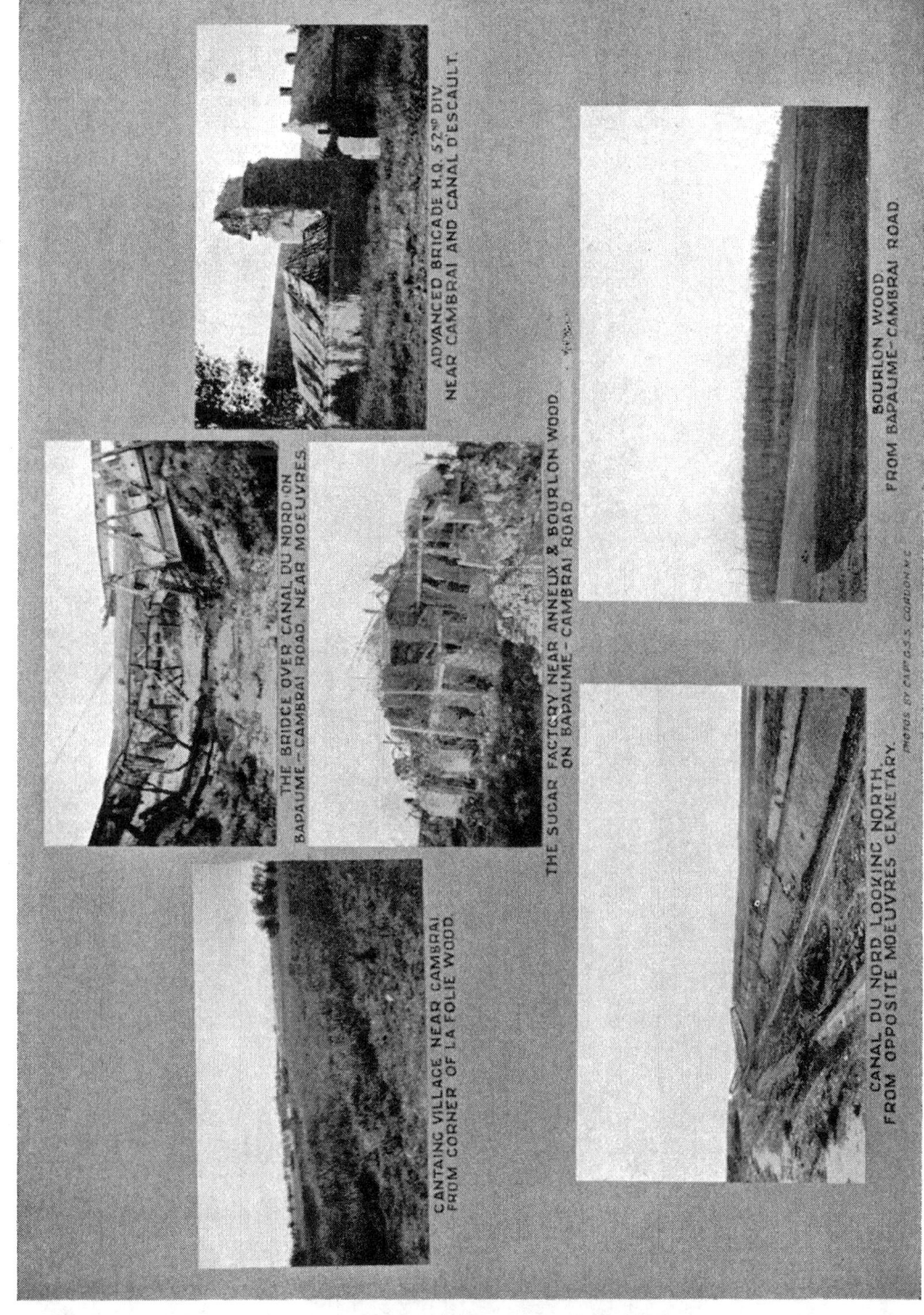

MASNAY ST JEAN.
H.Q. 17TH N'TH F'RS DARK BUILDING IN CENTRE.

MASNAY ST JEAN.
H.Q. BILLET ON LEFT.

QUEANT. TAKEN FROM THE SITE OF THE HINDENBURG LINE.

ABLAIN ST NAZAIRE, WITH NOTRE DAME DE LORETTES HILL IN THE DISTANCE.

ESCAULT CANAL, LOOKING PAST LA FOLIE WOOD TOWARDS CAMBRAI.

PHOTOS BY C.Q.M.S. T.M.HORSLEY.

PLATE XXI.

making, working downwards across the open ground between Moevres and Boursies towards the Bapaume-Cambrai road."

On 27th September the division attacked again. This was part of the Allies' final offensive, which extended from the Verdun and Champagne fronts right up to the coast. Opposite the Third Army the Huns were in their last line. If they were thrown out of the Hindenburg line, they had the unpleasant prospect of retreating over open country chased by their formerly despised enemies, therefore it was to be expected that the fighting would be severe, and so it proved; indeed at one time the issue on the 52nd's front was in doubt, but finally all objectives were carried.

These were to mop up the Hindenburg front line west of Canal du Nord, and all the area up to, but excluding, the Hindenburg support line east of the canal. The canal, although dry, was a serious obstacle to the advance of the guns and transport.

Three crossings were made by the Pioneers. The first, " A " Company's job, was ready for the artillery by 11 a.m. " C's " job was more arduous. The operation had been very carefully thought out, with the assistance of aeroplane photos and every contingency provided for as far as possible. The big bridge on the Bapaume-Cambrai road had been demolished, and a crossing had to be provided close by. It was foreseen that a great deal of material would be required for filling in, and a large number of fascines had been made and loaded on to transport wagons, to be brought up when called for.

" 27th, Friday.—Up at 2.39 a.m. Moved off to trench near Cambrai and right of Pronville. Arrived at 8 a.m. Twelve casualties on the way up (five killed, seven wounded)."

Captain Cole went on ahead with runners, to be sent back to bring up the company as soon as it was possible for the work to be started. They had to manœuvre a bit to avoid the machine-gun fire, but caught up the infantry, who were checked momentarily at the canal, though a passage had been forced on the left. The runners brought up the company No. 9 Platoon, C.S.M. Street heading the procession, not a bit depressed by the gruelling it had on the way up. Work was started, and Lieutenant Blair and the transport rolled up according to plan with the fascines, which were soon out of the wagons and in the canal along with every sort of stuff that could be found. The Hun had most thoughtfully left a well-stocked R.E. dump close by, which came in handy. In the middle of the business the Boche blew up a mine under the road some three hundred yards ahead, and a party had to be sent off to make a way round the crater.

A comic interlude was the sudden appearance from some dug-outs in a big spoil heap on the far side of the canal of a crowd of Boche with hands held high, shouting: " Kamerad! Kamerad! " The Company did not knock off work till 9 p.m. Eighteen and a half hours work.

" B " Company, commanded by Captain Smith, had orders to make good a crossing of the Canal du Nord in E.26.b, then to follow through E.27 and E.28, mopping up. This was done according to plan. Captain Smith was wounded, and Captain Douglas took over the company. Then followed a day of clearing up, " chiefly filling craters in roads, and burying dead Germans and horses. I fear that frequently three birds were killed with one stone."

The division halted the next three days to bury the dead and reorganize. The battalion was employed on improving the crossings over the canal and salvage work in the Moevres area. The casualties during September were: Killed, one officer and seven other ranks; wounded, two officers (Captain N. Smith on 27th) and twenty-two other ranks (one died).

During the first five days of October, the division had severe fighting near Cambrai, in which the attempt to seize the suburb known as Faubourg de Paris was unsuccessful owing to the fire of machine-guns concealed in the outskirts of the town and along the railway. The battalion was, as usual, busy on useful work. The Divisional " G " War Diary says: " Pioneers dug the trench from A.19.a to the redoubt A.27.a, and completed the work during the night 3rd/4th so that covered communication and a good trench existed the whole way to the redoubt. A second line of defence was also dug by them (assisted by the infantry), so that whether the attack succeeded or not there would be defence adequately organized against any counter-attack attempted from direction of Cambrai."

The following is " B " Company's account of the first job carried out: " Our work was to convert an old communication trench into a fire trench, east of the River Escaut. We left camp at dusk and passed by way of a sunken road into La Folie Wood. Crossing the canal by a broken bridge, we approached the ' site ' in extended order over some marshy ground. There was considerable shelling en route. We reached the trench and carried out our work satisfactorily. It was close to the front outpost line, and just over a mile outside the city of Cambrai. The city was in flames and presented an awe-inspiring sight, one which many of us will remember all our lives."

The second line was the work of " A " and half " C " with a hundred and fifty " Jocks." " The Huns seemed to be fully alive to our presence and gave us a good dusting."

The division was relieved by the 57th Division, and on the 7th it went back to the Le Caurey area. During the preceding month its casualties had been 80 officers and 1,561 other ranks, and it had taken 15 officers and 790 men alive, and 92 machine-guns, besides putting a great many Huns out of action in other ways. The battalion entrained at Vaulx Vraucourt at 3.30 p.m. on 7th, and arrived at Tinques at 1 a.m. on the 8th, and then marched six miles to Manin. "Here we stayed till 15th, doing various parades and playing football (and drinking vin blanc). Now got decent billets in houses, and it was a treat to sleep again in beds. In fact, what with having the Boche on the run, and good billets, the war was not so bad at this time." The rest of the month was spent working under the Chief Engineer of the 8th Corps. The companies were somewhat scattered. " C " was in Douai for some time working on bridges. The other two companies were on the roads from Izel till 20th, then " A " went on to bridging in Douai, and " B " to Raches for road repairs. The battalion came under the orders of the 52nd Division again on 29th October.

On the 31st the headquarters and transport moved to Vieux Condé. " A " was at Sars et Rosieurs, " B " at Lecelles and " C " at Bouvignies.

The casualties during the month are recorded as three killed and fifteen wounded.

CHAPTER X

FINALE

DURING the twenty days that had elapsed since the 52nd Division went out to rest and refit, much had occurred, and the enemy had been driven back along his whole line. On the 8th October the British First and Third Armies had forced him beyond the Selle-le-Château line, and two days earlier the French on the south had reached the Suippe. On the 9th, the Germans retreated from their positions near Laon, which had become untenable, and from the Scheldt to the Aisne their armies started for home. The Belgian Army and British Second Army (Plumer), under the command of King Albert, commenced their advance as early as 28th September, and at one bound recovered all the ground lost in the spring.

On 14th October they attacked from Dixmude to the Lys, and compelled the Huns to quit Lille. The Allied attacks from the south continued, and from Cambrai to the Scheldt the retreat almost became a rout.

The 52nd Division came back into the line on 27th October at Sameon, and the next day the 156th Brigade took over the front of the 12th Division along the Jard Canal, the east bank of which the enemy was holding with a strong rear-guard of all arms. He had broken down all the bridges, and his front was strengthened by inundations which only left three lines of approach open, and all these were closely watched. Fortunately the division was not called to turn him out by force, but only to watch him till the operations to the north and south took effect, and then to follow him as rapidly as possible.

These operations were not long delayed. On the north, the Belgian-British Forces, under King Albert, ejected the Germans from Zeebrugge and Bruges, Courtaii, Roubaix, and joined hands with the British Army on the Scheldt at Pecq on 1st November. On the south the great attack began on 1st November. The Americans opened the ball on the extreme right and broke clean through, never stopping till the Armistice. North of the latest arrivals, the French and British Forces proved that in spite of the long time they had been in play, they were, like Johnnie Walker, still going strong.

So when the 52nd came up, it was fairly clear that the enemy must soon abandon his positions on the far side of the Jard Canal, although he was still holding the eastern bank, and indeed had some posts in the narrow strip of land between the canal and the Scheldt. The 8th Division on the right had prepared rafts for the crossing, and the scheme of operations had been carefully worked out by the 8th Corps. The 157th Brigade relieved the 8th Division on the right of 156th Brigade on night of 4th/5th, and the same night gas was projected into Hergnies.

On the 4th the British First, Third and Fourth Armies gave the enemy a crushing blow, advancing five miles on a thirty-miles front from the Sambre to Valenciennes. The orders for the pursuit, which was to be launched as soon as the Huns started moving, were issued by General Hill on 5th November, and the code word selected to start the chase was " Hunt." Patrols were very active everywhere, but the enemy showed no sign of moving, and on the 6th his guns were very active. Prisoners captured on that day said that the retirement was fixed for that night, but the patrols found him still there on the 7th, and at dawn the next day also they were greeted with machine-gun fire from near Bruille, but a little later another patrol failed to draw fire, though showing itself recklessly. At 8.30 a.m. the long-waited-for word " Hunt " was sent out to the expectant troops. No time was lost; by 11.30 a.m. a covering party from 157th Brigade had been put across both the Scheldt and the canal, and had established itself from Bruyeres through Rieux de Conde to the outskirts of Vieux Condé, and back to the canal. The squadron of the 4th Hussars attached to the division and the Cyclist Company pushed on ahead, and formed a screen farther forward, and by nightfall the 6th H.L.I. formed a line of outposts through Lorette. The 156th Brigade, on the left, also got well over the canal, the only opposition met with being from a few snipers in Hergnies, who were speedily cleared out. Before dark, " A " Battery, 156th Brigade, R.F.A., was ready for action in Hergnies.

The rapid transfer of so large a force across the double obstacle formed by the River Scheldt and Jard Canal was no small feat, and the credit of it is due to the Field Companies and the Pioneers.

On the 9th the advance was continued to the line of the Antoing-Pommeroeul Canal, which was crossed by bridges left by the enemy, the inhabitants joyfully assisting the troops to repair them and make them fit for heavy transport. By nightfall the whole of the 157th Infantry Brigade and the 4th Royal Scots of 156th Brigade, together with the 9th Brigade R.F.A. were over the canal, and the Cyclists, pushing on ahead, fell into a machine-gun ambush near La Piquet. The high ground near Blaton on the right flank was occupied.

On 10th the advance was carried on. The enemy's rear-guard was found round Herchies, and an action was carried on till after midnight, and resulted in Erbaut and high ground between it and Jurbrise being captured. Two machine-guns and seventeen prisoners were taken.

On the 11th it was found that the Boche had left. The Nimy-Jurbrise road was occupied. The 155th Brigade captured three trains in Jurbrise. At 11 a.m. on the 11th November, when the Armistice came into force, the division halted along the road from Nimy to Jurbrise, the right flank being just north of the canal, and the left about half a mile north of Jurbrise, which town was entirely held. Thus ended three very strenuous days' pursuit, during which the division advanced over twenty miles in an air line. The enemy obtained a good start, owing to the delay inseparable from the passage of the Scheldt and the Jard Canal, and he further obstructed the roads in every conceivable way while himself having a clear line of retreat and every incentive to hurry, yet in spite of these difficulties the division brought him to action at Herchies, and took a final gleaning of prisoners.

In the War Diary of the General Staff of the division great credit is given to the Royal Engineers, Pioneers and the 185th Tunnelling Company. "It was by their untiring efforts that the rapid advance in a water-logged area which was traversed by several rivers and canals, and in which all bridges and nearly every culvert was destroyed, was made possible. Every road had a mine blown in it, especially to those east of the Jard Canal."

The Battalion Diarist, never very communicative, has by now become very war weary, and his record for these stirring times reads :

"8th November.—Battalion Headquarters to Mont-du-Proy J.28.c.1.9. 'A' to Q.2.B and worked on road approaches to bridges in flooded area in K.33. 'B' to Q.3b. on roads. 'C' to Haute Rive J.30.c. on road approaches to bridges.

"9th November.—Headquarters to Peruwelz L.2.d.7.9. 'B' to Peruwelz L.2.a.

"10th November.—To Crandglis G.6.c. Sheet 45 Battalion Headquarters to Sirault L.1.c. 1.b. 'A' to Happart H.4. 'B' and 'C' on roads.

"12th November.—'B' to Villerot, 'C' to Baudour, on roads."

You notice that no event on 11th appeared worthy of his notice. A correspondent in "B" tells us, "When the company was in Peruwelz another division (47th?) passed through, and a rumour was started about there being an Armistice proposed. It was not until the 12th November that we had official information that hostilities had ceased."

The contrast between the scenes of wild, joyous enthusiasm in Whitehall, and the placid ignoring of the Armistice in Peruwelz is striking.

A correspondent on Battalion Headquarters writes: "Peruwelz was reached at dusk on the night of 8th October. Few, if any, in the battalion will ever forget the first impression of entering the first occupied town. The 17th Battalion Northumberland Fusiliers were, with the exception of a small advance guard, the first troops to enter, marching in column of route; the people seemed to go simply mad with excitement, and lined the streets, waving lighted lamps and candles; flags were got out, and streamers were stretched across the road. After marching from early morn the men were practically done, but such a reception flung fatigue to the wind, and the thought, 'It's been worth it,' flew through everyone's mind. On settling down in billets the men began to inspect the town; at least after the civilians had finished with them. As soon as one appeared in the street the people simply took possession and insisted on one going into their houses to drink to the health of freedom and to the exit of the Germans, which had only taken place during the previous few hours."

Another correspondent notes that Peruwelz was the first place "B" Company struck which had not been wrecked "and which looked more like a civilized town," but "not a scrap of metal was to be found. The Germans had taken the whole lot, from nobs on the windows and door handles to church bells, for their own uses." The same informant tells us that on 9th November, while the company was employed on road work, "At one particular cross-road a party under a Sergeant was working, when the Corps Commander came up in a car, stopped the work, told the Sergeant to call his men around him, explained to them who he was, what they were doing, and generally gave them an explanation." Puzzle: Name the Corps Commander?

One unwelcome feature of post-armistice life which was cheerfully put up with was shortness and irregularity of rations, owing to supplies being diverted to feed the refugees "who commenced to stream through in thousands, and also to the inhabitants of certain villages which had been stripped by the Germans."

On the 19th, Battalion Headquarters moved to Château Milfort, where "the owner took several N.C.O.'s into his garden, where a man was busy digging up bottles of wine that had been buried under the garden path four years before. Various toasts were duly honoured. The same gentleman told us that the park of the château had been used a good deal during the war as a landing place for British aeroplanes to drop and pick up spies."

All this time the battalion was employed on erasing from the land the marks of the beast. Filling in craters blown in the roads, repairing bridges, and, in the intervals, training. Training for what? For the next war?

On 26th November the whole battalion was assembled in Masnuy St. Jean, a straggling village, only just big enough to hold it. Here the battalion settled down and was occupied with education classes, games, ceremonial parades, and other diversions, among which was a dance at Masnuy St. Pierre, which was attended by the inhabitants. The gay Pioneers found such favour in the eyes of the fair daughters of the land that the local swains left the ball-room in a huff, but some were persuaded to return later.

In December, a Divisional Inter-Company football tournament was played. The team of "A" Company having defeated in succession those of "B" and "C," represented the battalion and overcame various other teams, fighting its way into the final round, when, after a very hard fought game, it was beaten by a company of the 5th H.L.I. by one goal.

Those who have read so far will have realized that the battalion had not had much time during the three years in France to keep up its barrack square drill, so with two big ceremonial parades in the near future, a good deal of what we call in the Army "spit and polish" was necessary to ensure that it should earn on the parade ground the same high praise that it had already done in more useful but less showy spheres of activity.

The first big parade took place at Maisieres, the Mons drill ground, on 18th January, 1919, when the whole division paraded, and General Sir A. J. Godley, K.C.B., K.C.M.G., commanding 22nd Corps, presented distinctions which had been recently won. Lieutenant-Colonel King received the D.S.O., Captains Gordon and Watson the M.C., and Sergeant Vagg the D.C.M. All went off well and the battalion gained high commendation. The second ceremonial was the presentation of the King's Colour.

The presentation of Colours is a very beautiful sight if the battalion to receive them is very highly drilled and steady under arms, otherwise it is a sorry spectacle. The 17th Northumberland Fusiliers determined to acquit itself well, and worked hard. There were many rehearsals, and some amusing incidents occurred. The battalion not having a band at that time, borrowed that of the Royal Scots, which at one of the early rehearsals, either out of sheer light-

PLATE XXII.

THE RETURN OF THE CADRE.

LAYING UP OF COLOURS.

PLATE XXIII.

Unveiling of the War Memorial, York.

heartedness or from ignorance, played for the march past, not the British Grenadiers, but some rollicking Highland melody, and played it fast too, so that the companies went by in a " crescent formation " at a fast pace, the small men in the centre striving vainly to keep up with their taller comrades on the flanks. On another occasion, the rehearsal being over, the battalion started for home in column of route with bayonets still fixed. The attention of the " temporary Second " being drawn to this, he acted with promptness, issuing the orders " Battalion halt, order arms, unfix bayonets " all in one breath. The spectacle which followed is best left to the imagination, but the battalion was on the march again within sixty seconds, with bayonets securely stowed away. Pioneers are always resourceful folk. However, proficiency was soon gained, and after a final rehearsal, in which the Divisional Commander, representing the Corps Commander, presented a broomstick, ornamented with a dirty square of red cloth, representing the King's Colour, to Captain Wilkinson, representing the Senior Subaltern, the battalion felt itself quite ready for the ordeal.

The parade took place on 27th January at Jurbrise, some four or five kilometres from Masnuy St. Jean on the Mons-Soignies road. The ground was covered with hard frozen snow. The battalion was drawn up so as to form three sides of a square, in the centre of which the Colour rested against a pile of drums. The ceremony was brief but very impressive. The Senior Chaplain having given an address and dedicated the Colour, Sir Arthur Godley, the Corps Commander, advanced and handed the Colour to Captain E. R. Wilkinson, who received it on bended knee. Sir Arthur then made a stirring speech, in which he spoke of the good work done by the battalion during the three years that had passed since it landed in France. Colonel King replied, giving a brief account of the battalion's history. The battalion then re-formed line, and the Colour party turned about, Captain Wilkinson raised the Colour, and the battalion presented arms. The band played the National Anthem while the Colour party " took post," moving at the slow march to the space left for it in the centre of the line. The battalion then marched past the Corps Commander.

" The battalion marched past in fine style, and was complimented both by the Corps Commander and Divisional General on the bearing of the men and the splendid way in which they marched."

The battalion might well march back to its billets proud of having displayed a precision and steadiness throughout a difficult test, worthy of the highest traditions of the regiment to which it belonged.

This was a fitting ending to the Great Adventure. Three years of hard work and war had told its tale; some of the "green bunch" of 1916 lay farther back in France and Flanders, some were already back in Old England sick or wounded, but the remainder stood there all the better for all they had been through, a battalion that could go anywhere and do anything.

"Time now began to hang heavy on our hands.

"Games and easy exercises were the order of the day, and sports were organized both in the battalion and throughout the whole division.

"Boxing matches were also organized, and after a very interesting series of bouts, Privates Quinney and Soulsby, 'A' Company, and Private Ridsdale, 'C' Company, were, as usual, invincible and secured most of the divisional championships, both Quinney and Soulsby securing events in their own weights and in heavier weights.

"A cross-country event was also organized throughout the Army Corps, the teams being composed of members of one unit. The 17th Battalion team easily won the brigade heat. They then represented the brigade in the divisional match and carried off this event also, in which the team's victory was also distinguished by the fact that Captain J. R. Sadler and Private G. Downey were first and second man home respectively. The battalion team representing the division secured the Corps' trophy, Captain J. R. Sadler and Lieutenant J. Henderson being second and third man home respectively."

From this time onwards the strength of the battalion decreased very rapidly. Demobilization went on steadily, and on 15th February ten officers and seventy-six other ranks of the more recently joined were sent to the 36th Battalion of the regiment. The War Diary for February closes with the statement that "training ceases on account of lowness of strength from demobbing." On 20th March the remnants of the battalion removed to Soignies, a small market town situated about half-way between Mons and Brussels. Here the equipment was made up to Mob. Table and the strength of the battalion gradually dwindled until we were down to cadre strength of three officers and thirty-two men, the officers being Colonel King, Commanding, Captain J. R. Sadler, Adjutant, and Captain and Quartermaster A. G. Tindell.

"About the beginning of June, Colonel King left us and proceeded to England for demobilization, after which he returned to his former post in the Argentine. About a fortnight later the order came for the cadre battalion to move to Antwerp in order to embark for home."

"After loading the transport and equipment into sea-going barges at Antwerp, the officers and men were ordered to proceed to Newcastle via Boulogne. On arrival at Newcastle, we were received by the Mayor and other civic officials, at whose hands we received entertainment and hospitality during the few days which we spent there prior to proceeding to Ripon."

"At Ripon the members of cadre were demobilized with the exception of the two officers, Captains Sadler and Tindell, and Corporals Train and Eldon, who proceeded to Aintree to await the arrival of the transport and equipment. After a fortnight's waiting, these arrived intact from Richborough, where they had been landed, and after handing them over to the Ordnance at Aintree, the little party proceeded once more to Newcastle with the Colours."

"The Colour party were met at Newcastle by Mr. C. A. Lambert, the Divisional Goods Manager, and his assistant, Mr. Morley, and a number of the North-Eastern Railway Company's local officials, together with Major Cole and several of the old officers of the battalion."

"The party marched to the Cathedral Church of St. Nicholas,[1] where, in the presence of a large gathering of the men who had been with the battalion on active service, and who had been given special leave by the Railway Company and their employers for the occasion, the Colours were deposited in a place of honour in the church. Before the service, Mr. Lambert, on behalf of the North-Eastern Railway Company, entertained the officers who were present at luncheon, and welcomed the members of the battalion home."

"The next day the two officers and N.C.O.'s who were left, proceeded to Ripon for demobilization, and so closed the history of the 17th Northumberland Fusiliers (N.E.R.) Pioneers."

---

[1] The party was received at the Cathedral by the Vicar of Newcastle (Canon Newsom), Canon Kempson, the Rev. J. J. Pigg, the Rev. E. Dudley Clark, the senior verger, and the choral scholars. The service was conducted by the Vicar, who, in the course of an address, referred to the battalion as a well-tried and hard-fighting one, and expressed his pride at receiving the Colour into keeping.

EMBARKATION ROLL OF OFFICERS

Rank	Name	Date of Embarkation	Casualties	Remarks
Lieut.-Col.	Pears, M. L.	20.11.15	Died in England	C.M.G. 3.6.16. Mentioned in despatches 13.6.16.
Major	Compton, P. H.	,,		To 6th D.G. 16.8.16.
,,	Oxley, H. C.	,,		To 5th S.W. Borderers 15.10.16.
Capt.	King, W. D. V. O.	,,		Major 17.8.16. Lieut.-Col. 4.9.16. D.S.O. 1.1.19. Mentioned in despatches 4.1.17, 8.11.18.
,,	Philips, H. V.	,,		
,,	Taylor, G. S.	,,		Major 5.9.16. Military Cross 14.9.17.
,,	Mackenzie, A.	,,	K.	
,,	Ker, H. T.	,,		Major 23.11.16. To 11th Royal Berks 17.11.16.
,,	Kitching, J. E.	,,		Staff Captain. To D.G.T. (H.Q.) 25.11.16.
,,	Redmond, H. M. S.	,,		To R.E. (R.O.D.) 7.11.16.
Lieut.	Ellis, H. C.	,,		
,,	Smith, P.	,,		Transport Officer. Resigned 24.1.17.
,,	Cole, H. S.	,,		Capt. 5.9.16. Major 18.9.18. Mentioned in despatches 8.11.18.
,,	Plumptre, E. A. W.	,,	W.	
,,	Lakeman, R. M.	,,	W.	Capt. 1.9.16. Mentioned in despatches 8.11.18.
,,	Glendinning, P. B.	,,		Capt. 30.11.16. To R.E.
,,	Riddel, J. O.	,,	W.	To R.E.
,,	Douglas, G. V.	,,		Capt. 10.12.16. Military Cross 1.1.18. Mentioned in despatches 4.1.17.
,,	Gordon, G. S. S.	,,		Capt. and Adjut. 20.10.16. Military Cross 1.1.19.
,,	Reid, J.	,,		R.A.M.C.
Lieut. & Q.M.	Tindill, A. G.	,,		Capt.
2nd Lieut.	Mitchell, A. G.	,,		Lieut. 17.3.16. To G.H.Q. Egypt 20.10.17.

17th and 32nd (S.) Batts. Northumberland Fusiliers (N.E.R.) Pioneers

Rank	Name	Date of Embarkation	Casualties	Remarks
2nd Lieut.	Robertson, W. W.	20.11.15		Lieut. 1.9.16. To R.E.
,,	Young, H.	,,		To G.H.Q. (D.D.) 5.3.17.
,,	Mucklow, G. F.	,,	W.	
,,	Blair, J.	,,		Lieut. 1.9.16. Capt. 9.11.16.
,,	Locock, L.	,,		Lieut. 21.9.16. Capt. 3.11.16.
,,	Sadler, J. R.	,,		Capt. 28.11.16.
,,	Pattison, A. N.	,,		To D.G.T. 26.4.17.
Capt. & Adjut.	Martin, G. W.	,,	K. 17.9.18	Mentioned in despatches 13.6.16. Major 20.10.16. Quéant Cemetery.

DRAFTS

Rank	Name	Date of Embarkation	Casualties	Remarks
2nd Lieut.	Marple, R. G.	1.1.16		To Indian Army 1.6.17.
Lieut.	Dallin, R. de P.	10.3.16	W.	
2nd Lieut.	Garvie, J.	10.3.16		Capt. and Adjut. 4.10.18.
,,	Hope, N.	10.3.16		Lieut. R.T.O. 4.5.16.
,,	Jellicoe, J. A.	10.3.16		To Indian Army 23.5.17.
Lieut.	Willatt, A.	5.1.16		R.A.M.C.
2nd Lieut.	Donald, G.	11.3.16		To 19th N.F. 15.6.17.
,,	Fletcher, R.	11.3.16		To 18th N.F. 2.4.16.
Capt.	Wells, S. C.	27.3.16		To 18th N.F. 15.6.17.
2nd Lieut.	Drury, J. C.	13.5.16		Lieut. 1.7.17.
,,	Germain, H. G.	13.5.16	Missing 12.7.16	Death presumed on or after 12.7.16.
,,	Smurthwaite, O.	16.6.16		Lieut. 26.12.16. Killed with 18th N.F.
Lieut.	Glanville, L. S. H.	24.7.16		R.A.M.C.
2nd Lieut.	Brisley, F. de Bock	15.6.16		To Indian Army 23.5.17.
Capt.	Craggs, J. B.	25.8.16		To 19th N.F. 27.9.16.
2nd Lieut.	Smith, E. W.	25.8.16		Lieut. 26.11.17.
,,	Neville, G. R.	25.8.16		Transport Officer 25.1.17. Lieut. 26.11.17.
,,	Watson, N.	16.9.16	W.	Capt. 26.9.18. Military Cross.
Capt.	Child, W. N.	16.9.16		R.A.M.C.
Lieut.	Hutson, S.	16.9.16	W.	
Capt.	Matthews, J. A. V.	21.3.17	W.	R.A.M.C.
2nd Lieut.	Blaiklock, J. F. W.	1.5.17		Lieut. 25.4.18. To R.A.F. 25.9.18.
Lieut.	Phelan, A. E.	15.9.17		To 1st N.F.
,,	Gregory, T. W.	17.9.17		To 16th N.F.

Embarkation Roll of Officers

Rank	Name	Date of Embarkation	Casualties	Remarks
Lieut.	Dawson, F.	17.9.17		To 16th N.F.
2nd Lieut.	Piper, C. W.	18.9.17		To R.A.F. 20.9.18.
,,	Rutledge, C.	24.9.17		
,,	Maughan, W. D.	24.9.17	K. 19.11.17	Ypres.
,,	McKay, G.	17.9.17		
Lieut.	Cameron, W.	18.9.17		To R.F.C.
,,	Hutchinson, F. W.	18.9.17		
,,	Gaffney, B.	18.9.17		
,,	Wilkinson, E. R.	18.9.17		Capt. 10.10.18.
,,	Wardroper, A. K.	18.9.17		Capt.
2nd Lieut.	Harris, W. E.	18.9.17	W.	
,,	Basey, F. T.	18.9.17	W.	Lieut. 1.7.17.
,,	Tindall, G. W.	18.9.17		Lieut. 1.7.17. Capt.
,,	Marshall, C. B.	18.9.17		To R.F.C.
,,	Calvert, W. E.	18.9.17		
,,	Pickering, J. G.	18.9.17		
,,	Potts, J.	18.9.17	W.	
,,	Dinning, W.	10.12.17		Lieut. 1.7.17.
Lieut.	Maskell, R.	17.6.18		
Capt.	Martyn, S. R.	13.8.18		To 1st Monmouth Regiment 25.9.18.
Major	Bell, P.	24.8.18		
2nd Lieut.	Dixon, R. H.	25.9.18		
,,	Harvey, W.	25.9.18		
,,	Forbes, A. K.	25.9.18		
,,	Petch, J. W.	25.9.18		
,,	Redford, W. J.	4.6.18		
,,	Sumner, H.	11.10.18		
,,	Bowes, D.	26.10.18		
,,	Borland, W. D.	26.10.18		
,,	Cockayne, F.	26.10.18		
,,	King, E.	26.10.18		
,,	Parker, G. W.	26.10.18		
,,	Gilduff, E.	26.10.18		
,,	Hillhouse, J. P.	26.10.18		
,,	Petty, J. T.	26.10.18		
Lieut.	Cox, F. W.	4.6.18		
,,	Connell, M. W.	4.6.18		
,,	Harrison, A. C.	4.6.18		
,,	Heslop, N.	4.6.18		
,,	Laing, E. C.	30.8.18		

LIST OF OFFICERS WHO PASSED THROUGH THE 17TH BATTALION NORTHUMBERLAND FUSILIERS BETWEEN SEPTEMBER 1914 AND SEPTEMBER 1915, BUT WHO DID NOT SERVE WITH THE BATTALION ON FOREIGN SERVICE.

Colonel	D. B. Preston
Lieutenant-Colonel	M. Williamson
Major	A. C. Geddes
Major	A. H. B. Wright
Major	W. D. Rudgard
Major	E. St. J. Lawson
Captain	A. D. M. Napier
Captain	J. Bywell
Captain	P. E. Nobbs
Lieutenant	R. W. D. Reeves
Lieutenant	G. L. Thompson
Lieutenant	J. C. F. Irvine
Lieutenant	P. Smith
Hon. Lieutenant and Quartermaster	G. Pearce
Second-Lieutenant	W. L. Henderson
Second-Lieutenant	J. F. Cameron
Second-Lieutenant	J. M. F. Craven
Second-Lieutenant	W. McLellan
Second-Lieutenant	R. Nelson
Second-Lieutenant	T. M. Harrison
Second-Lieutenant	G. Paget
Second-Lieutenant	C. Cowley
Second-Lieutenant	R. McDougal
Second-Lieutenant	T. E. Cameron
Second-Lieutenant	W. B. Brown
Second-Lieutenant	A. Moncrieff
Second-Lieutenant	R. F. Stobart
Second-Lieutenant	F. A. Vernon
Second-Lieutenant	C. H. Pick
Second-Lieutenant	D. Clayton
Second-Lieutenant	N. B. Paddon
Second-Lieutenant	T. B. Hare
Second-Lieutenant	W. Maughan

ROLL OF MEN WHO SERVED WITH THE 17TH (S.) BATTALION NORTHUMBERLAND FUSILIERS PIONEERS 1914-1919

D. = Died Overseas—Sickness.
D.G. = Died of Gas.
D.W. = Died of Wounds.
E. = Embarked with Battalion.
G. = Gassed.
K. = Killed in Action.
T.B.E. = Transferred before Embarkation.
W. = Wounded.

Reg. No.	Name	Coy.	Rank	Casualties	Remarks
17/ 766	Abbey, T.	A	Private		E.
17/ 588	Abbott, A.	C	,,		E. R.O.D.
17/ 1279	Abbott, J.	A	,,	W.W.	E. R.O.D.
17/ 1105	Abbott, W. C.	B	,,		E.
17/ 1049	Adamson, F.	A	,,		E.
17/ 589	Addison, S.	B	,,	K.	E. 8.11.17, Ypres, Bard Cottage Cemetery.
17/ 1393	Aisbitt, T.	C	,,	W.	E.
17/ 591	Aislabie, J.	B	,,	W.W.	E. L/Cpl.
17/ 592	Aked, A.	C	,,	K.	E. 29.11.17, Ypres, 28th British Military Cemetery.
17/ 395	Akers, C. F.	B	,,	W.	E. Corporal.
17/ 1120	Alderson, J. G.	C	,,	W.	E.
17/ 66	Aldis, G. S.	D	,,	G.W.	E. Military Medal.
17/ 67	Allott, G. W.	D	,,		E.
17/ 484	Almond, H.	C	,,		E.
17/ 68	Ambler, J. J.	D	Corporal		E. Commission.
17/ 1380	Amey, E. J.	A	Private		E. Corporal Commission.
17/ 1342	Amos, W. F.	A	,,		E. R.O.D.
17/ 1469	Anderson, C.	C	,,	W.	E.
17/ 259	Anderson, H. W.	D	,,	G.	E.
17/ 257	Anderson, J.	A	,,	W.	E.
17/ 1335	Angus, T. S.	A	,,	W. W.	E.
17/ 1160	Annis, C. J.	C	,,	G.	E.
17/ 69	Anthony, N. G.	C	,,		E. Commission.
17/ 594	Appleby, C.	D	,,	G.	E.
17/ 485	Applegarth, F. T.	B	,,		E.
17/ 396	Arlington, T. D.	B	,,		E. R.O.D.
17/ 894	Armstrong, A.	A	,,		E.

17th and 32nd (S.) Batts. Northumberland Fusiliers (N.E.R.) Pioneers

Reg. No.	Name	Coy.	Rank	Casualties	Remarks
17/ 1389	Armstrong, A. E.	A	Private		E.
17/ 1470	Armstrong, J.	A	,,	W.	E.
17/ 1344	Armstrong, J. W.	A	,,		E. R.O.D.
17/ 595	Armstrong, T.	A	,,		E.
17/ 1401	Atkins, G. H.	B	,,		E.
17/ 70	Atkinson, H. G.	D	L/Cpl.	W.	E. Corporal.
17/ 399	Atkinson, J. G.	B	Private	W.W.	E.
17/ 260	Atkinson, W. E.	A	,,	W.	E. L/Cpl.
17/ 71	Audus, G. W.	D	,,		E.
17/ 597	Aungle, G. H.	A	,,		E.
17/ 1341	Auslow, T.	A	,,		E.
17/ 72	Ayres, A.	C	,,		E. To 11th N.F.
32/ 199	Abbott, T.	B	Private		
32/ 891	Abbott, T. C.	A	,,	W.	
32/ 907	Adams, C. L.	C	,,		To 36th N.F.
45208	Adams, T.	A	L/Cpl.		To R.F.C.
32/ 66	Airey, W.	D	Private	W.	
32/ 972	Alderson, F.	B	,,		
17/ 256	Alderson, J. T.	B	,,		
45196	Allchurch, T. H.	D	,,		To 6th N.F.
12872	Allen, W.	C	,,		
32/ 259	Allerston, G. R.	B	,,		
17/ 1527	Almond, H. T.	A	,,		
32/ 142	Alsop, T.	B	,,		
17/ 1528	Altringham, J.	A	,,		
32/ 882	Amos, J. E.	C	,,		To 36th N.F.
17/ 1459	Ampleford, A.	D	,,	W.	
32/ 67	Andrew, D.	B	,,		
45260	Andrews, W.	A	,,		
32/ 68	Argyle, F.	B	,,		To 10th N.F.
44278	Arnold, H.	B	,,		To 6th N.F.
45130	Arundel, S.	C	L/Cpl.		To 6th N.F.
45129	Ashford, C. S.	C	Private	K.	27.9.18, Canal du Nord, Cambrai.
45199	Ashworth, T.	C	,,	D.	2.1.18, Cimetière St. Sever, Rouen.
32/ 489	Atkin, J. W.	C	,,		L/Cpl.
32/ 927	Atkinson, J. W.	A	,,		
45122	Austin, J.	D	L/Cpl.		
17/ 1431	Abel, H.		Private		T.B.E.
17/ 590	Ainsly, J.		,,		,,

Reg. No.	Name	Coy.	Rank	Casualties	Remarks
17/ 1241	Alderson, J.		Private		T.B.E.
17/ 1242	Allison, B.		,,		,,
17/ 593	Alton, J.		,,		,,
17/ 767	Appleton, G. H.		,,		,,
17/ 397	Armitage, W.		,,		,,
17/ 596	Arridge, J.		,,		,,
17/ 183	Atkin, A.		,,		,,
17/ 1161	Atkinson, B.		,,		,,
17/ 1280	Atkinson, F.		,,		,,
17/ 398	Atkinson, H. V.		,,		,,
17/ 258	Atkinson, J.		,,		,,
17/ 1471	Badenock, W.	A	Private	W.	E.
17/ 1162	Bailey, A.	A	,,		E. L/Cpl.
17/ 486	Bailey, E.	C	,,		E.
17/ 1398	Bailis, S.	A	,,		E.
17/ 487	Bainbridge, J.	B	L/Cpl.		E. L/Sergt.
17/ 1067	Baker, P.	C	,,		E. Corporal.
17/ 1217	Baker, W. E.	D	Private	W.	E.
17/ 598	Baldwinson, T.	D	L/Cpl.	K.	E. 1.7.16. Somme, Bouzincourt Cemetery.
17/ 488	Ball, A. E.	A	Private		E.
17/ 599	Ball, W. N.	A	,,	W.W.	E.
17/ 768	Balmer, T.	A	,,		E.
17/ 1281	Banning, G. D.	D	,,	D.W.	E. 4.7.16. Somme, Cimetière St. Siver, Rouen.
17/ 2	Barber, A.	A	,,		E.
17/ 600	Barber, G. E.	B	L/Cpl.	W.W.	E. Corporal.
17/ 1218	Barker, C. E. A.	A	Private	W.	E.
17/ 601	Barker, E.	B	L/Cpl.		E. Corporal. Meritorious Service Medal.
17/ 769	Barker, E.	B	Private	K.	E. 2.11.17, Ypres, Bard Cottage Cemetery.
17/ 895	Barker, G. N.	B	,,	W.	E.
17/ 3	Barker, H. W.	D	,,	W.	E.
17/ 1042	Barker, R. W.	D	,,	W.	E.
17/ 1219	Barker, S.	A	,,	D.W.	E. 29.9.18, Cambrai 38 C.C.S.
17/ 966	Barker, W.	C	,,	W.	E.
17/ 75	Barrow, J. W.	D	,,		E.
17/ 189	Bartleson, P.	B	,,		E.

17th and 32nd (S.) Batts. Northumberland Fusiliers (N.E.R.) Pioneers

Reg. No.	Name	Coy.	Rank	Casualties	Remarks
17/ 770	Barwick, R.	A	Private	W.	E.
17/ 1074	Bassett, J. H.	A	,,		E.
17/ 896	Bateman, H.	B	,,		E. L/Cpl.
17/ 76	Bateson, G. E.	D	,,		E. ,,
17/ 1384	Batey, J. J.	A	,,	W.	E.
17/ 897	Batterbee, W. G.	D	L/Cpl.	W.	E. Corporal.
17/ 4	Batty, A.	C	Private		E.
17/ 771	Baxter, T. S.	A	,,		E.
17/ 77	Bays, F.	C	,,	K.	E. 1.7.16, Somme, Authuille Military Cemetery.
17/ 78	Beale, E.	D	Corporal		E.
17/ 1359	Bean, A.	C	Private	W.	E. R.O.D.
17/ 5	Bean, W. R.	D	L/Cpl.		E.
17/ 79	Beautiman, H.	D	Private		E.
17/ 1509	Beavers, W. G.	A	,,		E.
17/ 1108	Beck, E.	A	,,		E.
17/ 80	Bedford, C. T.	C	,,		E.
17/ 1472	Bell, F. J.	A	,,		E.
17/ 261	Bell, J. C.	A	,,	W.	E. L/Cpl.
17/ 968	Bell, R.	A	L/Cpl.		E. L/Sergt.
17/ 81	Bell, W.	D	Private		E.
17/ 604	Bell, W.	A	,,		E.
17/ 1220	Belton, R. J.	A	,,		E.
17/ 192	Bendelow, A. H.	C	L/Cpl.	W.	E. Sergt.
17/ 605	Benson, H.	B	Private		E.
17/ 1489	Berridge, W. T.	A	,,	W.W.	E.
17/ 1421	Beswick, A.	D	,,		E.
17/ 606	Bewick, J. L.	C	,,		E.
17/ 1221	Bicker, W. H.	A	,,		E.
17/ 401	Bickerton, C.	A	,,		E. Corporal.
17/ 899	Bilton, S. G.	D	,,		E.
17/ 1821	Birtle, A.	B	,,		E. R.O.D.
17/ 971	Bishop, J. T.	D	,,		E.
17/ 607	Black, J. H.	A	,,		E.
17/ 1345	Blackburn, A.	D	,,		E. R.O.D.
17/ 608	Blackburn, W.	A	,,	W.D.W.	E. 10.2.18, Poperinghe.
17/ 263	Blades, P.	D	L/Sergt.		E. Sergt. Commission.
17/ 264	Blair, G. W.	B	Private		E.
17/ 972	Blakey, G. C.	A	,,		E. L/Cpl. To R.E.
17/ 265	Blakey, W. E.	A	Sergt.		E. Military Medal. Commission.
17/ 609	Bland, W.	A	Private		E. Sergt.

Reg. No.	Name	Coy.	Rank	Casualties	Remarks
17/ 491	Blaxland, E. N.	D	L/Cpl.		E.
17/ 1282	Blenkinsopp, R. L.	A	Private		E. R.O.D.
17/ 772	Blewitt, E.	A	,,		E.
17/ 492	Boast, H. J.	B	Corporal	W.	E.
17/ 1078	Boddy, J. W.	A	Private		E. ,,
17/ 84	Bolton, J.	D	,,	K.	E. 10.7.16, Somme, Bouzincourt Cemetery.
17/ 610	Boocock, F.	D	L/Cpl.		E. Sergt.
17/ 1283	Boon, C. S.	D	Private		E.
17/ 194	Booth, W.	A	Corporal	W.	E. Sergt.
17/ 195	Boston, A.	C	Private	W.	E.
17/ 611	Bousfield, R. W.	B	,,		E.
17/ 773	Bousfield, S.	A	,,	W.	E. L/Cpl.
17/ 612	Bowerbank, A.	B	,,	W.	E.
17/ 6	Bowes, A. J.	C	,,		E. L/Cpl.
17/ 1331	Boynton, G. W.	A	,,		E. R.O.D.
17/ 196	Bradbury, G. L.	D	,,		E.
17/ 775	Bradley, J.	A	,,	K.	E. 27.9.18, Canal du Nord, Cambrai.
17/ 197	Bradley, T.	C	,,	W.W.	E.
17/ 1284	Bradley, W. H.	B	,,		E.
17/ 776	Bradshaw, H.	D	,,	W.	E.
17/ 494	Bray, S. B.	A	,,	G.	E.
17/ 1084	Brayshaw, S.	D	,,		E.
17/ 973	Breckon, R. H.	D	,,		E. L/Cpl.
17/ 85	Bricklebank, C. H.	D	,,		E.
17/ 777	Briggs, A. T.	B	,,	W.W.	E.
17/ 86	Briggs, R.	D	,,		E.
17/ 1350	Briggs, S. L.	C	,,		E.
17/ 267	Broadley, W.	A	,,		E.
17/ 613	Brook, G. L.	C	Sergt.		E.
17/ 1122	Brooks, F.	D	Private	K.	E. 19.11.17, Ypres, Bard Cottage Cemetery.
17/ 614	Broome, J. A.	B	,,	W.W.	E.
17/ 406	Brotton, A. E.	C	,,	W.	E.
17/ 1284	Brown, A.	B	,,	W.	E.
17/ 1458	Brown, C. E.	C	,,	W.W.	E.
17/ 778	Brown, E. S.	A	,,		E.
17/ 495	Brown, G.	D	,,	W.	E.
17/ 1166	Brown, H.	C	,,	W.W.	E.
17/ 1072	Brown, J.	A	,,	K.	E. 16.5.16, Aveluy.
17/ 407	Brown, P. E.	B	C.Q.M.S.		E. Commission.
17/ 467	Brown, P. R.	B	Private		E.

17th and 32nd (S.) Batts. Northumberland Fusiliers (N.E.R.) Pioneers

Reg. No.	Name	Coy.	Rank	Casualties	Remarks
17/ 1519	Bruce, G.	A	Private	K.	E. 1.8.16, Loos, Sains-en-Gohelle Cemetery.
17/ 1440	Bryan, G. W.	B	,,	W.	E.
17/ 779	Buckle, F.	B	,,		E.
17/ 1285	Bulmer, T.	A	,,		E. R.O.D.
17/ 974	Burbridge, S. G.	C	,,		E.
17/ 618	Burn, J.	A	,,		E.
17/ 7	Burnitt, J.	D	,,		E.
17/ 619	Burns, R.	C	L/Cpl.		E. Corporal.
17/ 976	Burns, T.	A	Private		E.
17/ 408	Burton, W. H.	D	,,	G.W.	E.
17/ 8	Burtt, J. M.	D	L/Cpl.	K.	E. 29.6.16, Somme, Authuille Military Cemetery.
17/ 1061	Busby, O.	C	Private		E.
17/ 1168	Bussey, G.	B	,,	W.	E.
17/ 270	Butcher, J.	B	L/Cpl.		E.
17/ 198	Butler, E. J.	D	Private	W.	E.
17/ 88	Butler, J. L.	D	,,		E.
17/ 780	Butler, J. R.	D	,,		E.
17/ 271	Byers, J.	B	,,	W.	E. Corporal.
17/ 89	Byers, J. D.	B	,,		E. ,,
17/ 90	Bywell, J. E.	A	R.Q.M.S		E.
17/ 486	Bailey, E.		Private		
17/ 1121	Baker, J. W.	D	,,		Corporal.
32/ 144	Balls, J. W.	B	,,		
17/ 200	Bancroft, J.	B	,,		
32/ 926	Barker, A. R.	B	,,		
32/ 327	Barker, C.	B	,,		
45174	Barr, J.	C	,,	W.	
32/ 871	Baxter, A.	A	,,	W.	
45213	Bayles, W. J.	C	,,		To 6th N.F.
17/ 602	Beautiman, J. E.	D	,,		Died of Wounds.
32/ 202	Beautiman, T.	D	,,		
32/ 394	Beckett, A.	B	,,		
32/ 940	Beckett, W. R.	B	,,		
28/ 10	Beckwith, G. W.	A	,,	W.	
44279	Beenham, A.	D	,,		
45177	Beever, H.	A	,,		To 6th N.F.
32/ 4	Bell, H.	A	,,		
17/ 400	Bell, H.	B	,,		
17/ 1081	Bell, J.	A	,,	W.	

Reg. No.	Name	Coy.	Rank	Casualties	Remarks
32/ 736	Bell, R. L.	A	Private	W.	
32/ 72	Benn, W.	B	,,		
44272	Bennett, F. J.	C	,,		To 6th N.F.
45150	Bennett, F. W.	C	,,		,, ,,
45808	Bennett, W.	C	,,		
17/ 1164	Benson, S. C.		,,		
17/ 490	Bentley, F.	D	,,		
17/ 1109	Besford, J. R.	C	,,	W.	
17/ 402	Bidewell, F.	D	,,	W.	
45143	Biggs, A. G.	A	,,		To 6th N.F.
45131	Bilbrough, G. V.	D	,,		
45223	Binns, L.	D	,,		To 6th N.F.
32/ 923	Birch, A. R.	A	,,		
17/ 403	Birch, F. W.	A	L/Cpl.		Corporal.
17/ 1554	Bird, A.	A	,,		,,
32/ 74	Bird, H.	B	Private		
26128	Birrell, J.	D	,,		
45113	Blackburn, W.	C	,,		To 6th N.F.
32/ 872	Boast, S.	B	,,		
32/ 77	Boggett, F.	A	,,		
17/ 902	Boocock, J. J.	C	,,		
45256	Booth, G. P.	D	,,		
32/ 861	Booth, J. T.	A	,,		
32/ 76	Bootyman, W.		,,		To 14th N.F.
17/ 774	Bowen, E.	B	,,		
32/ 660	Boxall, S. K.	A	,,		To 36th N.F.
45134	Boyd, W.	C	Corporal		To 6/7 Royal Scots Fus.
5648	Boynes, J.	C	Private		
44280	Boynette, T. W. C.	D	,,		To 6th N.F.
32/ 150	Brackstone, J. E.		,,		To 14th N.F.
45229	Bradbury, V. H.	A	,,		To 6th N.F.
45159	Brady, G.	A	,,		,, ,,
26142	Brewin, J.		L/Cpl.		To 14th N.F.
45217	Brice, S. M.	D	Private		To 36th N.F.
45232	Briggs, H. T.	A	,,		To 6th N.F.
32/ 203	Brison, G. W.	A	,,		
17/ 1849	Brittain, W. G.	C	,,	W.	
17/ 405	Brookes, J. C.	B	,,		R.O.D.
45140	Brown, R.	D	,,		To 6th N.F.
17/ 1495	Brown, R. E.	D	,,		
17/ 1529	Brown, T.	C	,,		
32/ 538	Brown, T. F.	C	,,		To 36th N.F.
32/ 680	Brownlee, C. M.	A	,,		

17th and 32nd (S.) Batts. Northumberland Fusiliers (N.E.R.) Pioneers

Reg. No.	Name	Coy.	Rank	Casualties	Remarks
45215	Buckel, W.	A	Private		To 6th N.F.
45185	Buckland, J. T.	D	,,		,, ,,
17/ 617	Burgoyne, J.	C	,,		
17/ 87	Burnan, J. H.	C	L/Cpl.		Corporal.
32/ 8	Burton, J.		Private		To 14th N.F.
17/ 270	Butcher, J.	B	,,		
32/ 207	Butler, J.	B	,,		
17/ 1121	Baker, J. W.		Private		T.B.E.
17/ 1	Baker, T.		,,		,,
17/ 1041	Ballantine, J.		,,		,,
17/ 965	Banks, W.		,,		,,
17/ 73	Bardy, C.		,,		,,
17/ 74	Barker, W.		C.S.M.		,,
17/ 967	Barnes, A. E.		Private		,,
17/ 190	Battle, J.		C.S.M.		,,
17/ 1163	Bee, J. T.		Private		,,
17/ 191	Beech, J.		,,		,,
17/ 1453	Bell, A.		,,		,,
17/ 400	Bell, H.		,,		,,
17/ 603	Bell, J.		,,		,,
17/ 969	Bell, T. P.		,,		,,
17/ 898	Bell, W.		,,		,,
17/ 262	Bellwood, J. A.		,,		,,
17/ 489	Benson, F. J.		,,		,,
17/ 193	Beswick, C. M.		,,		,,
17 82	Bilsby, H. H.		,,		,,
17/ 1412	Binns, T.		,,		,,
17/ 1321	Birtle, A.		,,		,,
17/ 404	Bishop, J.		,,		,,
17/ 83	Boland, T. B.		,,		,,
17/ 1553	Bond, E. W.		,,		,,
17/ 493	Bowering, G.		,,		,,
17/ 268	Broadley, W. S.		,,		,,
17/ 266	Briggs, A. D.		,,		,,
17/ 1165	Brown, E. F.		,,		,,
17/ 615	Brown, G.		,,		,,
17/ 616	Brown, H.		,,		,,
17/ 1441	Buckley, J.		,,		,,
17/ 1510	Burdy, A. J.		,,		,,
17/ 900	Burnand, R.		,,		,,
17/ 269	Burnip, R.		,,		,,
17/ 901	Buxton, F. B.		,,		,,

Reg. No.	Name	Coy.	Rank	Casualties	Remarks
17/ 9	Byrne, J.		Private		T.B.E.
17/ 781	Cade, P.	C	Private		E.
17/ 977	Cairns, J.	A	,,		E.
17/ 904	Callaghan, J.	A	,,		E. L/Cpl.
17/ 409	Calvert, S. H.	D	,,	W.	E.
17/ 410	Calvert, W. B.	A	Sergt.		E.
17/ 272	Cambridge, J.	B	Private	W.	E.
17/ 1086	Caminada, J.	B	L/Cpl.		E.
17/ 199	Cammidge, H.	C	Private	W.	E.
17/ 1201	Camp, G. W.	B	,,	W.	E.
17/ 1056	Campbell, H.	B	,,		E.
17/ 496	Carbert, A.	C	,,		E.
17/ 273	Carling, H.	B	,,		E.
17/ 274	Carlisle, R.	A	L/Cpl.		E. Corporal to 10th K.O.S.B.
17/ 1390	Carlson, T. H. F.	C	Private	W.	E.
17/ 1169	Carr, C.	A	,,		E.
17/ 903	Carr, T.	B	,,		E.
17/ 620	Carrigan, C. A.	A	,,	W.W.	E.
17/ 200	Carter, A.	C	,,	W.	E.
17/ 1123	Carter, S.	A	,,		E.
17/ 1511	Cartmell, C.	B	,,	W.W.	E.
17/ 13	Cass, S.	D	,,	W.	E.
17/ 782	Cassidy, J.	B	L/Sergt.		E. Sergt.
17/ 788	Cavanagh, J.	A	Private	D.W.	E. Ypres.
17/ 621	Chambers, J.	A	,,		E.
17/ 98	Chapleo, W.	C	,,		E.
17/ 1065	Charlton, W.	C	,,	W.	E.
17/ 1124	Chatt, C.	D	,,		E.
17/ 1125	Chatt, T.	D	,,	K.	E. 15.3.16, Somme, Aveluy Cemetery.
17/ 1222	Cheeseman, M. J.	B	,,		E.
17/ 1249	Chilton, T.	D	,,		E.
17/ 275	Clapham, T. W.	C	,,		E. L/Cpl.
17/ 980	Clark, A.	C	,,		E.
17/ 981	Clark, H. S.	C	,,		E.
17/ 94	Clark, T. L.	B	,,		E.
17/ 982	Clark, W.	C	L/Cpl.	W.	E. L/Sergt.
17/ 15	Clarke, F.	C	Private	W.	E.
17/ 1059	Clarke, W.	C	,,		E.
17/ 276	Coates, A. F. W.	B	L/Cpl.		E.

17th and 32nd (S.) Batts. Northumberland Fusiliers (N.E.R.) Pioneers

Reg. No.	Name	Coy.	Rank	Casualties	Remarks
17/ 1357	Coates, H.	B	Private		E. R.O.D.
17/ 1171	Coates, J. W.	D	,,		E. L/Cpl.
17/ 412	Cobb, G.	D	Private		E.
17/ 16	Cole, T. J. C.	D	L/Cpl.		E. Sergt.
17/ 1058	Cole, W.	C	Private	W.	E.
17/ 277	Colley, L. H.	A	L/Cpl.		E. L/Sergt.
17/ 1405	Colling, J. R.	B	Private	D.W.	E. 13.7.15, Somme, Wimereux Cemetery.
17/ 96	Consitt, A.	D	,,		E.
17/ 622	Cook, O.	B	,,	K.	E. 30.10.17, Ypres, St. Julien Cemetery.
17/ 414	Copeland, C. C.	B	,,		E. R.O.D.
17/ 203	Copeland, J. W.	C	,,	K.	E. 16.11.17, Ypres, Bard Cottage Cemetery.
17/ 623	Copp, R. K.	A	,,		E.
17/ 1172	Coulthard, G. L.	B	,,		E.
17/ 905	Coulthard, T.	B	,,		E.
17/ 279	Coutts, D.	A	,,	W.	E.
17/ 1445	Cowen, T. W.	B	,,		E.
17/ 1126	Cox, G. H.	D	,,	W.W.	E.
17/ 625	Craggs, R. H.	C	,,	D.W.	E. 13.11.17, Ypres, Mendingham Cemetery.
17/ 17	Craven, H.	D	,,	W.	E. L/Sergt.
17/ 18	Craven, W.	C	,,		E.
17/ 906	Crawford, R. H.	B	,,	D.S.	E. 14.6.18, Neuville St. Vaast.
17/ 627	Crews, C. R.	A	,,		E.
17/ 1287	Crinkley, C.	A	,,	W.	E.
17/ 1127	Crisp, W.	A	,,	K.	E. 8.7.16, Somme.
17/ 19	Croft, C.	C	,,		E. L/Cpl.
17/ 1090	Crooks, G. W.	C	,,		E.
17/ 498	Crosby, R.	B	,,	D.W.	E. 6.7.16, Somme, Cimetière du Bois, Haring Heilly.
17/ 1063	Crossling, H.	C	,,	W.W.	E.
17/ 626	Crossling, J. W.	D	,,		E.
17/ 499	Crundwell, G. H.	D	,,		E. L/Cpl.
45240	Caffrey, J. T.	D	Private		To 6th N.F.
45188	Campbell, L. C.	A	,,		,, ,,
43231	Carr, G. A.		,,		,, ,,
17/ 11	Carter, F.	D	,,		
45180	Carter, W.	C	Corporal		

Reg. No.	Name	Coy.	Rank	Casualties	Remarks
45123	Cassie, W.	A	L/Cpl.		To 6th N.F.
17/ 91	Cawkill, H.	D	Private	W.	
32/ 209	Cawkwell, A. A.	C	,,		
17/ 1079	Chadwick, W.	A	,,		
17/ 1170	Chambers, J. W.	B	,,	W.	
17/ 14	Chapman, J.	C	,,	W.G.	
32/ 967	Charlton, E.	B	,,	W.	
28/ 12	Charlton, W.	D	,,		
43279	Chatt, R.		,,		To 6th N.F.
32/ 434	Chipchase, J. E.	A	,,		To 36th N.F.
17/ 411	Chisman, G.	C	,,		
32/ 468	Clark, J.	B	,,		
45255	Clark, P. E.	D	,,		
45182	Clark, T. H.	C	Corporal		
17/ 1373	Clement, J.	C	L/Cpl.		
17/ 1433	Clifford, A. E.	D	Private		
17/ 1062	Clifford, G. S.	C	,,	K.	27.9.18, Canal du Nord, Cambrai.
57615	Clifton, W. H.	C	,,	K.	16.11.17, Ypres, Bard Cottage Cemetery.
17/ 1442	Close, M. S.		Private		
32/ 902	Coates, A.	C	,,		
45164	Cockcroft, E.	D	,,		To 6th N.F.
267787	Coleman, G. E.	A	,,	D.W.	4.4.18, Ypres.
32/ 153	Collinson, J. J.	B	,,	W.	
17/ 1492	Colton, J.	C	,,		
32/ 12	Comasky, T.	A	,,	W.G.	
32/ 212	Connor, E.	A	,,		
45251	Cook, W. A.	A	,,		To 6th N.F.
32/ 474	Cooper, E.	B	,,		
45171	Cooper, F. A.	D	,,		To 6th N.F.
17/ 2013	Cope, J.		Sergt.		A.O.C.
17/ 1488	Coulter, W. G.	C	Private		
17/ 624	Coulthard, R. H.	B	,,	D.W.	10.6.17, Ypres.
32/ 154	Cowens, R.	A	,,		
32/ 337	Craggill, C.	C	,,	W.	
45264	Crann, F.	D	,,		To 6th N.F.
32/ 497	Crawford, F.	B	,,		
44281	Crawford, J.	D	,,		To 6th N.F.
45533	Cresswell, A.	A	,,		,, ,,
45169	Crook, J.	D	,,		To 36th N.F.
32/ 14	Crooks, R. A.	C	,,	W.	
45175	Crosby, A. H.	C	,,		To York and Lancs.

17th and 32nd (S.) Batts. Northumberland Fusiliers (N.E.R.) Pioneers

Reg. No.	Name	Coy.	Rank	Casualties	Remarks
17/ 1358	Crossan, B.	B	Corporal		R.O.D.
45248	Crowther, E.	C	Private		To 6th N.F.
32/ 890	Cundall, J.	B	,,		
32/ 340	Cunneyworth, J.	B	,,		
32/ 156	Curley, D. C. H.		,,		To 14th N.F.
17/ 1174	Curry, F.		,,		,, ,,
17/ 1386	Calder, R. P.		Private		T.B.E.
17/ 10	Campion, W.		,,		,,
17/ 1044	Carlile, G. J.		Sergt.		,,
17/ 12	Cartwright, W.		Private		,,
17/ 92	Chambers, E. W.		,,		,,
17/ 621	Chambers, J.		,,		,,
17/ 1362	Chandler, J.		,,		,,
17/ 978	Chapman, C.		,,		,,
17/ 979	Charlton, A.		,,		,,
17/ 1408	Clark, J.		,,		,,
17/ 1286	Clark, J. W.		,,		,,
17/ 784	Clementson, J.		,,		,,
17/ 983	Clitheroe, J. W.		,,		,,
17/ 276	Coates, A.		,,		,,
17/ 1530	Coates, R.		,,		,,
17/ 201	Coates, T. N.		,,		,,
17/ 984	Cobb, J.		,,		,,
17/ 985	Cockburn, J.		,,		,,
17/ 1455	Cockin, B.		,,		,,
17/ 1058	Cole, W.		,,		,,
17/ 925	Colling, W. R.		,,		,,
17/ 278	Connar, E.		,,		,,
17/ 413	Cook, T.		,,		,,
17/ 1202	Cooper, R. H.		,,		,,
17/ 1243	Copeland, J. A.		,,		,,
17/ 95	Coulon, H. F.		,,		,,
17/ 1173	Crute, J.		,,		,,
17/ 628	Cundell, E.		,,		,,
17/ 1174	Curry, F.		,,		,,
17/ 97	Cuthbertson, J. W.		,,		,,
17/ 500	Dalby, E.	B	Private	K.	E. 1.7.16, Somme, Authuille Wood.
17/ 629	Dale, H.	B	,,	D.W.	E. L/Cpl. 16.7.16, Somme, Warloy-Baillon Cemetery.

Reg. No.	Name	Coy.	Rank	Casualties	Remarks
17/ 1096	Dale, J.	C	Private	W.W.	E.
17/ 443	Dale, W. E.	A	,,	W.	E. To 14th N.F.
17/ 501	Dalton, H.	C	,,	W.	E.
17/ 785	Dalton, J.	A	,,		E.
17/ 786	Dalziel, J. W.	A	Sergt.	W.	E. D.W. England.
17/ 1250	Daniels, T.	D	Private		E.
17/ 630	Davies, H.	B	,,		E. To R.E.
17/ 98	Davis, F.	D	,,		E.
17/ 280	Davis, G.	B	,,		E.
17/ 1128	Davison, A.	D	,,		E.
17/ 787	Davison, R. W.	A	,,		E.
17/ 631	Dawe, H. J.	C	,,		E. To R.E.
17/ 1228	Dawson, H.	D	,,	W.W. D.W.	E. 18.7.18, Neuville St. Vaast.
17/ 1320	Dawson, W. A.	D	,,		E.
17/ 1252	Dennis, J.	C	,,	W.	E.
17/ 632	Deyes, T.	D	,,		E.
17/ 281	Dickenson, A.	A	,,		E.
17/ 788	Dickson, A. J.	A	,,		E.
17/ 908	Dinning, J. T.	B	,,	W.	E.
17/ 102	Dinsdale, J. W.	C	,,		E.
17/ 502	Dinsdale, R.	C	Corporal		E. Sergt.
17/ 633	Dixon, H.	A	Private	W.	E.
17/ 789	Dixon, T.	D	,,	W.	E.
17/ 20	Dobson, E.	D	,,		E.
17/ 1289	Dobson, E.	D	,,		E.
17/ 909	Dodd, J. J.	A	,,	W.	E.
17/ 790	Dodds, L.	D	C.Q.M.S.		E. Commission.
17/ 1110	Dodsworth, R.	A	Private		E.
17/ 910	Donaldson, J. E.	B	,,		E.
17/ 282	Dorward, W.	A	C.Q.M.S.		E. C.S.M. Commission.
17/ 21	Douglas, H. C.	D	Private		E.
17/ 206	Downey, R.	C	,,		E.
17/ 283	Driver, J. C.	A	,,		E.
17/ 103	Dry, W. S.	D	,,	W.W.	E.
17/ 987	Dryden, J.	A	,,		E.
17/ 793	Dryden, T.	A	,,	W.	E. Died whilst P.O.W. 3.11.18, War Hospital, Gardilegen, Germany.
17/ 22	Duck, J. R.	C	,,	W.	E. Corporal.
17/ 416	Duery, T. B.	A	L/Cpl.		E. ,,
17/ 23	Duggleby, W. R.	A	Private		E.
17/ 635	Dunford, H. B.	C	,,		E.

17th and 32nd (S.) Batts. Northumberland Fusiliers (N.E.R.) Pioneers

Reg. No.	Name	Coy.	Rank	Casualties	Remarks
17/ 1176	Dunn, F.	D	Corporal	K.	E. L/Sergt. 20.4.18, Nieppe Forest, Ebblingham Cemetery.
17/ 634	Dunn, J.	B	Private	K.	E. 8.11.17, Ypres, Bard Cottage Cemetery.
17/ 1253	Dunn, J. W.	D	,,	W.	E.
17/ 1369	Dunn, T. H.	D	,,		E.
17/ 686	Dutton, H. E.	C	,,	W.G.	E.
17/ 286	Dyble, W.	A	Corporal	W.	E.
45205	Davies, A.	A	Private	W.	To 36th N.F.
32/ 196	Davison, A. W. S.		,,		To 14th N.F.
17/ 1531	Davison, G.		,,		,, ,,
32/ 650	Dawson, F.	A	,,		To 36th N.F.
17/ 99	Day, T.	D	Corporal		
17/ 100	Deakin, S. J.	C	Private		
45185	De Caux, H.	A	,,		To K.O.Y.L.I.
36097	Deighton, W.	C	Sergt.		
17/ 1288	Dennett, C.	D	Private		
18/ 1231	Derry, J. O.	D	,,		To 14th N.F.
45235	Dewhirst, W.	D	,,		To 36th N.F.
32/ 506	Dick, D.	B	,,		
17/ 1532	Dickens, W.		,,		To 14th N.F.
17/ 101	Dickenson, A.		Corporal		To Y. and L.
45242	Dickenson, J.	C	Private		
17/ 1327	Dixon, G.	B	,,		
32/ 954	Dixon, R. H.	B	,,	W.	
32/ 195	Dobby, H.		,,		To 14th N.F.
32/ 15	Dobson, A. W.		,,	W.	
44289	Dodd, F.	C	,,		To Y. and L.
17/ 1290	Dodsworth, W.		,,		
32/ 695	Donkin, H.	A	,,		To 36th N.F.
32/ 268	Douglas, W.		,,	W.	To R.E.
32/ 966	Dover, W.	B	,,		
45247	Driver, H.	A	,,		To 6th N.F.
32/ 696	Dudley, J. A.	A	,,		To 36th N.F.
17/ 1131	Dunn, J. J.	A	L/Cpl.	D.W.	20.10.16, Somme, Forceville Communal Cemetery.
32/ 158	Dunn, T.	B	Private		
17/ 285	Dutton, J. R.	B	,,		R.O.D.
45190	Dyer, S. J.	D	,,		

Reg. No.	Name	Coy.	Rank	Casualties	Remarks
17/ 415	Daley, C. L.		Private		T.B.E.
17/ 1129	Davison, T.		,,		,,
17/ 1429	Derbyshire, D.		,,		,,
17/ 907	Devine, P.		,,		,,
17/ 1175	Dewhirst, A. S.		,,		,,
17/ 986	Dick, T. M.		Corporal		,,
17/ 205	Dickenson, F.		Private		,,
17/ 1473	Dobbie, E. S.		,,		,,
17/ 1130	Dobby, A.		,,		,,
17/ 1290	Dodsworth, W.		,,		,,
17/ 1533	Douglas, E.		,,		,,
17/ 791	Downey, W. A.		,,		,,
17/ 792	Draper, J.		,,		,,
17/ 1117	Drayton, P.		,,		,,
17/ 284	Duckling, J.		Sergt.		,,
17/ 1422	Dunn, H.		Private		,,
17/ 911	Dunning, H. O.		,,		,,
17/ 1070	Earle, C.	C	Private	W.	E.
17/ 417	Easby, J. R.	C	Corporal		E. L/Sergt.
17/ 287	Easter, H. E.	C	Private		E.
17/ 637	Eastwood, W.	D	,,		E.
17/ 1235	Eccles, J. T.	D	,,	W.	E.
17/ 1263	Eddy, W.	A	,,		E.
17/ 988	Edgar, J.	A	,,		E.
17/ 418	Edington, J.	A	,,		E.
17/ 638	Edmond, W. H.	D	,,	W.	E.
17/ 1291	Edwards, G.	B	,,		E. To R.E.
17/ 104	Eldon, J. B.	D	,,		E. L/Cpl.
17/ 288	Elliott, A. J.	B	,,	W.	E.
17/ 989	Elliott, J. G.	A	,,		E.
17/ 1064	Elliott, J. H.	C	,,		E. L/Cpl.
17/ 1461	Elliott, R.	A	,,	W.	E.
17/ 640	Ellis, H. A.	D	,,		E.
17/ 794	Ellis, J.	A	,,		E.
17/ 105	Ellis, W. J.	C	Sergt.		E. C.Q.M.S.
17/ 912	Emmerson, E. T.	B	L/Cpl.		E. Corporal.
17/ 1474	Emmerson, G. L.	B	Private		E.
17/ 1178	Emmerson, J. J.	D	,,	W.	E.
17/ 289	Emmerson, R.	B	,,	W.W.	E. L/Cpl.
17/ 795	Emmerson, W. H.	B	L/Cpl.	W.	E. Corporal.
17/ 503	England, J. W.	D	Private		E.

17th and 32nd (S.) Batts. Northumberland Fusiliers (N.E.R.) Pioneers

Reg. No.	Name	Coy.	Rank	Casualties	Remarks
17/ 796	Erickson, J. C.	A	Private	W.	E.
17/ 1337	Errington, R.	B	,,		E. R.O.D.
17/ 1101	Esders, J. H.	D	,,		E.
17/ 207	Etheridge, W.	B	Corporal	W.	E. L/Sergt.
17/ 1460	Earle, J. W.	B	Private	D.W.	5.7.18, Neuville St. Vaast.
32/ 17	Easthill, J. W.	D	,,		
17/ 1107	Edgar, R.	C	,,		
17/ 639	Edmund, A.	D	,,		
32/ 216	Edwards, J.	A	,,		
45138	Elliott, L. F.		,,		To 6th N.F.
44271	Ellis, F. G.	C	,,		To Leicester Regiment.
45184	Ellis, J.	A	Sergt.		
32/ 217	Elstob, E.	A	Private		
32/ 218	Elsworth, W.	C	,,		
32/ 82	Etherington, H.	B	,,	K.	25.10.17, Ypres, St. Julien Cemetery.
17/ 1133	Evison, W.	D	,,		To 8th N.F.
17/ 964	Eden, R.		Private		T.B.E.
17/ 1416	Elliott, M.		,,		,,
17/ 1584	Elwick, J.		,,		,,
17/ 1177	Embleton, J.		,,		,,
17/ 1132	Emmerson, J.		,,		,,
17/ 641	Evans, A.		,,		,,
17/ 642	Fairless, W.	A	Private	W.	E.
17/ 1500	Farrar, F. R.	B	,,		E.
17/ 990	Farthing, S.	A	,,	W.	E.
17/ 797	Fawcett, A.	D	L/Cpl.	W.	E.
17/ 1134	Featherstone, W.	C	Private	W.	E. To 14th N.F.
17/ 643	Fent, T.	B	,,		E.
17/ 294	Ferguson, W. A.	C	Corporal		E. Sergt.
17/ 290	Fielding, G.	A	Private		E. L/Cpl.
17/ 799	Finch, G. W.	B	,,		E.
17/ 107	Firth, E. A.	D	,,		E.
17/ 800	Firth, G. P.	B	,,		E.
17/ 1332	Fleetham, M.	A	,,	W.	E.
17/ 644	Fletcher, R.	B	,,	W.	E.
17/ 646	Fletcher, W. W.	D	,,	W.	E.
17/ 291	Ford, G. E.	A	,,		E.
17/ 504	Forster, F.	A	,,		E.

Roll of Men Who Served

Reg. No.	Name	Coy.	Rank	Casualties	Remarks
17/ 208	Forster, G. A. N.	D	Private		E. To R.E.
17/ 1444	Forster, R.	A	,,		E. R.O.D.
17/ 292	Forster, U. F.	A	,,		E.
17/ 1501	Forster, W.	B	,,	K.	E. 15.7.16, Somme, Bouzincourt Military Cemetery.
17/ 991	Forsyth, J.	A	,,		E.
17/ 108	Foster, P.	C	,,		E. To D.L.I.
17/ 109	Fowler, H.	D	,,	W.	E. Sergt.
17/ 1057	Frankland, M. J.	B	,,	K.	E. 25.10.17, Ypres, St. Julien Cemetery.
17/ 505	Frazer, W. A.	C	,,		E.
17/ 648	Freeman, J. S.	C	L/Sergt.	W.	E. Sergt. Military Medal.
17/ 506	Furniss, J.	D	Private		E.
32/ 370	Fairbotham, H.	A	Private		To 36th N.F.
32/ 947	Fairhead, G. W. P.	B	,,	W.	
32/ 219	Falkner, H.		,,		To 14th N.F.
17/ 500	Farrar, F. R.	B	,,	W.	
32/ 688	Fawbert, T. E.	A	,,		To 36th N.F.
32/ 808	Fawcett, H.	B	,,		
17/ 1409	Featherstone, C.	C	,,		
32/ 160	Fell, H.	C	,,		
32/ 903	Fenton, A.	B	,,	W.	
45222	Fenwick, R. M.	D	,,		Commission.
17/ 1351	Ferguson, D. C.	C	L/Cpl.		To 14th N.F.
45198	Flanagan, W. H.	C	Corporal		Sergt.
45225	Flatow, J.	D	Private		
17/ 1462	Fletcher, J. H.	C	,,	W.	
32/ 841	Fogg, C. E.	B	,,		To 36th N.F.
32/ 18	Forbes, T.	D	,,		To 14th N.F.
32/ 448	Ford, C.	C	,,	W.	
32/ 197	Ford, W.	C	,,		
32/ 83	Forth, B.	A	,,		
17/ 1434	Foster, H.	B	,,		L/Cpl.
17/ 419	Foulger, E. A.	D	,,		,,
32/ 848	Fowler, J. S.	B	,,		
32/ 694	Frier, W. H.	B	,,		To 36th N.F.
32/ 161	Fussey, F. H.	C	,,	W.	
17/ 293	Fawcett, C. A.		Private		T.B.E.
17/ 1535	Fay, J.		,,		,,

17th and 32nd (S.) Batts. Northumberland Fusiliers (N.E.R.) Pioneers

Reg. No.	Name	Coy.	Rank	Casualties	Remarks
17/ 106	Fenn, J.		Private		T.B.E.
17/ 798	Fewster, A.		,,		,,
17/ 1292	Findlay, S.		,,		,,
17/ 1203	Firth, G.		,,		,,
17/ 1475	Fisher, W. G.		,,		,,
17/ 645	Fletcher, C.		,,		,,
17/ 801	Ford, F.		,,		,,
17/ 1179	Foster, F.		,,		,,
17/ 1293	Foster, W. H.		,,		,,
17/ 647	Fotheringham, J.		,,		,,
17/ 913	Franklin, W.		,,		,,
17/ 1551	Froughton, J.		,,		,,
17/ 649	Furness, J. T.		,,		,,
17/ 914	Gaines, J. H.	B	Private		E.
17/ 1050	Gallagher, G. E.	D	,,		E.
17/ 993	Gardiner, J. R.	B	,,		E.
17/ 507	Garvey, J. M.	A	,,	W.	E.
17/ 209	Gattenby, E.	C	,,		E.
17/ 1520	Gawthorpe, G.	B	,,		E.
17/ 650	Gent, V.	B	,,	K.	E. 4.7.16, Somme, Aveluy Military Cemetery.
17/ 652	Gibbon, W. H.	C	,,		E.
17/ 508	Gibson, G. H.	A	,,		E.
17/ 1419	Gibson, H.	D	,,		E.
17/ 296	Gibson, W.	A	,,		E.
17/ 651	Gibson, W.	A	,,		E.
17/ 994	Gilchrist, R.	A	,,		E.
17/ 110	Gill, A.	C	,,		E. L/Cpl.
17/ 1294	Gillard, F. C.	D	,,		E.
17/ 111	Gilliam, H.	C	,,		E.
17/ 1435	Gillham, R.	C	,,		E.
17/ 510	Gladwell, F. E.	B	,,	K.	E. 29.7.17, Ypres.
17/ 915	Gladwin, W.	C	,,		E.
17/ 511	Goding, C. H.	B	L/Cpl.		E.
17/ 653	Gooch, E. C.	B	Private		E.
17/ 655	Gordon, A.	D	L/Cpl.	W.	E. Sergt.
17/ 1181	Gospel, J. W.	B	Corporal	W.	E. ,,
17/ 802	Gowland, T.	B	Private		E.
17/ 995	Graham, F.	C	Sergt.	W.W.	E.
17/ 1521	Graham, J.	B	Private	W.	E. Corporal.

Roll of Men Who Served

Reg. No.	Name	Coy.	Rank	Casualties	Remarks
17/ 656	Graham, T.	C	L/Cpl.		E. To R.E.
17/ 298	Graham, T. P.	B	Sergt.	W.	E. C.Q.M.S. Mentioned in Despatches.
17/ 112	Gray, E.	D	Private		E.
17/ 113	Green, F.	D	,,		E.
17/ 916	Green, J.	A	,,		E.
17/ 658	Green, J. L.	B	,,		E. L/Cpl.
17/ 996	Green, W.	A	,,	W.	E.
17/ 512	Green, W. E.	B	L/Cpl.		E. L/Sergt.
17/ 1113	Greenley, W. A.	B	Private		E. L/Cpl.
17/ 115	Grewar, J. A.	D	,,	W.	E.
17/ 658	Grey, R.	B	,,		E.
32/ 963	Gallon, W. T.	B	Private		
46827	Galt, J.	B	,,	D.W.	25.10.17, Ypres, St. Julien Cemetery.
45172	Gardner, T. W.	D	,,		To 6th N.F.
17/ 1338	Garthwaite, C. E.	A	,,		R.O.D.
32/ 222	Gawthorpe, A.		,,		To 14th N.F.
45136	Gills, O.	C	,,		To 6th N.F.
32/ 943	Gladwin, S.	B	,,		To 36th N.F.
44273	Gogerley, J. C.	C	,,		To 6th N.F.
57583	Goldsbrough, G. W.	B	,,	K.	25.10.17, Ypres, St. Julien Corner Cot Stn.
17/ 1180	Goodchild, H.	A	,,		
45206	Goodwin, T. F.	C	,,		To 1/4 K.O.Y.L.I.
17/ 802	Gowland, T.	B	,,		
32/ 85	Graham, F.	B	,,		
17/ 1536	Grantham, C. H.		,,		To 14th N.F.
32/ 678	Gray, W.	B	,,		To 36th N.F.
45239	Greatorex, R. B.	C	,,		To 6th N.F.
17/ 114	Green, H.		,,		
45254	Green, V. E. H.	A	,,		To 12th K.O.Y.L.I.
45141	Green, W.	C	L/Cpl.		
32/ 971	Greener, J.	B	Private		To Labour Corps.
32/ 19	Greenwell, W.		,,		
17/ 1295	Greenwood, G.	B	,,		R.O.D.
45147	Greenwood, W.	C	,,		To 6th N.F.
32/ 87	Gregory, A.		,,		
45228	Gregson, W.	A	,,		To 6th N.F.
44276	Groome, W. H.	B	,,		,, ,,
45244	Grove, F. R.	C	,,		,, ,,
32/ 20	Guy, J. E.		,,	W.	To R.A.M.C.

17th and 32nd (S.) Batts. Northumberland Fusiliers (N.E.R.) Pioneers

Reg. No.	Name	Coy.	Rank	Casualties	Remarks
17/ 295	Gamester, J. J.		Private		T.B.E.
17/ 992	Garbutt, C.		,,		,,
17/ 297	Gill, R.		C.S.M.		,,
17/ 509	Gilling, R.		Private		,,
17/ 654	Good, W.		R.S.M.		,,
17/ 1135	Gould, J. M.		Private		,,
17/ 1365	Granger, B.		,,		,,
17/ 803	Grant, T.		,,		,,
17/ 1108	Grasby, H. A.		,,		,,
17/ 1224	Graves, J.		,,		,,
17/ 210	Gray, M.		,,		,,
17/ 657	Green, A.		,,		,,
17/ 1204	Grey, E.		,,		,,
17/ 660	Guy, G. W.		,,		,,
17/ 513	Haines, W. J.	C	Private		E. L/Cpl.
17/ 1296	Haldane, T.	B	,,		E. R.O.D.
17/ 514	Halder, E.	C	,,		E. Corporal.
17/ 116	Hall, A.	D	,,		E.
17/ 117	Hall, E.	D	L/Cpl.		E. Corporal.
17/ 299	Hall, E. D.	A	Private		E. ,,
17/ 24	Hall, F. C.	D	,,	W.	E.
17/ 805	Hall, G.	B	,,		E.
17/ 806	Hall, J. J.	B	,,		E.
17/ 300	Hall, J. T.	B	L/Cpl.		E. Sergt.
17/ 1112	Hall, R.	A	Private	W.	E.
17/ 1273	Hall, R. E.	C	,,		E.
17/ 1297	Hall, R. F.	A	,,	W.	E. To 10th N.F.
17/ 119	Hallam, F.	C	L/Cpl.	K.	E. 12.7.16, Somme, Bouzincourt Military Cemetery.
17/ 301	Hallam, R. W.	A	,,	G.	E.
17/ 302	Halliday, F. C.	A	Private		E.
17/ 807	Halls, J. H.	B	,,		E. R.O.D.
17/ 808	Hammond, J. H.	B	,,		E. L/Cpl.
17/ 120	Hancock, G. T.	D	,,		E.
17/ 809	Handley, J.	C	,,	K.	E. 27.9.18, Canal du Nord, Cambrai.
17/ 1225	Hanney, T. P.	B	,,		E.
17/ 121	Hanson, G.	C	,,		E.
17/ 211	Hardwick, H.	D	,,		E.
17/ 212	Hardy, A.	D	,,		E.

Reg. No.	Name	Coy.	Rank	Casualties	Remarks
17/ 811	Hardy, A.	B	Private	W.W.	E. L/Cpl.
17/ 812	Harkness, J. R.	A	,,		E.
17/ 664	Harland, J.	B	,,		E.
17/ 1407	Harland, W.	B	,,	W.	E.
17/ 421	Harpin, F.	A	,,	G.	E.
17/ 123	Harris, F.	C	L/Cpl.		E.
17/ 813	Harris, J.	B	Private		E. L/Cpl.
17/ 998	Harris, J.	B	,,		E.
17/ 1864	Harrison, A. L.	A	,,	W.	E.
17/ 304	Harrison, C.	C	,,	W.	E. Corporal.
17/ 516	Harrison, F. H.	B	,,	W.	E.
17/ 815	Harrison, H. C.	B	,,		E. L/Cpl.
17/ 1080	Harrison, S.	A	,,	W.	E.
17/ 816	Harrison, W. E.	B	,,		E.
17/ 422	Harrison, W. P.	B	,,		E.
17/ 1264	Hartas, F. W.	A	,,	W.	E.
17/ 662	Harvey, G. S.	D	,,		E.
17/ 517	Haslin, J.	C	,,		E.
17/ 817	Hauxwell, C. F.	A	,,		E.
17/ 919	Hawksby, G.	C	,,		E.
17/ 1069	Hawthorn, J. F.	A	,,		E.
17/ 917	Haxby, H.	B	,,	W.	E. L/Cpl.
17/ 518	Hay, S.	A	,,		E.
17/ 920	Henderson, R. T.	B	,,		E.
17/ 999	Hendrie, R.	A	,,		E.
17/ 921	Hepburn, G. H.	A	Sergt.	W.	E.
17/ 124	Herman, F. L.	D	Private	G.	E.
17/ 1244	Heslop, R.	D	,,		E.
17/ 666	Heward, T. R.	B	Corporal	W.	E.
17/ 214	Hewitt, W.	B	Private	W.	E.
17/ 215	Hewson, C. W.	C	,,		E.
17/ 922	Hey, S. W.	C	L/Cpl.	W.	E. Corporal.
17/ 1348	Hill, J. A.	D	Private		E.
17/ 1000	Hill, J. H.	C	,,	W.	E.
17/ 519	Hill, S. H. R.	B	,,	W.	E.
17/ 424	Hindley, E.	A	L/Cpl.		E. L/Sergt.
17/ 1115	Hird, R. E.	B	Private	W.	E.
17/ 521	Hitcham, J.	A	L/Cpl.		E. To R.E.
17/ 667	Hitcham, S.	C	,,		E. Corporal.
17/ 1001	Hodge, D. W.	A	Private		E.
17/ 1226	Hodges, H. E.	D	,,	W.	E.
17/ 1299	Hodgson, A.	A	,,		E. R.O.D.
17/ 27	Hodgson, F.	C	L/Cpl.		E.

134 17th and 32nd (S.) Batts. Northumberland Fusiliers (N.E.R.) Pioneers

Reg. No.	Name	Coy.	Rank	Casualties	Remarks
17/ 668	Hodgson, F. W.	B	Private		E.
17/ 522	Hodgson, R.	C	,,	K.	E. 27.1.16, Somme, Authuille Cemetery.
17/ 125	Hogben, H.	D	,,		E.
17/ 216	Hoggard, T.	C	,,	W.	E.
17/ 305	Hoggarth, W.	B	,,		E.
17/ 1236	Hoggett, J. W.	C	,,		E.
17/ 1206	Holliday, J. F.	D	,,		E.
17/ 28	Holmes, T. A.	C	,,	W.	E. L/Cpl.
17/ 217	Holmes, W.	D	,,	K.	E. 3.1.18, Ypres.
17/ 669	Holmes, W.	D	,,		E.
17/ 126	Holroyd, J. H.	D	,,	W.	E.
17/ 523	Hood, G. S.	B	,,	W.	E.
17/ 524	Hookway, J. R.	B	,,		E.
17/ 307	Hope, W. M.	A	,,		E.
17/ 673	Hopper, J. E.	B	,,	W.	E.
17/ 218	Hopwood, A.	C	,,		E. Corporal.
17/ 219	Hornby, T. W.	B	,,		E.
17/ 425	Horner, A. E.	D	,,		E.
17/ 128	Hotham, H.	D	,,	W.	E.
17/ 308	Howe, T. R.	B	,,	D.W.	E. 18.6.18, Neuville St. Vaast.
17/ 1387	Howey, A. E.	B	,,	K.	E. 5.8.17, Ypres.
17/ 129	Howland, E.	D	,,	W.	E. To 1st N.F.
17/ 1098	Hubbick, W.	B	,,		E.
17/ 1140	Hudson, T.	D	,,		E.
17/ 1383	Hudspith, H.	B	,,	W.	E. L/Cpl.
17/ 309	Hudspith, J. R.	A	,,	W.W.	E.
17/ 220	Hullah, J.	A	,,		E.
17/ 1382	Hulse, W.	D	,,		E.
17/ 526	Hutchinson, D. A.	B	,,		E. L/Cpl.
17/ 923	Hutchinson, G. O.	A	,,		E.
17/ 527	Hutchinson, R. N.	C	,,		E.
17/ 924	Hutchinson, R. W.	B	,,		E.
32/ 634	Hague, C. E.	D	L/Cpl.		
45224	Hainsworth, B.	D	Private		To 6th N.F.
32/ 89	Halder, M.	C	,,		
32/ 571	Hall, A.	D	,,		
45204	Hall, A.	C	,,		To 6th N.F.
32/ 22	Hall, W.		,,		To 14th N.F.
45137	Hammond, H.	D	,,		
32/ 162	Hancock, W.		,,		To 14th N.F.

Reg. No.	Name	Coy.	Rank	Casualties	Remarks
32/ 398	Hansell, J.	C	Private		
17/ 810	Harcourt, W. E.	C	,,	W.	To 12th D.L.I.
32/ 91	Hardwick, W.	D	,,	W.	
17/ 303	Hardy, A. H.	B	,,	W.	
17/ 997	Harker, T. F.		,,		To 14th N.F.
17/ 1512	Harlow, A.	C	,,		
45237	Harris, T. H.	C	,,		To 6th N.F.
32/ 226	Harrison, M.		,,		To 14th N.F.
17/ 1275	Harrowing, B. N.		,,		To 12th K.O.Y.L.I.
17/ 1136	Hart, R. L.	B	,,	W.	
32/ 693	Hartley, C.	B	L/Cpl.		
32/ 929	Hatfield, O.	B	Private		
45253	Haydon, H. S.	D	,,		To 6th N.F.
32/ 400	Hayles, T. T.	B	,,		To R.A.S.C.
32/ 92	Hedley, O.		,,		To 14th N.F.
45138	Hemming, P. W.	C	,,		
32/ 580	Hepworth, G. A.	B	,,		
17/ 124	Herman, F. L.	D	,,		
28/ 1	Hewitt, J. H.	D	,,		
17/ 214	Hewitt, W. R.	B	,,		L/Cpl.
17/ 1298	Hewson, H.	C	,,		
17/ 1336	Hickson, J.		,,		R.O.D.
32/ 163	Hill, E. A.	C	,,	D.W.	5.10.18.
45160	Hill, L.	A	,,		To 6th N.F.
45162	Hill, L. R.	D	,,		To 6th N.F.
32/ 165	Hillyer, E.		,,		To 14th N.F.
32/ 166	Hind, W.		L/Cpl.		,, ,,
32/ 894	Hinton, H.	B	Private		To 36th N.F.
32/ 946	Hodgson, T.	B	,,		,, ,,
57534	Hodgson, T.	B	,,	K.	30.10.17, Ypres, St. Julian Cemetery.
32/ 25	Hogarth, R.	C	,,	W.	
238066	Holborn, H. R.	C	,,		
32/ 276	Holdsworth, W. E. R.	C	,,	K.	27.9.18, Canal du Nord, Cambrai.
45151	Holmes, F.	C	,,		To 6th N.F.
45218	Honey, G. E.	A	,,		,, ,,
45246	Honeycombe, P. G.	A	,,		,, ,,
32/ 94	Hornby, J. W.	C	,,	W.	
32/ 227	Hornby, P.	A	,,		
17/ 1539	Horner, J. C. E.		,,		To 14th N.F.
45126	Horner, L.	D	,,		To 6th N.F.
202580	Horsley, T. M.	C	Sergt.		C.Q.M.S.

17th and 32nd (S.) Batts. Northumberland Fusiliers (N.E.R.) Pioneers

Reg. No.	Name	Coy.	Rank	Casualties	Remarks
32/ 911	Houlden, R. W.	B	Private		Corporal.
17/ 1002	Houlden, W. E.	D	,,	W.	
32/ 552	Howe, T.		,,		To 14th N.F.
17/ 1254	Hudson, G. S.	D	,,		
17/ 525	Hudson, M.	C	,,	D.W.	1.11.17, Ypres, Bard Cottage Cemetery.
17/ 1381	Huffam, J. H.	B	Sergt.		Commission.
32/ 95	Hughes, C.		Private		To 14th N.F.
17/ 426	Hullah, E.	B	,,		R.O.D.
30063	Hume, J.	D	,,	W.	
45211	Hume, R. G.	C	,,		To 36th N.F.
32/ 933	Hunt, G. S.	B	,,		
17/ 1265	Hunter, W.		,,		To 14th N.F. D. of W.
17/ 804	Hall, A.		Private		T.B.E.
17/ 113	Hall, J.		,,		,,
17/ 1502	Hall, J. T.		,,		,,
17/ 1137	Halliday, G.		,,		,,
17/ 1828	Hamilton, W. M.		,,		,,
17/ 1476	Hanney, F.		,,		,,
17/ 1205	Hardcastle, F.		,,		,,
17/ 1428	Hardcastle, G.		,,		,,
17/ 665	Hargrave, R. W.		,,		,,
17/ 515	Harland, H.		,,		,,
17/ 122	Harmer, W. E.		,,		,,
17/ 1043	Harrington, W. E.		,,		,,
17/ 661	Harris, A. H.		,,		,,
17/ 918	Harris, S. P.		,,		,,
17/ 213	Harrison, A.		,,		,,
17/ 814	Harrison, A. E.		,,		,,
17/ 663	Hart, W. E.		,,		,,
17/ 1491	Hawkins, W.		,,		,,
17/ 1846	Hazel, F. J.		,,		,,
17/ 25	Hedge, F. E.		L/Sergt.		,,
17/ 1182	Heron, E.		Private		,,
17/ 423	Heskett, W.		,,		,,
17/ 26	Hewitson, R.		,,		,,
17/ 1522	Hick, W.		,,		,,
17/ 520	Hird, J. W. B.		,,		,,
17/ 1856	Hogg, E.		,,		,,
17/ 670	Holborn, H. R.		,,		,,
17/ 306	Hollinshead, M. H.		,,		,,
17/ 671	Honour, E.		,,		,,

Reg. No.	Name	Coy.	Rank	Casualties	Remarks
17/ 1097	Hope, D. W.		Private		T.B.E.
17/ 672	Hope, F. L.		,,		,,
17/ 1537	Hope, J.		,,		,,
17/ 1538	Hope, R. J.		,,		,,
17/ 926	Hopkins, A. W.		,,		,,
17/ 818	Horner, J. T.		,,		,,
17/ 1138	Horner, W.		,,		,,
17/ 127	Horsley, R. A.		,,		,,
17/ 1227	Houlsby, J.		,,		,,
17/ 1496	Houlsby, R. S.		,,		,,
17/ 1139	Howells, J. L.		,,		,,
17/ 674	Howitt, G.		,,		,,
17/ 129	Howland, E.		,,		,,
17/ 1251	Hudson, G. S.		,,		,,
17/ 310	Hunter, J. W.		,,		,,
17/ 427	Husbund, W.		,,		,,
17/ 1099	Hutchinson, H.		,,		,,
17/ 1188	Hutchinson, W.		,,		,,
17/ 221	Ibbotson, H.	D	Private		E.
17/ 927	Iley, W.	D	Sergt.		E. Commission.
17/ 1003	Iredale, R.	A	Private	W.	E.
17/ 1045	Irving, W.	A	Sergt.		E.
17/ 820	Irwin, E. H.	D	Private		E.
17/ 928	Ingleby, E.		Private		T.B.E.
17/ 819	Innes, J.		,,		,,
17/ 428	Irwin, J. W.		,,		,,
17/ 1468	Isley, T.		,,		,,
17/ 311	Jackson, C.	B	Private		E.
17/ 1370	Jackson, G.	D	,,		E.
17/ 429	Jackson, H.	D	,,		E.
17/ 1503	Jackson, H.	B	,,	W.	E.
17/ 130	Jackson, J.	D	,,		E. To 2nd W.Y.
17/ 312	Jackson, J.	A	,,		E.
17/ 676	Jackson, J. W.	D	,,		E. L/Cpl.
17/ 313	Jackson, R.	A	,,		E.
17/ 29	Jackson, R. S.	C	,,		E. Commission.
17/ 431	Jackson, T. A.	B	L/Cpl.		E. Corporal.
17/ 131	Jacobson, J.	B	Private	D.W.	E. L/Cpl. Ecurie.

17th and 32nd (S.) Batts. Northumberland Fusiliers (N.E.R.) Pioneers

Reg. No.	Name	Coy.	Rank	Casualties	Remarks
17/ 528	James, R.	A	Private	W.	E. Corporal.
17/ 1004	Jameson, H.	C	,,		E.
17/ 30	Jefferson, T. H.	D	Sergt.		E. Commission.
17/ 1464	Jeffrey, R.	D	Private		E. L/Cpl.
17/ 677	Jeffrey, W. A.	B	Sergt.	D.W.	E. 20.4.18, Nieppe Forest, Ebblingham Cemetery.
17/ 1005	Jennison, A.	B	Private		E.
17/ 31	Johnson, E. W.	C	L/Cpl.		E. Corporal.
17/ 1228	Johnson, H.	A	Private		E. To K.O.Y.L.I.
17/ 1095	Johnson, J. F.	B	,,	D.W.	E. 13.1.17, Somme, Mailly Wood Cemetery.
17/ 433	Johnson, L. R.	A	,,		E.
17/ 1266	Johnson, R.	C	,,	W.	E. L/Cpl.
17/ 316	Johnson, R. W.	C	L/Cpl.	W.	E.
17/ 1326	Jones, G.	D	Private		E.
17/ 182	Jubb, H. S.	C	Sergt.	W.	E. Mentioned in Despatches.
45191	Jackson, A.	D	Sergt.		To 6th N.F.
32/ 959	Jackson, G.	B	Private		
44282	Jarvis, R.	B	,,		To 6th N.F.
32/ 282	Jefferson, R. M.	B	,,		
32/ 29	Jeffrey, B.		,,		To 14th N.F.
17/ 1477	Jeffreys, N.	A	,,		
45133	Jewkes, S.	D	,,	W.	
18/ 1648	Jobson, G. C.	D	,,		
32/ 283	Johnson, A.	B	,,		
32/ 96	Johnson, E.		,,	G.	
45179	Johnson, J.		Corporal		To 2nd O. and B.L.I.
32/ 284	Johnstone, R.	C	Private	W.	
44283	Jordan, G.	C	,,		
17/ 529	Jowett, J. H.	C	,,		
17/ 675	Jackson, A.		Private		T.B.E.
17/ 430	Jackson, J. W.		,,		,,
17/ 314	Jacques, A.		,,		,,
17/ 432	Jagger, J. B.		Sergt.		,,
17/ 1353	James, E.		Private		,,
17/ 1540	Johnson, C. E.		,,		,,
17/ 315	Johnson, D.		,,		,,
17/ 1228	Johnson, H.		,,		,,
17/ 1141	Jones, J. R.		,,		,,

Reg. No.	Name	Coy.	Rank	Casualties	Remarks
17/ 484	Joules, S.		Private		T.B.E.
17/ 222	Kelly, W. H.	C	Private		E.
17/ 530	Kemp, A. E.	B	,,	W.	E. L/Cpl.
17/ 317	Kendra, J. W.	B	,,		E.
17/ 1006	Kennedy, W. T.	A	,,		E. Corporal.
17/ 1528	Kenny, A.	B	,,	W.	E.
17/ 531	Key, T. H.	A	,,		E.
17/ 582	Kidd, E. R.	A	,,		E.
17/ 485	Kidd, F.	D	L/Sergt.		E.
17/ 1076	King, F.	C	Private		E.
17/ 823	Kirk, D.	B	,,		E.
17/ 533	Kirkby, F. B.	D	,,		E.
17/ 678	Kirkwood, C.	D	,,		E. Sergt.
17/ 1184	Knaggs, T.	D	,,		E.
17/ 319	Knox, R.	A	,,	W.	E. Corporal.
17/ 1323	Kay, H.		L/Cpl.		To 14th N.F. (K.)
32/ 30	Ketteringham, C.	A	Private		
19/ 1819	King, J. A.	D	L/Cpl.	W.	
32/ 98	King, T. W.	C	Private		R.O.D.
32/ 169	Kirk, C.	B	,,	W.	
32/ 99	Kleiser, L. C.		,,		To 14th N.F.
17/ 1208	Knowles, A.	D	,,		Died in England, 15.7.16.
45170	Knowles, J.	C	,,		To 6th N.F.
17/ 1207	Keyworth, A. T.		Private		T.B.E.
17/ 822	Kilvington, J. N.		Sergt.		,,
17/ 133	Kirkwood, T.		Private		,,
17/ 1300	Knight, W. H.		,,		,,
17/ 318	Knightson, W.		,,		,,
17/ 930	Lamb, F.	A	Private		E.
17/ 534	Lamb, J.	C	,,		E.
17/ 1446	Lambton, J.	A	,,		E. R.O.D.
17/ 1438	Lamming, W.	C	,,	K.	E. 26.1.16, Somme, Authuille Cemetery.
17/ 535	Lancaster, J. W.	D	,,		E. R.O.D.
17/ 680	Langdale, A.	D	,,		E. Corporal.
17/ 1007	Lawson, A.	B	,,		E.
17/ 1391	Lazenby, E. W.	B	,,	W.	E.

17th and 32nd (S.) Batts. Northumberland Fusiliers (N.E.R.) Pioneers

Reg. No.	Name	Coy.	Rank	Casualties	Remarks
17/ 436	Lea, C. E.	B	Sergt.		E. C.Q.M.S.
17/ 32	Leake, A. B.	C	L/Cpl.		E. Commission.
17/ 681	Leaske, B.	B	,,		E. Corporal.
17/ 1447	Leckonby, H. G.	A	Private		E. R.O.D.
17/ 437	Ledran, A.	D	L/Cpl.	W.	E.
17/ 1102	Lee, G. W.	D	,,		E. Sergt.
17/ 1142	Lee, H.	A	Corporal		E. Commission.
17/ 682	Lee, R.	B	Private		E. L/Cpl.
17/ 1366	Lee, R.	C	,,		E.
17/ 321	Leeming, S.	B	,,	D.G.	E. 16.7.16, Somme, Puchevillers British Cemetery.
17/ 825	Levitt, E.	C	Corporal	W.G. W.W.	E. Sergt. Mentioned in Despatches.
17/ 536	Liddle, N. A.	A	Private		E.
17/ 1148	Lile, A.	B	,,	D.W.	E. 11.6.17, Ypres.
17/ 322	Little, H.	A	,,	K.	E. 20.10.16, Somme, Englebelmer Military Cemetery.
17/ 328	Littlefair, T. W.	D	Sergt.		E. C.Q.M.S.
17/ 1089	Lloyd, W.	D	Private		E.
17/ 134	Lockton, C. A.	D	,,		E.
17/ 826	Lockwood, R. W.	C	L/Cpl.	W.	E. Corporal.
17/ 224	Lofthouse, F.	C	,,		E. ,,
17/ 225	Longfellow, H. R.	C	Private		E.
17/ 686	Longstaff, G. L.	B	,,		E.
17/ 685	Longstaff, R.	B	,,	D.G.	E. 17.7.16, Somme, Puchevillers British Cemetery.
17/ 1415	Longstaff, W.	B	,,		E.
17/ 226	Lonsbrough, R.	A	C.S.M.		E. Commission.
17/ 827	Lumley, E.	B	L/Cpl.		E. Corporal.
17/ 1301	Lunn, W.	D	Private		E. R.O.D.
17/ 1497	Lynn, J. J.	B	,,		E.
17/ 1185	Lacey, W.	C	,,	G.	
82/ 170	Laing, W.	D	,,		
45168	Lammin, A. E.	C	,,		To 6th N.F. Corporal.
82/ 171	Lamplugh, S. H.	D	,,		
82/ 172	Langhorn, A.	A	,,	D.W.	15.6.17, Ypres.
45258	Laughton, G. A.	A	,,		
17/ 1391	Lazenby, E. W.	B	,,		
17/ 1186	Leach, A.	A	,,		
82/ 101	Leach, J.	B	,,		

Reg. No.	Name	Coy.	Rank	Casualties	Remarks
32/ 874	Leak, E.	B	Private		To 36th N.F.
32/ 348	Lee, A.	A	,,	W.	
45167	Lennox, W.	D	,,		To 6th N.F.
44284	Lindsay, J.	D	,,		,, ,,
32/ 550	Lindsley, J.		,,		To 14th N.F.
32/ 951	Liversedge, W. J.	B	,,	W.	
17/ 1457	Livingstone, J.	A	,,	D.W.	21.3.18, Ypres.
17/ 1420	Lofthouse, G.	A	,,	W.	
32/ 256	Lomax, E. M.	D	,,		
32/ 102	Long, G.		,,		To 14th N.F.
17/ 1541	Longstaff, J.		,,		To 14th N.F. K. 16.7.16.
45257	Lyle, A. E.	D	,,		To 6th N.F.
45238	Lynn, C. W.	A	,,		,, ,,
17/ 1497	Lynn, J. J.	B	,,		
17/ 929	Lace, W.		Private		T.B.E.
17/ 1185	Lacy, W.		,,		,,
17/ 1077	Lamb, J. G. W.		,,		,,
17/ 824	Langford, E.		,,		,,
17/ 679	Lavin, P.		,,		,,
17/ 1186	Leach, A.		,,		,,
17/ 1454	Leake, S. H.		,,		,,
17/ 1404	Leckey, W.		,,		,,
17/ 683	Ledder, J. P.		,,		,,
17/ 320	Lee, A.		,,		,,
17/ 223	Liddle, A.		,,		,,
17/ 537	Lloyd, G.		,,		,,
17/ 1008	Lodge, M.		,,		,,
17/ 931	Lowes, A.		,,		,,
17/ 687	Luty, H.		,,		,,
17/ 542	MacDonald, J.	B	Corporal		E. Sergt.
17/ 324	Mack, R.	A	Private	K.	E. 2.10.17, Oost Dunkerke.
17/ 538	Mapplebeck, H.	C	,,	W.	E.
17/ 1010	Maquire, T.	B	,,		E. To R.E.
17/ 1524	Marsh, C.	C	,,		E.
17/ 33	Marson, E. C.	D	,,	D.W.	E. 23.12.15, Somme, Meaulte Military Cemetery.
17/ 539	Mason, H.	B	,,		E.
17/ 540	Mason, J.	D	L/Cpl.	W.	E.

17th and 32nd (S.) Batts. Northumberland Fusiliers (N.E.R.) Pioneers

Reg. No.	Name	Coy.	Rank	Casualties	Remarks
17/ 828	Massheder, J. W.	B	L/Cpl.	K.	E. Corporal. 15.8.18, Ecurie.
17/ 439	Masterman, J. R.	B	Private	W.W.	E.
17/ 695	Mathieson, G. S.	A	L/Cpl.		E. To R.E.
17/ 694	Maude, F.	C	Private		E.
17/ 932	Maude, L.	B	,,		E.
17/ 541	Maughan, J.	A	,,		E.
17/ 34	Mawson, F.	C	,,		E.
17/ 1478	McCall, G.	B	,,	K.	E. 9.5.18, Nieppe Forest.
17/ 1009	McCulloch, J.	A	,,		E.
17/ 229	McDermott, P.	D	,,		E.
17/ 690	McGregor, J.	D	,,		E.
17/ 327	McGuinness, C.	A	,,		E.
17/ 1399	McKenney, A.	C	,,	W.	E.
17/ 1114	McLaren, W.	B	,,	D.G.	E. 15.7.16, Somme, Bouzincourt Cemetery.
17/ 1052	McManus, P.	B	,,	W.	E.
17/ 136	McMartin, W.	D	,,		E.
17/ 984	McNichol, A.	B	,,		E.
17/ 329	McVeigh, F. J.	A	,,		E. L/Cpl.
17/ 137	Mekin, J. A.	D	,,		E.
17/ 330	Merrifield, J.	B	,,	W.	E.
17/ 1145	Metcalfe, C. J.	D	,,		E.
17/ 1303	Metcalfe, R. C.	D	,,	W.	E.
17/ 440	Milburn, A.	B	Sergt.		E.
17/ 231	Milburn, C. P.	D	Private		E. To R.E.
17/ 1402	Mileham, W.	B	,,	W.W.	E.
17/ 35	Miller, C.	C	Sergt.	G.	E.
17/ 698	Millington, W. T.	D	Private	W.	E.
17/ 331	Milne, S. B.	D	L/Sergt.		E. Sergt. Commission.
17/ 36	Mitchell, H.	C	Private		E.
17/ 139	Mitchell, H.	D	,,		E.
17/ 332	Mitchell, H. H.	B	L/Sergt.		E. Sergt. Commission.
17/ 140	Mitchinson, J. A.	D	Private		E.
17/ 1505	Mitchinson, J. S.	C	,,		E.
17/ 831	Mitchinson, R. J.	A	,,		E. L/Cpl.
17/ 1506	Mitchinson, T. B.	C	,,	W.	E. ,,
17/ 697	Moat, H.	B	C.S.M.		E.
17/ 1012	Mole, J.	A	Private		E.
17/ 832	Moody, G.	A	,,	W.	E.
17/ 1513	Moor, J. H.	C	,,		E.
17/ 232	Moore, H.	B	,,		E.

Reg. No.	Name	Coy.	Rank	Casualties	Remarks
17/ 544	Moore, J.	D	L/Cpl.		E. Sergt.
17/ 333	Moore, O.	A	Private		E.
17/ 1276	Moore, R.	B	,,		E. L/Cpl.
17/ 1480	Moore, R.	C	,,		E. To 12th D.L.I.
17/ 1116	Moore, S. A.	D	,,		E.
17/ 1014	Moore, T.	D	,,		E.
17/ 334	Moore, W. L.	A	,,		E.
17/ 37	Morfitt, H. J.	C	,,		E.
17/ 834	Morgan, W.	A	,,		E.
17/ 141	Morley, A.	B	,,		E.
17/ 835	Morrill, G.	C	,,		E.
17/ 1013	Morris, A.	D	,,		E.
17/ 142	Morris, E.	C	,,		E.
17/ 335	Morris, P. A.	A	Sergt.	W.	E. Commission.
17/ 336	Morris, S. K.	B	,,	D.W.	E. 10.7.16, Cimetière du Bois, Haring Heilly.
17/ 441	Morris, W. C.	D	Private		E.
17/ 836	Morrison, A.	C	,,	W.	E.
17/ 1376	Mortimer, G.	C	,,		E.
17/ 1229	Morton, J.	B	,,	D.S.	E. 18.6.18, Neuville St. Vaast.
17/ 698	Mounsey, J.	B	L/Cpl.		E.
17/ 1100	Mounsey, J.	A	Private		E.
17/ 546	Mullen, F.	D	,,		E.
17/ 699	Murray, G.	B	,,		E.
17/ 1414	Musgrave, J. L.	B	,,		E.
17/ 837	Myers, H. D.	A	,,		E.
32/ 408	Maddison, R. L.	A	Private		Commission.
32/ 173	Magson, T.	D	,,		To 8th N.F.
17/ 1209	Main, A.		Sergt.		To 14th N.F.
17/ 692	Malham, B.	D	Private		
17/ 135	Mann, J. E.		,,		To 14th N.F.
17/ 325	Manning, D.	D	,,	W.	
17/ 1187	Mark, T. J.	D	,,		
45144	Markham, W. H. J.	C	,,		Commission.
45268	Marks, E. H.	D	,,		
45209	Marsh, L.	C	,,		Commission.
32/ 105	Marston, W. J.	A	,,	W.	
32/ 288	Martin, J.	D	,,		
17/ 1189	Masland, J.	A	,,		
17/ 1542	Mason, R.	A	,,		
32/ 860	Mason, W.	B	,,	K.	5.10.18.

17th and 32nd (S.) Batts. Northumberland Fusiliers (N.E.R.) Pioneers

Reg. No.	Name	Coy.	Rank	Casualties	Remarks
32/ 518	Mason, W. H.	B	Private		To 36th N.F.
32/ 928	Massey, W. E.	B	,,		,, ,,
17/ 1525	Matthers, G. E.		,,		To 14th N.F.
17/ 326	Matthews, J.	B	,,		
32/ 900	McDonald, H.	B	,,		
17/ 1479	McDonald, H.		,,		To 14th N.F.
32/ 106	McDonald, T. P. F.	B	L/Cpl.	G.	
45187	Meek, A. O.	A	Private		
17/ 965	Meggitt, E.	B	,,		
32/ 985	Meggitt, E.	B	,,		
45219	Merrell, C. W.	C	,,		To 6th N.F.
17/ 696	Merryweather, R. W.	B	,,	G.	To 14th N.F.
45142	Miller, E.	A	,,		To 6th N.F.
45220	Millward, F. H.	C	,,		,, ,,
17/ 1210	Mirfield, C. H.	D	,,		
32/ 291	Mirfin, H.	D	,,		
32/ 85	Mitchell, G. W.	D	,,		R.O.D.
32/ 292	Mitchell, W.	A	,,	W.	
45149	Mitchell, W. J.	C	,,		To 6th N.F.
45761	Montague, E. D.	B	,,	W.	,, ,,
17/ 545	Moore, E. J.		Sergt.		
32/ 422	Moore, F. J.	D	Private		
45152	Moorhouse, G.	C	,,	W.	
17/ 1071	Morland, T. O.	C	,,		
44998	Morris, J.	D	,,	G.	
45265	Mortimer, H. E.	B	,,		To 6th N.F.
17/ 1385	Moses, J. G.	B	,,		
17/ 699	Murray, G.	B	,,		
45197	Muskett, W. L.	C	Corporal		To 6th N.F.
32/ 110	Myers, W. H.	A	Private	K.	Accidentally. 1.7.17, Ypres, Poperinghe New Cemetery.
17/ 1822	Mack, J. G.		Private		T.B.E.
17/ 1802	Makin, J.		,,		,,
17/ 325	Manning, D.		,,		,,
17/ 1188	Markham, A.		,,		,,
17/ 227	Marplesden, L. F.		,,		,,
17/ 228	Marshall, A.		,,		,,
17/ 438	Marshall, J. F.		,,		,,
17/ 691	Marshall, W.		,,		,,
17/ 933	Masterman, J. E.		,,		,,
17/ 1504	Maughan, P. W.		,,		,,

Reg. No.	Name	Coy.	Rank	Casualties	Remarks
17/ 829	Maughan, T. W.		Private		T.B.E.
17/ 830	McConnell, M.		,,		,,
17/ 543	McDonald, E.		,,		,,
17/ 688	McDonald, P.		,,		,,
17/ 1144	McInteer, H.		,,		,,
17/ 689	McKechnie, W. R.		,,		,,
17/ 1363	McKenzie, J.		,,		,,
17/ 328	McLeod, N.		,,		,,
17/ 985	Medd, H.		,,		,,
17/ 230	Metcalfe, E.		,,		,,
17/ 138	Milner, J. W.		Sergt.		,,
17/ 1011	Mitchell, E.		Private		,,
17/ 833	Moody, J. W.		,,		,,
17/ 986	Moore, W.		,,		,,
17/ 1360	Morrell, E.		C.Q.M.S.		,,
17/ 442	Mortimer, W.		Private		,,
17/ 337	Moss, A.		,,		,,
17/ 546	Mullin, J.		,,		,,
17/ 338	Munster, T.		Sergt.		,,
17/ 937	Muroe, J.		Private		,,
17/ 700	Myers, W. D.		,,		,,
17/ 340	Nattrass, A. L.	C	L/Cpl.		E. Sergt.
17/ 1190	Neasham, W.	C	Private		E.
17/ 148	Needham, G.	D	,,		E.
17/ 702	Nelson, T. W.	A	,,	W.	E.
17/ 339	Nesbitt, W. F.	A	Corporal		E. Sergt.
17/ 888	Nevin, W.	A	Private		E.
17/ 547	Newlove, F.	D	,,		E.
17/ 839	Newsham, G. E.	D	,,		E.
17/ 548	Nichol, M.	A	L/Cpl.		E. Corporal.
17/ 840	Nichol, T.	A	Private		E.
17/ 144	Nichols, B. J.	A	R.S.M.	W.	E. Meritorious Service Medal.
17/ 443	Nichols, J. T.	D	Private	W.	E.
17/ 1092	Nichols, W. J. W.	B	L/Cpl.	D.G.	E. 16.7.16, Somme, Puchevillers Military Cemetery.
17/ 38	Nicholson, R.	B	Private		E. Commission.
17/ 1465	Noble, N. G.	B	,,		E.
17/ 841	Noble, R.	B	,,		E. L/Cpl.
17/ 842	Normington, G.	C	,,	W.	E.

17th and 32nd (S.) Batts. Northumberland Fusiliers (N.E.R.) Pioneers

Reg. No.	Name	Coy.	Rank	Casualties	Remarks
45178	Napper, H. W.	C	Private		
17/ 701	Nash, W.	A	,,		
32/ 232	Neale, W.	C	,,	W.	
32/ 873	Needham, W.	D	,,	D.W.	26.4.18, Nieppe Forest, Ebblingham Cemetery.
17/ 234	Nelson, A.	C	,,		
32/ 869	Ness, R. W.	B	,,	K.	25.10.17, Ypres, St. Julien Cemetery.
32/ 140	Nettleton, J. G.	C	,,	W.	
32/ 111	Newton, M.		,,		To 14th N.F.
32/ 175	Nichol, N.	B	,,		
32/ 112	Nicholson, A.	A	,,	W.	
32/ 430	Nicholson, H.	B	,,		To 36th N.F.
46511	Nicholson, J.	B	,,		
45216	Nicholson, W. H.	D	,,		To 6th N.F.
10231	Noonan, C.		,,		To 14th N.F.
32/ 389	North, T. A. C.	D	,,	W.	
17/ 1543	Naylor, F.		Private		T.B.E.
17/ 1211	Nettleton, H. E.		,,		,,
17/ 235	Neve, W.		,,		,,
17/ 1304	Newton, J. W.		,,		,,
17/ 444	Nicholson, T. W.		,,		,,
17/ 1015	Noble, G.		,,		,,
17/ 236	Nowell, H.		,,		,,
17/ 1191	Nuttall, J. T.		,,		,,
17/ 710	O'Connell, J.	A	Private	W.	E.
17/ 1355	Oliver, E.	B	,,		E. R.O.D.
17/ 341	Oliver, J. R.	A	Sergt.	W.	E. Military Medal.
17/ 342	Ord, E. D.	D	Private	D.W.	E. 20.4.18, Nieppe Forest, Ebblingham Cemetery.
17/ 1068	Ord, J.	B	Private	W.	E. L/Cpl.
17/ 445	Ord, W. H.	B	,,		E. R.O.D.
17/ 447	Overton, J.	D	,,		E.
17/ 448	Oxtoby, J. W.	B	,,	D.G.	E. 15.7.16, Somme, Bouzincourt Cemetery.
45155	Oddie, W.	D	Private		To 6th N.F.
32/ 38	Oliver, R.	D	,,		
17/ 446	Ornsby, J.		,,		To 14th N.F.

Reg. No.	Name	Coy.	Rank	Casualties	Remarks
17/ 549	Osleton, J. R.	A	Private	W.	
17/ 1544	Outhwaite, F.	A	,,	W.	
42547	Overend, J. W.	D	,,		
32/ 235	Oxley, T. C.	B	,,		
17/ 1448	Palmer, T. S.	A	Private		E. R.O.D.
17/ 938	Parias, D.	A	,,		E.
17/ 843	Parker, A.	D	L/Cpl.		E.
17/ 844	Parkin, A.	B	Private		E.
17/ 345	Parkin, J. V.	B	,,	W.	E.
17/ 344	Parkins, H. L.	A	,,		E.
17/ 237	Parnaby, J. T.	D	,,	W.	E.
17/ 1192	Parsley, G.	C	,,		E. Corporal.
17/ 146	Patient, T.	C	,,		E.
17/ 1267	Patterson, A.	A	,,		E.
17/ 346	Patterson, J.	D	Corporal		E. Commission.
17/ 1193	Pattison, W. Y.	B	Private		E.
17/ 1087	Pawlett, T.	B	,,		E.
17/ 1305	Payne, A. W.	C	,,		E.
17/ 40	Pea, P.	D	,,	W.	E.
17/ 41	Peacock, L.	C	,,		E. To R.E.
17/ 316	Peal, E.	A	,,		E.
17/ 1230	Pealing, F.	C	,,		E.
17/ 705	Pears, A.	D	,,		E.
17/ 1083	Pears, C.	D	,,		E.
17/ 347	Pearsall, A.	B	,,		E.
17/ 707	Pearson, E. S.	B	,,		E.
17/ 238	Pearson, F. J. H.	C	C.S.M.	W.W.G.	E. Meritorious Service Medal.
17/ 239	Pearson, H.	C	Private	W.W.	E.
17/ 348	Pearson, J.	B	,,		E. To 1/4 K.O.Y.L.I.
17/ 706	Pearson, W.	B	,,		E. L/Cpl.
17/ 1306	Pearson, W. N.	C	L/Cpl.		E. Commission.
17/ 449	Peart, T.	B	Private	W.	E.
17/ 1212	Peck, R. A.	A	,,		E.
17/ 350	Philipson, E. R.	A	,,	W.	E.
17/ 551	Pigg, A.	C	C.Q.M.S.	W.	E. Commission.
17/ 450	Pinder, E.	D	Private	W.	E.
17/ 1146	Porteous, G. P.	D	,,		E. To K.O.Y.L.I.
17/ 849	Porthouse, D.	A	L/Cpl.		E. Sergt.
17/ 940	Posgate, T.	A	,,	W.	E. Corporal.
17/ 709	Potter, R. G.	C	Private		E.

17th and 32nd (S.) Batts. Northumberland Fusiliers (N.E.R.) Pioneers

Reg. No.	Name	Coy.	Rank	Casualties	Remarks
17/ 1016	Potter, W. J.	B	Private	D.W.	E. 15.8.17, Ypres.
17/ 1498	Priestman, J.	C	,,	W.	E.
17/ 42	Pullan, T.	D	L/Cpl.		E. L/Sergt.
45156	Palmer, A. E.	D	Private	W.	To 6th N.F.
45243	Palmer, A. E.	A	,,		,, ,,
17/ 1545	Parker, J.		,,		To 14th N.F.
17/ 343	Parkin, B.	B	,,		L/Cpl.
17/ 1546	Parkinson, C.	D	,,		
45192	Parsonage, J.	D	,,		
17/ 550	Parvin, F.	C	,,		
17/ 1547	Patterson, H.	A	,,	W.	
48138	Patterson, R. Y.		,,		To 6th N.F.
17/ 1111	Patterson, T.	A	,,		
17/ 39	Pawson, B. C.	A	,,		
32/ 948	Pearce, G. W.	B	,,		
17/ 847	Pearson, W.		,,		To 14th N.F.
17/ 708	Pemberton, J. G.	B	,,		
45166	Petty, C. E.	D	,,		Commission.
45173	Piggott, S.	A	,,		
32/ 115	Pimp, T. A.	B	,,		
17/ 450	Pinder, E.	D	,,		
32/ 39	Place, W.		,,		To 14th N.F.
45241	Platts, F. C.	C	,,		To York and Lancs.
17/ 1231	Pocklington, F.	D	Corporal		
45124	Pollard, F. G.	C	Private		
44285	Powell, H. W.	D	,,		To 6th N.F.
45236	Priestman, E.	C	,,		,, ,,
17/ 145	Padley, A.		Private		T.B.E.
17/ 704	Parker, F. J.		,,		,,
17/ 343	Parkin, B.		,,		,,
17/ 939	Parkinson, T. G.		,,		,,
17/ 1514	Patrick, J. W.		,,		,,
17/ 703	Patterson, J. R.		,,		,,
17/ 1548	Pattinson, H. M.		,,		,,
17/ 1193	Pattison, W. Y.		,,		,,
17/ 846	Peam, T. F.		,,		,,
17/ 1494	Pearson, A. L.		,,		,,
17/ 349	Peel, E.		,,		,,
17/ 848	Pipe, J. H.		,,		,,
17/ 1245	Preston, C.		,,		,,

Roll of Men Who Served

Reg. No.	Name	Coy.	Rank	Casualties	Remarks
17/ 1246	Quinney, F.	A	Private		E.
17/ 1466	Rae, T.	D	Private	G.	E. L/Cpl.
17/ 1334	Raine, G.	B	,,		E. R.O.D.
17/ 944	Randall, T. P. L.	D	C.S.M.		E.
17/ 711	Rankin, D.	A	Private		E.
17/ 941	Ratcliffe, J. E.	B	,,	K.	E. 7.8.16, Bethune, Town Cemetery.
17/ 1119	Raw, A. E.	A	Cook Sgt.		E.
17/ 451	Readman, T. A.	D	L/Cpl.		E. Corporal.
17/ 240	Readman, W. R.	C	,,		E. To R.E.
17/ 552	Reader, C.	D	,,	W.	E. Commission.
17/ 1481	Reay, G.	C	Private	K.	E. 30.11.17, Somme, British Military Cemetery.
17/ 1195	Reay, G. E.	C	,,	W.	E.
17/ 1196	Reay, R.	A	,,		E. L/Cpl.
17/ 1467	Reid, A.	C	,,	K.	E. 27.1.16, Somme, Authuille Cemetery.
17/ 554	Reid, W.	A	,,	W.	E.
17/ 850	Remner, G. A.	B	L/Cpl.	W.	E. To W. Yorks.
17/ 43	Richardson, A.	D	,,	W.	E. L/Sergt.
17/ 351	Richardson, A. F.	C	Private		E.
17/ 241	Richardson, C. H.	D	,,		E.
17/ 352	Richardson, E. J.	A	,,		E.
17/ 712	Richardson, F.	C	,,		E.
17/ 353	Richardson, G.	B	,,	W.	E.
17/ 1060	Richardson, J.	C	,,	W.G.	E.
17/ 713	Richardson, T.	A	,,	W.	E.
17/ 1526	Richmond, W. R.	C	,,	G.K.	E. 30.11.17, Ypres, British Military Cemetery.
17/ 851	Ridley, J. T.	B	L/Sergt.	W.	E. C.Q.M.S.
17/ 556	Ridley, W.	A	Corporal	W.	E. Sergt.
17/ 557	Ridsdale, W. G.	C	L/Cpl.	W.W.	E.
17/ 715	Rigg, S.	C	Private		E.
17/ 452	Riley, R.	D	L/Cpl.	W.	E. Corporal.
17/ 356	Ripley, J. C.	B	,,		E. ,,
17/ 147	Rippingale, J. A.	D	Private		E.
17/ 1396	Ritchie, T.	B	,,	K.	E. 8.11.17, Ypres, Bard Cottage Cemetery.
17/ 1018	Ritchie, W.	A	,,		E.

17th and 32nd (S.) Batts. Northumberland Fusiliers (N.E.R.) Pioneers

Reg. No.	Name	Coy.	Rank	Casualties	Remarks
17/ 558	Riva, J. W.	D	Private	W.	E.
17/ 149	Roberts, A. A.	D	,,	W.	E.
17/ 357	Robertson, R.	A	,,	W.	E.
17/ 243	Robinson, A. G.	C	,,	W.	E.
17/ 1019	Robinson, B.	A	,,		E. To R.E.
17/ 1054	Robinson, C. N. B.	B	,,		E. To R.E.
17/ 1197	Robson, A.	C	,,	G.	E.
17/ 359	Robson, F.	C	,,	W.	E.
17/ 852	Robson, G.	A	,,	W.	E.
17/ 1255	Robson, J. R. H.	C	,,	W.	E.
17/ 360	Robson, S.	A	,,	W.	E.
17/ 561	Rochester, W. H.	A	,,		E.
17/ 718	Roe, H. J.	B	,,		E.
17/ 1432	Rogers, J.	D	,,	W.	E.
17/ 1147	Rooks, T.	C	,,		E.
17/ 454	Rothwell, W.	B	,,		E. R.O.D.
17/ 853	Rowe, F. W.	A	,,		E.
17/ 720	Rowntree, J. W. D.	B	,,	W.W.	E.
17/ 1198	Rushton, J.	D	,,	W.	E.
17/ 1199	Rutherford, R.	A	,,		E.
17/ 1330	Rutter, A.	B	,,		E. R.O.D.
29857	Radcliffe, F.	B	Private	W.	To 6th N.F.
17/ 1324	Railston, F.	C	Corporal		
57510	Randall, W.		Private	K.	16.11.17, Ypres, Bard Cottage Cemetery.
17/ 1194	Ransom, J.		,,	D.W.	30.10.17, Ypres, Bard Cottage Cemetery.
32/ 297	Renton, W. L.	A	,,	W.	
28/ 14	Reynolds, J. W.	D	,,		
45252	Richards, A. E.	A	,,		To 6th N.F.
32/ 40	Richardson, J.	A	,,		
17/ 354	Richardson, J.	A	,,		
33529	Richardson, R. H.		,,	D.S.	23.12.16, Etaples, Military Cemetery.
37944	Richardson, S.		Corporal		
45202	Richardson, W. H.	D	L/Cpl.		Corporal.
32/ 119	Riches, A.		Private		To 14th N.F.
17/ 1055	Ridley, J.	B	,,		
32/ 899	Rigg, E.	A	,,		To 36th N.F.
32/ 41	Rigg, T.		,,		To 14th N.F.
32/ 193	Ringwood, R. E.	D	,,	W.	
32/ 332	Robbins, E.	A	,,	W.	

Roll of Men Who Served 151

Reg. No.	Name	Coy.	Rank	Casualties	Remarks
45163	Roberts, F.	D	Private		To 6th N.F.
45249	Roberts, H.	A	,,		,, ,,
32/ 2	Roberts, H. P.		,,		To 14th N.F.
32/ 181	Robertson, A.		,,		,, ,,
32/ 649	Robinson, A.	C	,,	W.K.	16.11.17, Ypres, Bard Cottage Cemetery.
17/ 716	Robinson, A. W.	B	,,	W.	
32/ 962	Robinson, C. F.	B	,,		
32/ 298	Robinson, E.	D	,,		
17/ 717	Robinson, G. H.	C	,,		
32/ 42	Robinson, G. W.	D	,,		
17/ 1148	Robinson, J.	D	L/Cpl.	W.	
17/ 358	Robinson, J. G.	D	Private	W.	
17/ 1237	Robinson, W.		,,		
28/ 7	Robson, F. W.		,,		To 14th N.F.
32/ 120	Robson, J. W.	D	,,	D.W.	12.11.17, Ypres.
32/ 121	Rogers, T. R.		,,		To 14th N.F.
45210	Rose, R. W.	C	,,		To 6th N.F.
32/ 299	Rosier, A.	D	,,		
17/ 719	Routledge, H.	C	,,		L/Cpl.
45186	Rowe, F.	B	L/Cpl.		To 6th N.F.
17/ 721	Rowe, J.	A	Private		
39237	Rowland, J. W.	A	Sergt.		
44286	Roxby, E. L.	B	Private		To York and Lancs.
32/ 122	Ruddam, W. H.		,,		
32/ 44	Ruddick, J. P.	D	,,		
32/ 901	Rush, T. W.	B	,,	W.	
32/ 182	Rymer, J.	D	,,	W.	
17/ 1395	Radford, J.		Private		T.B.E.
17/ 1277	Rapp, E.		,,		,,
17/ 553	Redhead, T.		,,		,,
17/ 1017	Reid, E. F.		,,		,,
17/ 351	Richardson, A.		,,		,,
17/ 352	Richardson, E. J.		,,		,,
17/ 555	Richardson, S.		,,		,,
17/ 242	Richardson, T.		,,		,,
17/ 355	Richardson, T. S.		,,		,,
17/ 714	Ridsdale, S.		,,		,,
17/ 148	Riscam, J.		,,		,,
17/ 559	Robinson, J.		,,		,,
17/ 358	Robinson, J. G.		,,		,,
17/ 560	Robson, H.		,,		,,

17th and 32nd (S.) Batts. Northumberland Fusiliers (N.E.R.) Pioneers

Reg. No.	Name	Coy.	Rank	Casualties	Remarks
17/ 453	Robson, J.		Private		T.B.E.
17/ 1549	Robson, J. G.		,,		,,
17/ 1020	Rostron, J.		,,		,,
17/ 942	Rotherham, T.		,,		,,
17/ 454	Rothwell, W.		,,		,,
17/ 361	Rowell, H.		,,		,,
17/ 1021	Rowland, F.		,,		,,
17/ 854	Rowland, J. W.		,,		,,
17/ 722	Rowland, R.		,,		,,
17/ 1022	Ruddick, J. C.		,,		,,
17/ 362	Rutherford, T.		,,		,,
17/ 363	Sanderson, T. W.	A	Private		E. L/Cpl. To R.E.
17/ 855	Saunders, F. W.	A	,,		E.
17/ 150	Sawdon, A. R.	D	,,		E.
17/ 725	Sawkhill, S.	C	,,		E. L/Cpl.
17/ 1091	Schofield, T.	D	,,	W.	E. To 14th N.F.
17/ 562	Scott, F.	D	,,		E.
17/ 1047	Scott, F.	A	,,	W.	E.
17/ 563	Scott, J.	A	,,	W.	E.
17/ 1487	Scott, J. E.	A	,,		E.
17/ 364	Scott, J. G.	A	,,		E.
17/ 858	Scott, W.	B	,,		E.
17/ 943	Scrafton, W.	B	,,		E. L/Cpl.
17/ 1425	Seaman, G.	B	,,		E.
17/ 1149	Searle, H. W.	C	,,		E.
17/ 945	Seaton, J. T.	B	L/Cpl.	K.	E. Corporal. 12.11.17, Ypres, Bard Cottage Cemetery.
17/ 44	Seller, C. L.	B	Private		E. Commission.
17/ 153	Sellers, H.	D	,,	W.	E.
17/ 45	Serginson, B. W.	C	,,		E.
17/ 455	Serginson, W.	A	,,	W.	E. Military Medal.
17/ 365	Seymour, F. W.	B	L/Cpl.		E. Corporal.
17/ 1023	Shannon, J.	A	Private	W.	E.
17/ 1256	Sharp, J. W.	B	,,		E. R.O.D.
17/ 1515	Shaw, R. W.	C	,,	W.	E.
17/ 46	Shearsmith, H.	C	,,		E. L/Sergt.
17/ 1257	Shepherd, G.	C	,,		E.
17/ 48	Shinn, J. W.	D	,,		E.
17/ 366	Short, F.	A	L/Sergt.		E.
17/ 727	Simpson, A.	A	Private	W.	E.

Reg. No.	Name	Coy.	Rank	Casualties	Remarks
17/ 859	Simpson, A.	A	Private		E.
17/ 1490	Simpson, A. M.	C	,,	W.	E.
17/ 728	Simpson, F. S.	C	,,	W.	E.
17/ 729	Simpson, F. W.	B	,,		E.
17/ 1417	Simpson, G. H.	B	,,		E.
17/ 1888	Simpson, J.	C	,,		E.
17/ 1258	Simpson, J. W.	C	,,	W.	E.
17/ 1153	Simpson, W.	D	,,		E.
17/ 1053	Singleton, W.	B	,,		E.
17/ 730	Sissons, J. H.	D	,,		E.
17/ 1024	Skea, J.	A	,,		E.
17/ 1426	Skelton, A. E.	B	,,		E.
17/ 566	Skelton, H. E.	D	Corporal	W.	E. Sergt.
17/ 456	Smailes, J.	C	,,		E. ,,
17/ 1329	Smare, A.	B	Private		E. R.O.D.
17/ 860	Smith, A.	B	,,	G.	E.
17/ 1268	Smith, A.	B	,,		E.
17/ 567	Smith, A. R.	A	,,	D.W.	E. Died in England.
17/ 155	Smith, C. H.	B	,,	W.	E.
17/ 734	Smith, E. S.	A	Sergt.	W.	E.
17/ 861	Smith, F.	B	Private	W.	E.
17/ 1308	Smith, F.	B	,,		E.
17/ 1392	Smith, G.	C	,,		E.
17/ 1151	Smith, G. D.	C	,,		E.
17/ 569	Smith, G. E.	D	,,		E.
17/ 1238	Smith, H. G.	C	,,	G.	E.
17/ 368	Smith, J.	C	L/Cpl.	W.	E. Corporal.
17/ 1309	Smith, J.	B	Private	W.W.	E.
17/ 1394	Smith, R. H.	C	,,		E.
17/ 457	Smith, P.	A	,,	W.	E. To York and Lancs.
17/ 1025	Smith, R.	C	,,		E.
17/ 1269	Smith, S.	B	,,		E.
17/ 862	Smith, T.	D	,,		E. L/Cpl. Military Medal.
17/ 1118	Smith, T. L.	C	,,	W.	E.
17/ 52	Smith, W.	C	Sergt.	W.W.	E. Military Medal. Meritorious Service Medal.
17/ 571	Smith, W.	D	Private		E.
17/ 863	Smith, W.	A	,,		E.
17/ 1424	Smith, W.	C	,,		E. L/Cpl.
17/ 156	Smith, W. J.	D	,,	W.	E.
17/ 735	Smithson, A. P.	D	,,		E. L/Cpl.

17th and 32nd (S.) Batts. Northumberland Fusiliers (N.E.R.) Pioneers

Reg. No.	Name	Coy.	Rank	Casualties	Remarks
17/ 1368	Smurthwaite, F. J.	C	L/Cpl.		E.
17/ 736	Smurthwaite, J.	C	Private		E.
17/ 870	Snowden, R.	A	,,		E.
17/ 157	Snowdon, A.	C	,,		E.
17/ 572	Sonley, R.	B	,,	W.	E.
17/ 731	Soulsby, E. W.	A	,,	W.	E.
17/ 1418	Spearey, A.	D	,,		E.
17/ 158	Spenceley, J.	D	Sergt.	P.O.W.	E.
17/ 461	Spensley, A.	B	Private		E.
17/ 1259	Squires, W.	C	L/Cpl.		E. Corporal.
17/ 787	Stafford, J.	A	Private	W.	E.
17/ 738	Staples, J.	D	,,	K.	E. 1.7.16, Somme, Bouzincourt Cemetery.
17/ 1310	Steele, G.	D	,,		E. To York and Lancs.
17/ 864	Stephenson, A. E.	B	,,	W.	E. To 1st N.F.
17/ 1339	Stephenson, D.	D	,,		E. R.O.D.
17/ 1026	Stephenson, J. T.	A	,,		E.
17/ 865	Stephenson, R. W.	A	,,		E.
17/ 244	Stevenson, C.	C	,,		E.
17/ 872	Stewart, J.	A	L/Cpl.	W.	E.
17/ 373	Stobart, D. D.	B	Private		E. To R.E.
17/ 866	Stobbart, J. R.	C	,,	W.W.	E. Corporal.
17/ 1312	Stobbs, A. H.	D	,,		E. R.O.D.
17/ 1027	Stockdale, A. E.	B	,,		E.
17/ 573	Stockdale, E. R.	C	,,		E.
17/ 740	Stockdale, T.	D	,,	W.G.	E.
17/ 464	Stone, F. N.	B	,,	W.	E.
17/ 463	Street, G. C.	A	Sergt.	W.	E. C.S.M.
17/ 1347	Stringer, H.	D	Private		E.
17/ 374	Strong, R. R.	A	O.R. Sgt.		E. Colour Sergt.
17/ 375	Stuart, D. B.	A	Private		E.
17/ 376	Stubbs, T.	B	,,		E.
17/ 1088	Suffell, A.	D	,,	W.	E.
17/ 53	Sumner, H.	A	Sergt.		E. C.S.M. Commission.
17/ 867	Sutheran, N.	B	Private		E.
17/ 1232	Sutton, H.	D	,,		E.
17/ 1413	Swainson, H.	C	,,	K.	E. 26.1.16, Somme, Authuille Cemetery.
17/ 377	Swales, J.	D	Sergt.	W.	E. Commission. M.C.
17/ 868	Sweeney, J. R.	B	Private		E.
17/ 1340	Sweeney, P. E.	C	,,		E. R.O.D.
17/ 741	Swidenbank, J.	D	,,		E.
17/ 378	Sykes, E.	B	,,		E. L/Cpl.

Roll of Men Who Served

Reg. No.	Name	Coy.	Rank	Casualties	Remarks
17/ 574	Symonds, F.	D	Private		E. Corporal.
17/ 1427	Syrat, E. M.	C	,,		E.
32/ 931	Sanderson, A. F.	B	Private		
45121	Scace, J. H.	A	,,		
32/ 390	Scarffe, J. H.	A	,,		
57518	Scott, J. A.	D	,,	K.	2.11.17, Ypres.
32/ 302	Scriven, O.	B	,,		
32/ 920	Self, C. W.	A	,,	K.	29.9.18, Cambrai.
32/ 803	Sellars, T. W.	D	,,		R.O.D.
45119	Sexby, W. G. H.	C	,,		To 6th N.F.
45148	Sharpe, C. E.	C	,,		,, ,,
32/ 910	Shaw, D.	B	,,		To 36th N.F.
32/ 124	Shaw, F.		,,		To 14th N.F.
32/ 184	Shearson, G.	D	,,		
17/ 47	Shepherdson, A.	D	Sergt.		C.S.M.
17/ 49	Shipman, A. B.	D	Corporal		Sergt.
45231	Shuttleworth, E. H.	A	Private		To 6th N.F.
45107	Sims, H. C.	B	,,		To 1/5th Y. and L.
17/ 367	Sisson, F. W.	A	Corporal		Commission.
17/ 1410	Sloane, J. W.	A	Private		
45108	Smith, A. G.	A	,,	W.	
45183	Smith, C. E.	C	,,	W.	To 6th N.F.
17/ 51	Smith, E.	C	,,		To 14th N.F.
32/ 904	Smith, J.	B	,,	W.	
17/ 1824	Smith, J.	A	,,		
17/ 1152	Smith, S.		,,		
32/ 974	Smith, T.	B	,,		To 36th N.F.
32/ 186	Smith, V.		,,		To 12th K.O.Y.L.I.
32/ 878	Smith, W.	A	,,		To 36th N.F.
17/ 458	Smithson, J. W.		,,		
32/ 779	Smithson, W.	B	,,		
45110	Snell, L. G.	A	,,		To 6th N.F.
44287	Souter, G. A.	D	,,		To 6th N.F.
32/ 461	Spavin, J. M.	D	,,		
32/ 619	Spivey, H. E. W.	B	,,		
32/ 240	Spooner, T. L.	A	,,		
32/ 242	Sproates, T. W.		,,		To 14th N.F.
32/ 187	Stamp, W.		,,		To 12th K.O.Y.L.I.
32/ 244	Staveley, A. O.		,,		R.O.D.
45127	Stavens, A.	C	,,		
17/ 1811	Stephenson, J. R.		,,		To 14th N.F.
17/ 1260	Stockhill, H.		,,	W.	

17th and 32nd (S.) Batts. Northumberland Fusiliers (N.E.R.) Pioneers

Reg. No.	Name	Coy.	Rank	Casualties	Remarks
17/ 1270	Stoker, T.	A	Private		
45132	Stokes, W.	C	,,	D.W.	7.10.17, Oost Dunkerke.
17/ 1155	Stone, A.		,,		
47705	Stout, J.	B	,,	W.	
45234	Streeton, C. W.	D	,,		To 6th N.F.
18/ 268	Stuart, J. W.	D	,,		
32/ 53	Sunley, C. W.	A	,,	W.W.	
45233	Swain, T. S.	D	,,		To 6th N.F.
32/ 377	Swann, H. F.		,,		To 12th K.O.Y.L.I.
32/ 129	Sweeting, A.	C	,,	D.W.	27.9.18, Cambrai.
17/ 724	Sambrook, J. A.		Private		T.B.E.
17/ 856	Saunders, F. W.		,,		,,
17/ 1307	Scanlon, J.		,,		,,
17/ 151	Scott, T.		,,		,,
17/ 857	Scott, V.		,,		,,
17/ 152	Scott, W.		,,		,,
17/ 187	Sealing, W.		,,		,,
17/ 726	Senior, J.		,,		,,
17/ 154	Shepherd, A. H.		,,		,,
17/ 565	Shomler, A. W.		,,		,,
17/ 564	Short, A. C.		,,		,,
17/ 1150	Shrouder, J.		,,		,,
17/ 1888	Simpson, J.		,,		,,
17/ 946	Sissons, J. G.		Corporal		,,
17/ 50	Skilbeck, H.		Private		,,
17/ 1278	Skilbeck, S. F.		,,		,,
17/ 568	Smith, C.		,,		,,
17/ 948	Smith, C. D.		,,		,,
17/ 1247	Smith, C. H.		,,		,,
17/ 947	Smith, E. L.		,,		,,
17/ 949	Smith, J. G.		,,		,,
17/ 570	Smith, L.		,,		,,
17/ 459	Snaith, T.		,,		,,
17/ 869	Snowden, J. H.		,,		,,
17/ 732	Sowerby, W.		,,		,,
17/ 460	Speight, J. H.		,,		,,
17/ 733	Spence, H.		,,		,,
17/ 462	Spray, H.		,,		,,
17/ 1154	Stead, R.		,,		,,
17/ 951	Steel, G.		Sergt.		,,
17/ 1451	Stephenson, E.		Private		,,
17/ 789	Stephenson, H. F.		,,		,,

Reg. No.	Name	Coy.	Rank	Casualties	Remarks
17/ 871	Stephenson, J. W.		Private		T.B.E.
17/ 1449	Stobbs, J. W.		,,		,,
17/ 1155	Stone, A.		,,		,,
17/ 950	Straughan, W.		,,		,,
17/ 159	Sturgeon, A.		,,		,,
17/ 54	Suthering, J.		,,		,,
17/ 1261	Swann, J. H.		,,		,,
17/ 869	Swinburn, G.		L/Cpl.		,,
17/ 1213	Sykes, T.		Private		,,
17/ 870	Tait, E.	A	Sergt.		E.
17/ 871	Taplin, A.	A	Private	K.	E. 8.11.16, Somme, Aveluy Military Cemetery.
17/ 742	Tate, A.	A	,,	K.	E. 2.10.18. L/Cpl.
17/ 1028	Tate, G.	A	,,		E.
17/ 952	Tattersdill, S.	B	,,		E.
17/ 467	Taylor, E.	A	,,		E.
17/ 744	Taylor, G. H.	B	,,	W.	E.
17/ 1271	Taylor, V.	C	,,	D.W.	E. 17.11.17, Ypres.
17/ 745	Taylor, W. B.	B	,,		E.
17/ 1377	Taylor, W. C.	C	,,		E. R.O.D.
17/ 576	Taylor, W. H.	D	,,	W.	E.
17/ 1030	Teasdale, W.	B	Sergt.	W.K.	E. 4.8.17, Ypres.
17/ 746	Tebb, P. R. A.	D	Private		E.
17/ 379	Terry, J.	C	Sergt.	W.	E. Commission.
17/ 873	Terry, M.	C	Private		E.
17/ 168	Thackrah, A. E.	C	,,	W.	E.
17/ 747	Theakstone, F. S.	C	L/Cpl.		E. To R.E.
17/ 380	Theasby, T.	B	Private		E.
17/ 1085	Thomas, D. L.	B	,,		E. R.O.D.
17/ 1156	Thomas, F. W.	C	,,		E.
17/ 1031	Thomas, W.	C	,,	W.	E. To York and Lancs.
17/ 874	Thompson, B.	A	,,		E.
17/ 955	Thompson, G.	B	,,	W.	E. Sergt.
17/ 748	Thompson, H. V.	C	,,	W.	E.
17/ 246	Thompson, S.	C	,,		E.
17/ 165	Thompson, W.	D	Sergt.		E.
17/ 1374	Thorley, L.	C	Private		E.
17/ 1239	Tiffany, P. F.	A	,,		E.
17/ 1082	Tinn, H. G.	A	L/Cpl.		E. Sergt.
17/ 167	Tose, G.	C	Private		E.

158 17th and 32nd (S.) Batts. Northumberland Fusiliers (N.E.R.) Pioneers

Reg. No.	Name	Coy.	Rank	Casualties	Remarks
17/ 1082	Toward, J. W.	A	Private	W.	E.
17/ 1507	Towse, G. H.	C	,,		E.
17/ 381	Trainor, R.	A	,,	W.	E.
17/ 1313	Trembath, T.	D	,,	W.	E.
17/ 470	Trewick, E.	A	,,		E.
17/ 248	Turpin, J.	C	,,	W.	E.
17/ 1314	Tye, C.	C	,,		E. R.O.D.
57573	Tait, J.	C	Private	K.	16.11.17, Ypres, Bar Cottage Cemetery.
45158	Tallant, W. B.	D	,,		Commission.
45189	Taylor, F. W.	C	,,		To 6th N.F.
32/ 247	Taylor, G.		,,		To 12th K.O.Y.L.I.
45261	Taylor, H. J.	A	,,		To 6th N.F.
17/ 575	Taylor, J.	B	,,	W.	
45112	Taylor, R.	A	Sergt.		
32/ 349	Taylor, T. E.		Private		To 12th K.O.Y.L.I.
32/ 909	Taylor, T. R.	A	,,		To 36th N.F.
201798	Taylor, W. C.	D	,,		
45267	Taylorson, W. W.	C	,,		To 6th N.F.
32/ 877	Thames, J. W.	B	,,		
17/ 164	Thomas, H.	C	,,		
45263	Thompson, P. E.	D	,,		To 6th N.F.
238068	Thompson, P. O.	C	,,		
32/ 55	Thompson, R. J.		,,		To 12th K.O.Y.L.I.
45154	Thomson, H. G.	D	,,		To 6th N.F.
32/ 56	Tibbett, H. C.	C	,,		R.O.D.
17/ 1075	Todd, G.	A	,,	W.	
17/ 166	Tomlinson, W. H.		,,		To 12th K.O.Y.L.I.
32/ 57	Tong, E.		,,		To 14th N.F.
44288	Tonsley, R.		,,		To 13th N.F.
17/ 1233	Towler, R. H.		,,		
45145	Townend, H. V.	D	,,		
202877	Towns, J. R.	C	Sergt.		
34168	Towns, W.	D	L/Cpl.		Corporal.
32/ 308	Train, E.		Private		Corporal.
44277	Trees, J. G.	D	Sergt.	W.	
45114	Tregonning, W.	B	Private		To 6th N.F.
17/ 1157	Tunningley, E.	D	,,		
17/ 168	Tupling, T.	C	,,		
32/ 132	Turnbull, A.		,,		To 12th K.O.Y.L.I.
32/ 913	Turnbull, J. H.	A	,,		
32/ 419	Turpin, T.	C	,,	W.	

Reg. No.	Name	Coy.	Rank	Casualties	Remarks
19/ 1785	Twentyman, J. A.	D	Private		
17/ 169	Tyler, W. J.		,,		To 1/4 K.O.Y.L.I.
17/ 1262	Tasker, G. T.		Private		T.B.E.
17/ 1325	Tasker, J. W.		,,		,,
17/ 160	Tather, G. E.		,,		,,
17/ 55	Taylor, C.		,,		,,
17/ 1214	Taylor, C.		,,		,,
17/ 743	Taylor, D.		,,		,,
17/ 161	Taylor, E.		,,		,,
17/ 1029	Taylor, H.		,,		,,
17/ 953	Taylor, L.		,,		,,
17/ 56	Taylor, W. H. F.		,,		,,
17/ 954	Thompson, C. E.		,,		,,
17/ 245	Thompson, F.		,,		,,
17/ 577	Thompson, H. J.		,,		,,
17/ 1550	Thompson, J. C.		,,		,,
17/ 749	Thompson, J. J.		,,		,,
17/ 57	Thompson, P. R.		,,		,,
17/ 247	Thrift, G.		Sergt.		,,
17/ 1251	Todd, E.		Private		,,
17/ 1094	Tomlinson, J. W.		,,		,,
17/ 578	Tomlinson, T. W.		,,		,,
17/ 468	Tooth, A. J.		,,		,,
17/ 469	Trees, A.		Sergt.		,,
17/ 875	Tuffnel, W. I.		Private		,,
17/ 876	Turnbull, A.		Sergt.		,,
17/ 1437	Underwood, G. C.	C	Private		E.
17/ 1051	Underwood, W. H.	B	L/Cpl.		E. Cpl. Commission.
17/ 877	Urwin, G.	A	Private		E.
17/ 465	Ulliott, W.		Private		T.B.E.
17/ 466	Urwin, C. S.		,,		,,
17/ 170	Vagg, W. E.	C	Sergt.		E. Distinguished Conduct Medal.
17/ 1436	Verity, G. C.	C	Private		E.
17/ 249	Vokes, A. E.	C	,,		E.
17/ 764	Vokes, H.	B	,,		E.

17th and 32nd (S.) Batts. Northumberland Fusiliers (N.E.R.) Pioneers

Reg. No.	Name	Coy.	Rank	Casualties	Remarks
17/ 765	Vosper, J.	D	Private		E.
32/ 945	Varley, C. H.	B	Private		
17/ 171	Vernon, G.	C	,,	W.	
45115	Viles, R. W.	B	,,		To 6th N.F.
17/ 172	Voase, E.	D	,,		
32/ 249	Vollans, H.		,,		To 12th K.O.Y.L.I.
17/ 1093	Varey, W. G.		Private		T.B.E.
17/ 1493	Vokes, G. W.		,,		,,
17/ 58	Wade, S.	B	Corporal	K.	E. 5.2.16, Somme, Authuille Cemetery.
17/ 1379	Wain, G.	A	Sergt.	W.	E.
17/ 1215	Wakelin, C.	D	Private	W.W.W.	E. L/Cpl. Military Medal.
17/ 1516	Wakenshaw, R.	C	,,	W.	E.
17/ 383	Walker, A.	A	,,	W.	E.
17/ 1815	Walker, A.	C	,,		E. R.O.D.
17/ 750	Walker, C. M.	B	,,		E.
17/ 579	Walker, F.	A	,,		E.
17/ 250	Walker, G.	D	,,	W.	E.
17/ 1875	Walker, H. W.	D	,,		E.
17/ 878	Walker, J.	C	L/Cpl.	W.	E. Commission.
17/ 1240	Walker, J.	C	Private	W.	E.
17/ 1104	Walker, J. M.	C	,,		E.
17/ 1403	Walker, J. W.	B	,,		E.
17/ 174	Walker, S.	D	,,		E.
17/ 1517	Walker, W.	C	,,		E. To R.E.
17/ 754	Wallace, J. J.	B	Corporal		E. Sergt. Military Medal.
17/ 1333	Wallinger, T.	C	Private		E. R.O.D.
17/ 471	Wallis, J.	B	L/Cpl.	W.	E. L/Sergt.
17/ 1316	Wallis, J. E.	D	Private		E. R.O.D.
17/ 1248	Walton, F.	A	,,		E.
17/ 581	Walton, H.	C	,,	K.	E. 27.9.18, Cambrai, Canal du Nord.
17/ 880	Walton, J. G.	A	Sergt.		E. Pioneer Sergt.
17/ 881	Wanless, W. A.	B	Private		E.
17/ 1317	Ward, G. H.	C	,,	W.	E. R.O.D.
17/ 384	Ward, J. G.	B	,,		E.
17/ 582	Ward, S. O.	D	,,	W.	E. To 10th N.F.

Roll of Men Who Served

Reg. No.	Name	Coy.	Rank	Casualties	Remarks
17/ 882	Wardle, J. J.	A	Private		E.
17/ 957	Warner, H.	B	,,	K.	E. 15.8.16, Bethune, Town Cemetery.
17/ 1371	Waterhouse, F.	D	,,		E. L/Cpl.
17/ 583	Waters, G.	D	L/Cpl.		E.
17/ 956	Watson, C. B.	B	Private		E.
17/ 883	Watson, E.	C	Sergt.		E.
17/ 584	Watson, H.	C	Private		E.
17/ 1456	Watson, W.	C	,,		E.
17/ 755	Watson, W. F.	A	,,	W.	E.
17/ 1272	Weatherall, F.	C	,,	W.	E. L/Cpl.
17/ 175	Weatherill, P.	C	,,	W.	E.
17/ 472	Webster, J.	C	,,		E.
17/ 176	Webster, S.	D	,,		E. L/Cpl.
17/ 958	Webster, T. W.	B	,,	D.W.	E. 6.7.16, Somme, Cimetière du Bois, Haring Heilly.
17/ 1483	Wellburn, G. W.	C	,,		E.
17/ 60	Welburn, W. S.	D	,,		E. L/Cpl.
17/ 473	Welch, J. F.	C	,,		E.
17/ 386	Welsh, H.	A	Sergt.	W.	E.
17/ 1073	Welsh, J.	A	Private		E.
17/ 884	Westnadge, H. O.	A	,,		E.
17/ 388	Whaley, R. A.	B	,,	W.	E. D.W. with 10th N.F., 1.10.16.
17/ 474	Wharram, G.	A	,,		E.
17/ 178	Whipp, C. P.	C	,,		E.
17/ 389	White, A.	A	,,		E.
17/ 252	White, B.	C	,,		E.
17/ 885	White, F.	A	,,		E.
17/ 390	White, J. J.	A	,,	W.	E.
17/ 1450	White, J. R. W.	B	,,		E. R.O.D.
17/ 179	Whitehead, J. W.	B	,,	G.	E.
17/ 180	Whitehurst, G. W.	D	,,	W.	E.
17/ 475	Whitleton, T. S.	D	,,		E. L/Cpl.
17/ 1035	Whyatt, T.	A	,,		E. Corporal.
17/ 959	Wilkinson, A.	B	,,		E.
17/ 1484	Wilkinson, J.	C	,,	W.G.	E.
17/ 886	Wilkinson, W.	A	,,	W.	E.
17/ 1485	Willans, G. H.	C	,,	K.	E. 27.1.16, Somme, Authuille Cemetery.
17/ 761	Williamson, S. J.	C	Corporal		E. Sergt. Commission.
17/ 1499	Wills, J. T.	C	Private		E. L/Cpl.

17th and 32nd (S.) Batts. Northumberland Fusiliers (N.E.R.) Pioneers

Reg. No.	Name	Coy.	Rank	Casualties	Remarks
17/ 62	Wilson, A.	C	Private		E.
17/ 960	Wilson, A. E.	A	,,	W.W.	E.
17/ 63	Wilson, B.	B	L/Cpl.		E. To R.E.
17/ 183	Wilson, F.	D	Private		E.
17/ 758	Wilson, F.	B	Sergt.		E.
17/ 1348	Wilson, F. C.	B	Private		E. R.O.D.
17/ 1452	Wilson, H.	D	,,		E. L/Cpl.
17/ 760	Wilson, H. A.	C	,,	W.W.	E.
17/ 476	Wilson, J.	D	,,	K.	E. 2.11.17, Ypres, Bard Cottage Cemetery.
17/ 253	Wilson, J. W.	B	,,	G.	E.
17/ 477	Wilson, M. W.	B	L/Cpl.		E. Corporal.
17/ 478	Wilson, T.	D	Private		E. R.O.D.
17/ 759	Wilson, W. H.	C	Corporal	W.	E.
17/ 889	Winn, J.	C	Private		E.
17/ 961	Winter, C. H.	D	,,	W.	E.
17/ 391	Winward, A.	B	,,		E.
17/ 64	Wise, E.	C	L/Cpl.	W.W.	E. Sergt.
17/ 1216	Wood, A.	D	Private	W.	E.
17/ 1439	Wood, A. E.	C	,,	W.	E.
17/ 185	Wood, J.	D	,,		E.
17/ 1486	Wood, T. W.	C	,,		E.
17/ 254	Woodhall, W.	C	L/Cpl.		E. Sergt.
17/ 481	Worrall, A. C.	D	Private		E. R.O.D.
17/ 1354	Worthy, J. C.	C	,,		E. R.O.D.
17/ 255	Wright, A.	B	,,		E. L/Cpl. To R.E.
17/ 587	Wright, B.	C	,,	W.W.	E.
17/ 482	Wright, G.	A	,,		E.
17/ 1037	Wright, G.	D	,,	D.W.	E. 2.4.16, Somme, Nouvean Amiens.
17/ 1274	Wright, J. V.	D	,,		E.
17/ 1038	Wright, L. A.	D	,,		E.
17/ 762	Wright, T.	A	,,	W.	E.
17/ 891	Wright, W. H.	D	,,		E.
17/ 763	Wylie, R.	B	,,		E. L/Cpl.
32/ 449	Waind, J.	C	Private	D.W.	12.11.17, Ypres, Fozingham Cemetery.
45201	Wainwright, F.	A	,,		To 6th N.F.
45198	Wakley, H. G.	A	Corporal		Commission.
17/ 1158	Walker, C. H.	D	Sergt.		,,
17/ 1552	Walker, E. C.	A	Private		R.O.D.
16/ 50	Walker, H.	C	,,		

Roll of Men Who Served

Reg. No.	Name	Coy.	Rank	Casualties	Remarks
43148	Walker, R.		Private		To 6th N.F.
17/752	Walker, T.	A	,,		
17/879	Wall, W.		,,		To 12th K.O.Y.L.I.
32/564	Wallis, J. W.		,,		To 14th N.F.
32/325	Walton, H.	C	,,		
32/378	Walton, J. W.	B	,,		
32/61	Warren, J.		,,		To 14th N.F.
32/896	Warrener, B. B.	A	,,		L/Cpl.
57526	Waterman, F.	D	,,	K.	2.11.17, Ypres, Bard Cottage Cemetery.
45195	Watkins, J. C.	C	,,		To York and Lancs.
32/252	Watson, E.	C	,,		
34814	Watson, G.	C	,,		
32/527	Watson, H.	A	,,	W.	
40307	Watson, T. E.	A	,,	W.	
18/263	Watson, W.	B	L/Cpl.		
45189	Watson, W.	C	Private		To 10th N.F.
45221	Watts, A.	D	,,		To 6th N.F.
45214	Watts, B. A.	C	,,		,, ,,
17/756	Weatherald, A.		,,		
45280	Weatherhead, F. R.	C	,,	W.	Commission.
45203	Webb, W. H.	B	,,	W.	
32/862	Webster, G.	A	,,	W.	
32/864	Weighell, C.	D	,,		
17/385	Welford, C.	A	,,		
32/860	Wellburn, C. H.		,,		To 12th K.O.Y.L.I.
266085	Welsh, R.	B	,,		
58312	Wesson, C. H.	B	,,		
32/917	Wheatley, A.	B	,,		
31744	Wheeler, W.	A	,,		
32/186	White, R.	B	,,	G.	
17/1468	White, W. D.	C	L/Cpl.		
32/866	Whitehead, C. H.	A	Private	W.W. D.W.	20.4.18, Nieppe Forest, Ebblingham Cemetery
45146	Whitely, J. S.	A	,,		To 6th N.F.
32/310	Whitfield, R. W.		,,		To 12th K.O.Y.L.I.
17/181	Whitley, C.		,,		
43172	Whittaker, J. B.		,,		
44274	Wickens, F.	B	,,		
32/366	Wickham, A.		,,		To 12th K.O.Y.L.I.
32/396	Wilkinson, F.		,,		,, ,,
17/1423	Wilkinson, J. R.	A	,,		
45116	Willey, F. J.	D	,,		

17th and 32nd (S.) Batts. Northumberland Fusiliers (N.E.R.) Pioneers

Reg. No.	Name	Coy.	Rank	Casualties	Remarks
45120	Williams, A.	D	Sergt.		
45181	Williams, M. H.	D	L/Cpl.		Corporal.
32/ 312	Williamson, T.		Private		To 12th K.O.Y.L.I.
32/ 318	Wilsher, G. W.		L/Cpl.		,, ,,
45245	Wilson, F. C.	D	Private		To 6th N.F.
17/ 1086	Wilson, G.	A	,,	W.	
37760	Wilson, G.	C	,,	W.	
32/ 137	Wilson, S. W.		,,		To 12th K.O.Y.L.I.
32/ 345	Wilson, T.		,,		,, ,,
17/ 1318	Windle, H.	D	,,		Corporal.
32/ 698	Winship, A. E.	A	,,	W.	
16/ 738	Winship, T.	A	,,		
17/ 184	Winter, W. W. C.		,,		To 14th N.F.
45157	Wollen, A. G.	D	,,		To 6th N.F.
45118	Wood, E. G.	B	,,		,, ,,
17/ 480	Wood, F.	D	,,	W.	
18/ 437	Wood, J.	A	,,	W.	
45117	Wood, S. H.	A	,,		To 6th N.F.
17/ 1319	Woodmansey, M. W.	D	,,		
45262	Woolnough, A. W.	D	,,		To 6th N.F.
32/ 895	Woods, P. V.	A	,,		
28/ 497	Wordingham, T. H.	A	Sergt.		
45227	Worthington, W.	D	Private		
17/ 1361	Wright, A.	D	,,		
17/ 1406	Wright, G.	D	Corporal		Sergt. Commission.
17/ 890	Wright, G. C.		Private		
43299	Wright, W.		,,		To 6th N.F.
17/ 1033	Waine, H.		Private		T.B.E.
17/ 173	Walker, A.		,,		,,
17/ 751	Walker, E.		,,		,,
17/ 580	Walker, T.		,,		,,
17/ 59	Walkington, A.		,,		,,
17/ 753	Wallace, H.		,,		,,
17/ 1378	Waller, J.		,,		,,
17/ 1352	Wappitt, J. W.		,,		,,
17/ 1482	Watson, T. E.		,,		,,
17/ 1106	Watson, W.		,,		,,
17/ 387	Welch, W.		,,		,,
17/ 385	Welford, C.		,,		,,
17/ 61	Wells, L. J.		,,		,,
17/ 177	Westoby, W.		,,		,,
17/ 1034	Whitfield, S. J.		,,		,,

Reg. No.	Name	Coy.	Rank	Casualties	Remarks
17/ 757	Whitfield, T. A.		Private		T.B.E.
17/ 182	Wilcock, E.		Sergt.		,,
17/ 959	Wilkinson, A.		Private		,,
17/ 585	Wilkinson, H.		,,		,,
17/ 1430	Wilkinson, J.		,,		"
17/ 1159	Wilson, E.		,,		,,
17/ 887	Wilson, E. D. O.		,,		,,
17/ 183	Wilson, F.		,,		,,
17/ 888	Wilson, J.		,,		,,
17/ 1372	Wintersgill, T.		,,		,,
17/ 586	Wood, E.		,,		,,
17/ 1518	Worth, J. H.		,,		,,
17/ 1411	Wright, G. W.		,,		,,
17/ 1508	Wright, J.		,,		,,
17/ 392	Yarroll, L. J. C.	A	Private		E.
17/ 1048	Yarrow, W. T.	A	Sergt.		E. C.Q.M.S.
17/ 186	Yates, F. J.	D	Private		E. R.O.D.
17/ 1089	Yellowley, T.	A	,,	G.	E. L/Cpl.
17/ 488	Young, A. R.	B	Corporal	W.	E. Sergt.
17/ 893	Young, C. D.	A	Private		E.
17/ 1400	Young, J.	C	,,	W.	E. L/Cpl.
17/ 892	Young, R. W.	B	Corporal	W.	E. Sergt.
17/ 1040	Younghusband, W.	B	Private	W.	E.
45226	Yeo, H. B.	D	Private		
45200	Young, G. A.	B	,,	W.	
32/ 328	Younger, J. P.		,,		To 12th K.O.Y.L.I.

APPENDICES
APPENDIX I
CONGRATULATORY MESSAGES

In addition to the appreciative remarks of those under whom the battalion served, which have already been given, the following show that the battalion maintained its high standard to the very end:

L.R.644-17/7424.

LIEUTENANT-COLONEL D. O. KING,
    Commanding 17th Battalion Northumberland Fusiliers
        (N.E.R.) Pioneers.

I wish to express to you, and to all your officers, my regret at losing your services on light railways in this Army, and my appreciation of the work which you have done.

Our relations have always been cordial, and I am extremely sorry to lose you.

The work which you are going to do, however, is of greater importance, and I wish you all God-speed, a steady hand, and a good target.

(Signed) H. L. BODWELL, *Lieutenant-Colonel*,
A.D.L.R.II.

SECOND ARMY,
    13*th April*, 1918.

HEADQUARTERS,
11*th May*, 1918.

COMMANDING OFFICER,
    17th Northumberland Fusiliers Railway Pioneer Battalion.

The Divisional Commander desires me to express his appreciation of the excellent work which has been done by your battalion while it has been attached to this Division.

All work allotted to the battalion has been thoroughly carried out with a fine spirit.

He has taken steps to bring this under the notice of higher authority.

(Signed) T. A. BLAMEY, *Colonel*,
General Staff, 1st Australian Division.

XV CORPS No. 128/19 G,
11*th May*, 1918.

29TH DIVISION.

The attached letter from 1st Australian Division is forwarded for communication to 17th Northumberland Fusiliers Railway Pioneer Battalion.

I am to add the Corps Commander's appreciation of the good work performed.

(Signed) H. KNOX, *Brigadier-General*,
General Staff.

XV CORPS,
    11*th May*, 1918.

Appendices

XV Corps No. 128/23/G,
29th May, 1918.

17TH NORTHUMBERLAND FUSILIERS (PIONEERS).

The Corps Commander directs to convey to you his appreciation of the good work carried out by the battalion while in the 15th Corps. He thanks all ranks for their efforts, and wishes the battalion all good luck in the future.

(Signed) H. KNOX, *Brigadier-General*,
General Staff.

XV CORPS,
28th May, 1918.

17TH N.F. 5485.

HEADQUARTERS,
XV Corps G.S.

With reference to XV Corps letter No. 128/23/G. dated 29th May, 1918, the Corps Commander's remarks and good wishes are much appreciated by all ranks of the battalion under my command.

(Signed) D. O. KING, *Lieutenant-Colonel*,
Commanding 17th Battalion Northumberland Fusiliers
(N.E.R.) Pioneers.

1st *June*, 1918.

The 52nd Divisional Pioneers (17th Battalion Northumberland Fusiliers) showed great activity in the repair of roads, particularly in the 52nd Divisional Area east of the Jard Canal. Their work was characterized by very considerable thoroughness and power of organization, and it was invariably found that subaltern officers of this battalion employed, for instance, on repair or renewal of a road culvert had a sound engineering knowledge of all technical details involved.

During these operations the reconnaissance of enemy dumps and collection of materials therefrom was quickly and efficiently carried out.

I consider that the work done reflects great credit on the C.R.E. and the units under his command.

(Signed) A. H. CAREY, *Brigadier-General*,
Chief Engineer, VIII Corps.

HEADQUARTERS, VIII CORPS,
17th November, 1918.

A.1/3459.

52ND DIVISION.

I am directed by the Corps Commander to express his appreciation of the good work performed by the Field Companies, R.E., and Pioneer Battalion of the 52nd Division.

Within about eighteen days this Divisional R.E. constructed seventeen bridges, all of which have proved of great assistance in operations; especially satisfactory was the work performed during the construction of the heavy lorry bridge carrying the Douai-Raches road over the road near Douai railway station about 29th/31st October, and the erection of the Hopkins' steel girder bridge near Courcelles.

The work of the 52nd Division Pioneers (17th Battalion Northumberland Fusiliers) on the roads in the Divisional Area has throughout been characterized by much thoroughness and resource.

The Corps Commander says that the work done reflects much credit on the C.R.E. of the 52nd Division, and the units under his command and direction.

(Signed) A. A. McHARDY, *Brigadier-General*,
D.A. and Q.M.S.

19th *November*, 1918.

PLATE XXIV.

W. Officers and N.C.O.'s of 32nd Northumberland Fusiliers.

PLATE XXV.

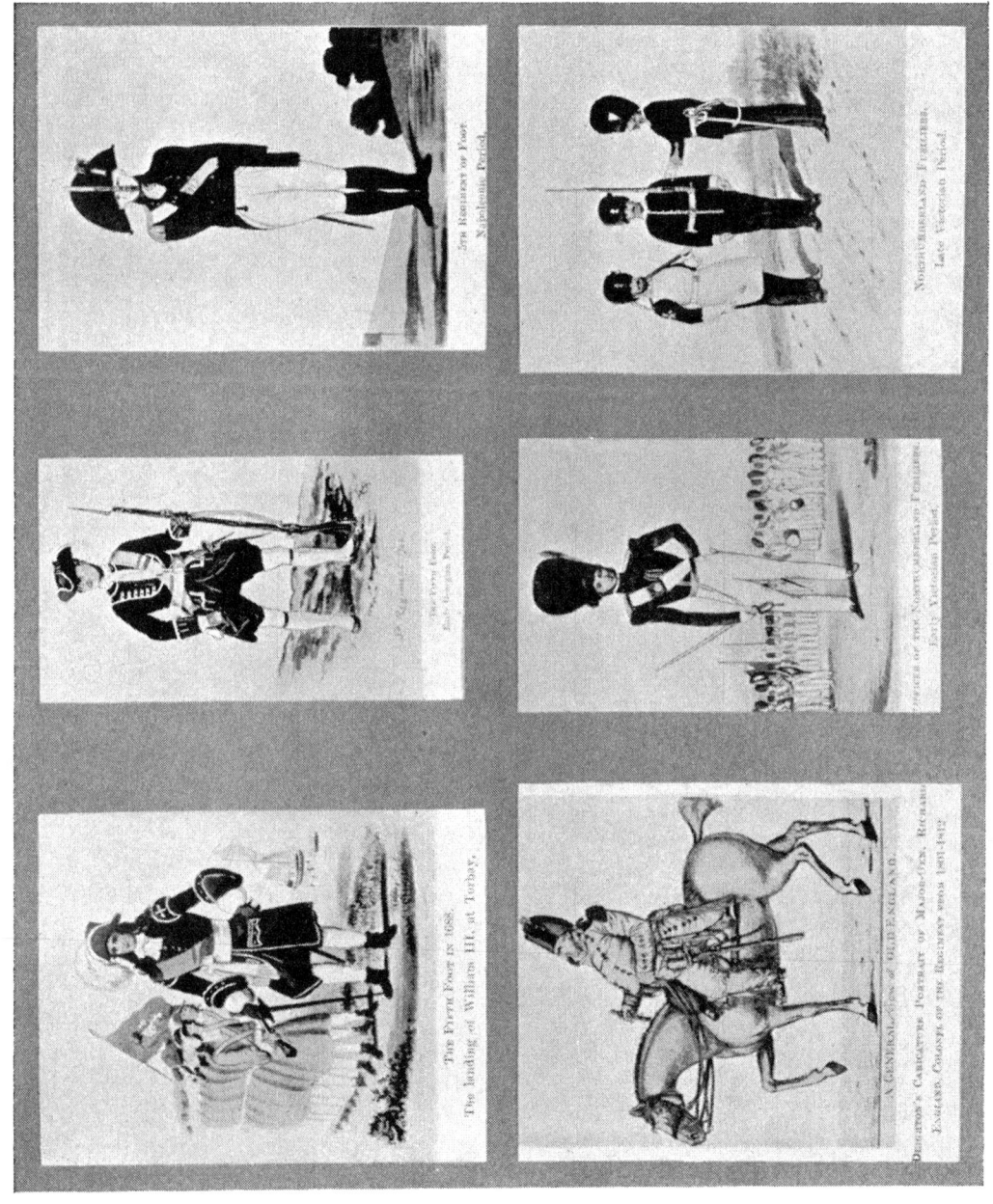

TYPES OF UNIFORM WORN BY NORTHUMBERLAND FUSILIERS.

APPENDIX II

THE THIRTY-SECOND NORTHUMBERLAND FUSILIERS

As soon as the necessary number of men had been recruited to complete the 17th Northumberland Fusiliers, measures were taken to form a Reserve Battalion. The men enlisted for this were at first formed into " E " and " F " Companies, and formed part of the battalion.

When the battalion moved to Catterick in the middle of June, 1915, the two Reserve Companies stayed behind in Hull, under command of Major A. H. B. Wright. The other officers with them were Captain G. Leonard Thompson, Lieutenants Dallin, Harrison, Blair, Vernon, Paddon, Hare, and others.

At this time these two companies were but little, if anything, behind the others in efficiency; in fact at the St. George's Day parade, 1915, " E " Company had won the prize for the best section in marching order.

The Reserve Companies stayed at Hull till 24th July, when they moved by train to Cramlington. " We reached Cramlington the same day (doubtless the N.E.R. were on their metal, having so many competent critics aboard)."

At Cramlington they lived in tents, and found themselves in the same camp with the Reserve Companies of the 16th, 18th and 19th Battalions of the regiment. About the 10th of August all these Reserve Companies were formed into the 28th Northumberland Fusiliers under command of Lieutenant-Colonel Fawcus.

Shortly before this, Major Wright secured a staff appointment in Newcastle, and was succeeded by Major E. St. J. Lawson, who, together with Second-Lieutenant Paget, joined from the 17th Battalion, and Second-Lieutenants Maughan and Pick joined on first appointment.

About the end of August the Reserve Battalion moved to Bardon Moor and camped among the heather.

Here Second-Lieutenant Beattie Brown " came into some prominence on account of the assistance he was able to give. Second-Lieutenant Hope came to us from the 17th Northumberland Fusiliers, and Second-Lieutenants Garvie and French joined."

Bardon Moor was a pleasant, healthy spot in summer, but as the autumn drew on it was found rather " parky " at nearly a thousand feet above sea-level, at which altitude the camp was situated.

The 28th Battalion was now split up, and the Reserve Companies of the N.E.R. Pioneers were formed into the 32nd Northumberland Fusiliers, and became the special reserve of the 17th Battalion. They were moved into huts at Ripon on 2nd November, which was hailed with delight by all concerned.

Shortly after this Lieutenant-Colonel B. O. Fyffe, of the Gloucester Regiment, who had been invalided home from France, where he had commanded the 10th Battalion Essex Regiment, was appointed to command the battalion, and Major Lawson was made Second-in-Command.

On 22nd December another move was made to Harrogate, where they were billeted in hotels, houses and other places. Here they were also very comfortable, and got on well with the inhabitants, as British soldiers always do. One kind lady, who said it did not matter about her name, having noticed that the sentry's hands were uncovered, left a pair of mittens for him at the orderly-room, which, needless to say, he brought into immediate use. Were these mitts handed over to the next sentry? History does not relate.

Appendices

The Dragon Lodge of the Order of Buffaloes invited some fifty of the battalion to its annual dinner, which was followed by a concert. The battalion had done a good long route march that day, so the men were just in trim to do justice to the good fare provided by their host and hostess, Mr. and Mrs. Beeforth. The little difference between the Titular Saint of the soldiers and the Dragon does not seem to have marred the harmony of the evening, which closed with a flood of oratory, the speakers being Mrs. Beeforth, R.S.M. W. Barker, C.S.M. J. Steel, Mr. Symington, R.Q.M.S. R. Gill, and Mr. Morgan.

February, 1916, saw the battalion again moved, this time to Newcastle, where they were billeted in schools, etc., and in the intervals of training were called upon for various guard duties.

Major Lawson left the battalion about this time, and was succeeded by Major G. L. Thompson, who in turn was succeeded in the Adjutancy by Lieutenant T. B. Hare.

In May, 1916, a move was made to the salubrious pit village of Usworth, where the battalion went under canvas. Here intensive training was undertaken, and drafts prepared for the 17th Battalion.

Occasionally we had news of the parent battalion, and were visited by some of their officers, notably Captains Phillips, Reeves and Ellis, who naturally were welcomed with open arms.

The 32nd Battalion subsequently became the 80th Training Reserve Battalion, and after that recruits other than N.E.R. men were enrolled.

The 80th Training Reserve was finally disbanded about Christmas, 1917, when still under the command of Lieutenant-Colonel Fyffe, though it is doubtful if there were many others of the original 32nd Battalion still serving under him at that time.

APPENDIX III

A BRIEF OUTLINE OF THE REGIMENT'S HISTORY

This short account of the Northumberland Fusiliers is added at the suggestion of Major Shenton Cole to give those who served in the 17th Battalion of that regiment some idea of the origin of the gallant corps, the honour of which they so well upheld. The few illustrations give some idea of the costumes their predecessors wore, which, if more showy, were certainly not as comfortable to fight in as the khaki we all wore.

I am indebted for the material on which this account is based to Mr. Alfred Brewis, who is a collector of prints and medals of the Fifth Foot. We have much to thank him for, and my only regret is that space prevents my re-printing his article word for word.

The Battle Honours of the Northumberland Fusiliers 1762-1899

Wilhelmstahl, St. Lucia 1778, Roleia, Vimiera, Corunna, Busaco, Ciudad Rodrigo, Badajoz, Salamanca, Vittoria, Nivelle, Orthes, Toulouse, Peninsula, Lucknow, Afghanistan 1878-80, Khartoum, Modder River, South Africa 1899-1902.

The above nineteen "Honours" were gained, thirteen in Europe, two in India, three in Africa, and one in the West Indies. They remind us of this regiment's large share in the Army's work of building up the British Empire.

Appendices

In 1674 a British division was raised in Holland to help the Prince of Orange in his great struggle with Louis XIV., King of France. The division consisted of two English, one Scotch, and an Irish regiment. The last was raised by Daniel O'Brien, Viscount Clare. In the next year the command was given to John Fenwick, and many English gentlemen now began to be given commissions in the regiment, so the designation " Irish " was dropped; probably it was at this time that the regiment adopted St. George as its badge, and perhaps also the motto, " Quo Fata Vocant." The regiment formed part of the British brigade, which showed desperate courage at the siege of Maestricht, when Colonel Fenwick was wounded. He shortly after left the regiment owing to some misunderstanding with the Prince of Orange. It is said that this inclined Sir John Fenwick to take part in a plot to assassinate William after he had become King of England, which led to his being executed in 1679.

The regiment fought at Monte-Cassel in 1677 and at Mons in 1678. In 1685 it, with the other British regiments, was brought from Holland to England to aid in putting down rebellions against James II. It now came on to the English establishment, and was known as the *Fifth* Regiment of Foot. It returned to Holland the same year, but on the 5th November, 1688, the Fifth landed at Torbay as part of the Army which escorted William of Orange and his wife Mary to London, where they ascended the throne without bloodshed, James II. having fled. The Fifth Foot fought for William at Boyne in 1690, at Athlone and Limerick in the following year.

The year 1694 saw the Fifth at Bruges and in the Lys district. The next year it assisted at the siege and capture of Namur, after which it was encamped on the sandhills near Nieuport. Thus does history repeat itself. Having fought in Spain in 1709, the Fifth went to Gibraltar in 1713, and stayed there fifteen years, sharing in the hardships of the great siege of " The Rock."

In 1755, after a long spell of service in Ireland, the Fifth took part, not without loss, in several " cut and run " expeditions across the Channel, landing in France, doing all the damage possible, then re-embarking without undue delay.

In 1760 the Fifth formed part of a force of some thirty-two thousand British troops under command of the Marquis of Granby, which was sent to Hanover to help the Prussians against the French; the British contingent distinguished itself at Warburg on 31st July, 1761, and the following year, on 24th June, at Wilhelmstahl, the victory was decided by Granby's contingent, which after a fierce fight destroyed the pick of the French Army. The Fifth, commanded by Lieutenant-Colonel Marlay, lead the attack, and forced the surrender of nearly a whole division. The regiment here won its first honour, and as a mark of distinction was allowed to exchange their three-cornered hats for the French Grenadier caps, and wore this style of headgear for many years; it was not till May, 1836, that the Fifth or " Northumberland Regiment of Foot " became the " Northumberland Fusiliers." The title " Northumberland " regiment was given in compliment to Earl Percy, who commanded the regiment for sixteen years (1768-84), but though the Earl made efforts to recruit in Northumberland, it is doubtful whether the regiment had even a small percentage of north-country men in its ranks.

During the eighteenth century the regiment had only spent seven years in England, forty-nine in Ireland, eleven on the Continent, fifteen at Gibraltar, and eighteen in North America and West Indies. It took part in the American War of Independence, was at Bunker's Hill, where it behaved best and suffered most; it distinguished itself at Long Island and Germantown; also after the French joined the Yankees, at St. Lucia, for the capture of which island (29th December, 1779) the Fifth won the privilege of wearing a white plume in the cap instead of the red and white tuft which was worn then by other regiments of the line.

After six years in Ireland, from 1780, the regiment returned to North America and served for a few years in Canada, recruiting among the settlers; before its return to England in 1797 all the Corporals and Privates were transferred to the 24th Foot, the Officers and Sergeants only returning home, and the regiment was recruited, not in Northumberland, but in Lincolnshire.

In 1799 two battalions of the regiment went to Holland with other British troops to attempt, with the help of Russian and Dutch allies, to drive out the French. The expedition failed, the troops suffered many hardships, and the two battalions formed the rear-guard of the British force in the withdrawal.

From 1808 to 1814 the regiment was fighting in the Peninsular War, where it gained the name of " The Old and Bold." The first battalion landed in Portugal, and the first invasion of Spain ended at Corunna. The second Fifth were with Picton's fighting division, and gained high praise from Lord Wellington; he wrote of their conduct as affording " a memorable example of what steadiness and discipline of the troops and their confidence in their officers can effect in the most difficult and trying situations." In 1811, at El Boden, this battalion charged with bayonet the French cavalry, and re-took the Portuguese guns which had been captured.

At Badajoz Colonel Ridge was killed in the moment of victory, when at the head of the Fifth he had scaled the castle walls, which were eighteen to twenty-four feet high, and had driven the garrison with terrible slaughter into the town.

After Salamanca the 2nd Battalion returned to England, and was disbanded in 1816. It left its effective Privates with the 1st Battalion, which had also been in the battle. The 1st Battalion took part in the great victory of Vittoria in 1813, and all the battles that followed it up to Toulouse, the crowning victory of the Peninsular War. The Fifth missed being at Waterloo owing to its services being required in Canada, where the war with America continued till Christmas Eve, 1814. On Napoleon's escape from Elba the Fifth was hurried home, but did not reach Europe till 11th July, 1815. It marched to Paris and formed part of the Army of Occupation, being at Bapaume in 1817 and Cambrai the following year.

Then followed forty years of peace service, which did not lower the efficiency of the regiment, for during the trying operation in India against the mutineers of the native army, the Fifth did good service for two years, and very early in the war a Sergeant and two Privates won the V.C., which had only been instituted shortly before.

While the Fifth was at Lucknow in 1857 authority was received to raise a 2nd Battalion in Newcastle, and Lieutenant-Colonel Vasey Kirland quickly raised 1,068 approved men. The 1st Battalion took part in the Afghan War, 1878, and the Soudan Campaign, 1898. The 2nd Battalion gained high praise from Sir Frederick Roberts for its services in the " Black Mountain " expedition in 1888. " There is not a better regiment in Her Majesty's service than the Northumberland Fusiliers." Both battalions were engaged in the Boer War. Two more battalions were raised in 1900, the Militia Battalion became the 5th Battalion, and formed part of the garrison of Malta during the war. The Volunteer Battalions sent several excellent companies to the front, which fought alongside their comrades of the Line Battalions.

During the Great War the number of battalions was raised to forty-two, of which twenty-five were actively engaged. There were eleven Reserve Battalions, three Garrison Battalions, and three battalions of young soldiers raised to form part of the Army of Occupation at the close of the war.

The " Honours " gained during the Great War are as follows; only those printed in heavy type are carried on the Colours.

Mons, Le Cateau, Retreat from Mons, **Marne 1914**, Aisne 1914, '18, La Bassée 1914, Messines 1914, '17, '18, Armentières 1914, **Ypres 1914**, **'15**, **'17**, **'18**, Nonne Bosschen, Gravenstafel, **St. Julien**, Frezenberg, Bellewaarde, Loos, **Somme 1916**, **'18**, Albert 1916, '18, Bazentin, Delville Wood, Pozières, Flers-Courcelette, Morval, Thiépval, Le Transloy, Ancre Heights, Ancre 1916, Arras 1917, '18, **Scarpe 1917**, **'18**, Arleux, Pilckem, Langemarck 1917, Menin Road, Polygon Wood, Broodseinde, Passchendaele, Cambrai 1917, '18, St. Quentin, Bapaume 1918, Rosières, Lys, Estaires, Hazebrouck, Bailleul, Kemmel, Béthune, Scherpenberg, Drocourt-Quéant, Hindenburg Line, Epéhy, Canal du Nord, St. Quentin Canal, Beaurevoir, Courtrai, **Selle**, Valenciennes, Sambre, France and Flanders 1914-18, **Piave**, Vittorio, Veneto, Italy 1917-18, **Struma**, Macedonia 1915-18, **Suvla**, Landing at Suvla, Scimitar Hill, Gallipoli 1915, Egypt 1916-17.

The battles in which the 17th Northumberland Fusiliers Pioneers took part were:

Somme Offensive, 1916
    Battle of Albert.
    Battle of Bazentin Ridge.
    Battle of Ancre Heights.
Flanders Offensive, 1917
    Battle of Pilckem Ridge.
    Battle of Langemarck.
    Second Battle of Passchendaele.
The Battles of the Lys
    Battle of Hazebrouck, 1918.
The Second Battle of Arras
    Battle of the Scarpe, 1918.
    Battle of Drocourt-Quéant Line, 1918.
Breaking of the Hindenburg Line
    Battle of the Canal du Nord, 1918.
The Final Advance
    Battle of Valenciennes, 1918.

APPENDIX IV

THE CONSTRUCTION OF THE BERGUETTE LIGHT RAILWAY DEPOT

Contributed by Captain J. Garvie, *17th (S.) Battalion Northumberland Fusiliers Pioneers*

The work carried out by the battalion consisted in setting out and being responsible for the erection of the light railway workshops, together with the construction of the necessary branch line leading to the workshops, and the siding accommodation.

The work was carried out under the direction of Lieutenant-Colonel John Bowden, O.B.E., D.A.D.L.R., and when the site was taken over by the battalion it was under cultivation with no preparation whatever. The branch line was taken off the main French line from Berguette station, and was one and a half miles long. The sidings were over forty in number, with a mileage of over twenty miles, necessitating the construction of seventy points and crossings. These lines, of course, were of ordinary gauge, the material used being mostly track which had been taken up at home and shipped to France.

The workshops consisted of two main buildings and four smaller ones. The largest, 300 feet by 200 feet, was for a main erecting shop 200 feet by 50 feet, with a smaller machine shop, a motor repair shop and storage accommodation. The other large building was 300 feet by 50 feet, and was for a sawmill and wagon repair shop. All of the buildings were made of timber, having been made in sectional parts, and barged direct to the site of the works, the walls and roofs being covered with corrugated iron. The main buildings were in bays of 25 feet span, and 12 feet high to the under-side of the roof trusses, except the erecting shop, which had a clear span of 50 feet, and a height of 25 feet. The roof trusses were carried on timber stanchions at 10 feet centres and, as the whole had to fit and be bolted together without alteration, much credit is due to Mr. W. E. A. Brown, F.R.I.B.A., who was responsible for the design in London, in that nothing had to be altered. The foundations of the stanchions were made of concrete into which rag bolts were fixed for holding these stanchions. As this work was always well ahead, and carried out independently of the fixing of the stanchions, much credit is due to the men who set the templates for these foundations, as any slight error in the setting out would have been difficult to rectify.

In no part had any adjustment to be made, and no trouble was experienced in fitting either the transverse or longitudinal parts. The accuracy of the work shows what the 17th were capable of doing, and no one is higher in their praise than Mr. Brown, who, sent out to supervise the erection of the buildings, says that " his work was very considerably lightened by the very able technical officers in the battalion, and the practical tradesmen in the ranks."

The subsidiary works carried on at the same time were the construction of several miles of 60 cm. gauge railway track in and around the workshops, the preparation of the foundations for the machinery in the various shops, and the erection of huts for the permanent staff. A road 200 yards long was also constructed. To obtain the ballast for the railway track and shop floors a siding was laid down at a coal mine at Estree Blanche, eight miles away, so that wagons could be loaded direct from the waste heaps of the mine earth and brought to the works. All this was carried out by the battalion, who only for the latter part of the time had the services of a company of German prisoners for spreading and levelling the mine earth.

The progress was greatly hampered by the excessive spell of frost which lasted about three weeks, the ground being so hard that picks had no effect. The barges were held up by the frozen canals delaying the arrival of the material, so that the actual working time was much curtailed. There was also an absence of tools and plant, especially scaffolding, so that much ingenuity had to be used, particularly in raising into position the large roof trusses which weighed over half a ton each, not to mention the difficulty of off-loading the barges without the use of a crane.

When the battalion left, the main constructional work was completed and the shops ready for occupation.

It might be added, that, before the war was over, some members of the battalion who were able to re-visit the site had the mortification of seeing the whole of their labours undone, as the workshops had had to be moved elsewhere owing to the unwelcome attention of Jerry's long-range guns.

APPENDIX V

THE BATTLEFIELDS RE-VISITED

[The following account of a visit to well-remembered places was written some little time after the cessation of hostilities, by Mr. T. M. Horsley, who served with the 17th, and was with them during all the later stages of the war, and to whom we are also indebted for several of our illustrations.]

We were making our way up from Amiens to Arras, which place we thought would be the best centre to get at some of the old spots well known to the 17th Northumberland Fusiliers, and although we were told when leaving Amiens that the train was going round by Doullens, we very soon found ourselves at Albert, and as the train was a stopping one we were able to notice quite a lot of interesting spots round about the Valley of the Ancre. Albert itself is, of course, very desolate-looking, but fairly well rebuilt, although there is a very large proportion of army huts in this quarter. The same remarks apply to Aveluy and Authuille. Aveluy Wood is still very much of a wilderness, although there is a good deal of undergrowth, but the stark tree-trunks still give it a very warlike look. The Ancre River does not seem to have returned to its pre-war state, as what was apparently the river bed is dry and covered with weeds, etc., and we noticed several rowing boats lying high and dry. Thiépval Ridge is very easily picked out by reason of the Ulster Tower, which was erected there some time ago as a memorial to the Ulster Division. After leaving the Ancre Valley at Miraumont the country is not so badly knocked about, except that at Achiet-le-Grand, which has a very battered look. As we had only two or three days in Arras, we decided that the first day should be spent north of the town, and the second day south of it.

The first place we stopped at of interest was Ecurie, and the change here from the war-time appearance is very noticeable. The corrugated-iron huts on the right side of the Arras road, that were used for stables when the 17th were there, are being put to the same use by a farmer, who has erected a big lot of farm buildings on the other side of the road, where the Quartermaster Stores used to be. The actual camp just in behind the Wood is still waste ground, the huts having been cleared away and the ground apparently being too broken-up to be utilized as yet. The sunken road which ran down behind the camp to Neuville St. Vaast has been filled in, and there is a large brick factory on the side immediately south of the camp, next to what used to be the stables. The artillery dug-outs towards the Labyrinth, which used to provide good cover when the camp was getting its nightly shells, are still intact, and are in the middle of a large beet field. The large dug-out at La Targette cross-roads, which was used by General Petain during the French offensives of 1915, has been preserved in its entirety, and is one of the show spots of the neighbourhood. It is about seventy feet deep, and the passage leading down to it is well timbered. The dug-out itself consists of three large chambers and a kitchen, each of these chambers being capable of accommodating two or three hundred men—the ventilating shaft being in the kitchen. Neuville St. Vaast is completely rebuilt, with the exception of a few houses on the north side, where Cellar Camp was. All the huts at Cellar Camp have been dismantled except two, the one nearest the road, which " C " Company used as Headquarters for a time and " B " Company's kitchen on the other side of Mangin Track, and the sunken road, which ran along the bottom of the camp, has been filled in.

We walked up from the village to Zivvy Dump, which has a particularly desolate look, and we noticed one hut there which still had a Canadian mark on it (Maple Leaf Hut), and a complete light railway train was drawn up opposite to what used to be the Control Office, complete even to the inevitable Baldwin engine, which was red with rust. The track was still there, except where wooden sleepers had been used, as these had been pulled up for fuel. Very little attempt seems to have been made to rebuild Souchez, where the famous Sugar Works still remain a pile of rubbish, although next door, Ablain St. Nazaire, has been pretty well rebuilt. From Souchez we went on to Lens, which town seems to have been occupied more with getting the pits in working order, rather than putting up elaborate houses. We noticed whole streets here consisting of nothing but Armstrong and Nissen huts. All the pit-heads which have been rebuilt are of reinforced concrete. Certain of the villages round about Lens, including Bully-Grenay, do not seem to have got on so quickly with the rebuilding; in fact, in this area, the only people who seem to have rebuilt on a solid scale are the Banks and Insurance Companies. Colliery Companies seem to be content to have the pits put in order rather than the offices. The Lens Mining Company's Offices were just a row of Armstrong huts. Annequin was the next place we noticed with a certain amount of interest, it being entirely rebuilt. We returned to Arras in the late afternoon through Loos, passing over Hill 70, which does not appear to be any different to what it was during the war. We noticed several parties of men here busy collecting barbed wire, corrugated iron, etc.

As we had not seen anything of Vimy, we decided to go there first thing next day. The craters on the top of Vimy Ridge are still as they were during the war, and no attempt seems to have been made to clear this particular area. Farbus, Petit Vimy and Vimy present an extraordinary sight, Vimy itself being a hive of industry with several factories whose tall chimneys dominate the landscape and give the place a very prosperous look.

We turned south here, and after passing through Oppy, Gavrell, Roeux and Monchy, soon got down into the Sensee area round about Henin and Croisilles. The area between Fouchy and Roeux on the Scarpe is still very battered looking, and in several places no rebuilding at all has been attempted. In Croisilles, too, very little rebuilding of a permanent nature has been done, most of the people there being content with huts. The trees above St. Leger village which were used as O.P.'s during the war are still there. Quéant has altered very much, and although little rebuilding has been attempted near the old Abbey the new village has been built farther towards the station.

The Hindenburg Line, which started from the main road at Quéant, and where the 17th were camped for a while, has been completely filled in, and it is very difficult indeed to trace the line of trenches; in fact, one would hardly believe that trenches ever existed there. The site of the Quartermaster Stores on the Bapaume Road, about five hundred yards out of Quéant, was very easily picked out, otherwise there were no traces whatever of the war. The valley between Quéant and Lagnicourt, which the writer remembers very vividly before the attack on the Canal du Nord in September, 1918, being filled to overflowing with tanks, artillery, infantry, etc., had a most peaceful appearance, the whole of the land being under the plough.

Whilst in this area we intended to have a look at Bapaume, but found the time was getting rather short, so after striking the main road at Ervillers, we turned straight back to Arras. It was quite dark when we passed through Mercatel, which was rather a pity, as we would like to have explored Blaireville, Ficheux, and other places in that area, through which the battalion passed during August, 1918.

The general impression conveyed after a visit of this kind is that the French have been extremely quick in reconstruction work. Reinforced concrete has been used to a very great extent, particularly for railway bridges, station buildings, telegraph poles, fencing, etc. Certain areas have got on very much quicker than others, but generally speaking, most of the villages we visited are by now pretty well rebuilt.

The work of clearing away the debris and filling in the trenches was mostly done by the Chinese Labour Corps, the inhabitants themselves pushing on with the building operations. The Chinese remained in the country up to the beginning of this year, and at Neuville St. Vaast we were told that they had only left there in May this year. All the trenches have been filled in, and in many cases form part of a cultivated field. In fact, it was very difficult indeed to realize that there have ever been such things as trenches. The barbed wire has been all collected, and the method adopted in this case seems to have been to collect the wire and dump it alongside either side of the nearest road, which has had the effect of forming two large hedge-like mounds, which are now rapidly being covered with grass. All the villages are very much alike in one sense; where the place was so badly damaged as to make rebuilding impossible on the old site, the whole village has moved two or three fields away, and with the exception of the Ancre area, there are very few temporary buildings to be seen, all the new houses being of brick. We seemed to pass a brick factory about every five hundred yards along the road, and everyone was busy building in one way and another. In particular, when we were going through Croisilles, we noticed an old man, who must have been about seventy years old, assisted by his wife, who was certainly no younger, putting the floor into a house. It certainly seems pretty plucky to start building a house under these conditions at such an age.

We had made up our minds to visit Masnuy St. Jean, and managed to get there after changing at Douai, Valenciennes and Mons, to say nothing of being bundled out of the train at the French Frontier Station and again at the Belgian Station to be put through our paces by the Customs. The thing that seemed to bother them most was the writer's camera. The Belgians were particularly polite and informed us that if we were English they would not examine our luggage, but would be satisfied if we showed our passports. Masnuy St. Jean has very pleasant recollections of the time the 17th was billeted there, and although we were only able to stay there overnight we were given a most hearty welcome, and were assured that the same welcome would be given to any of the old battalion who would care to re-visit the village.

APPENDIX VI

POTTED PIONEERING

HERE is an artist's impression of the multifarious duties which fell to the lot of the stout lads of the 17th Northumberland Fusiliers Pioneers during their sojourn overseas, not so long ago, when there was a little dispute on the Continent in which they felt it incumbent upon themselves to take the weaker side.

The sobriquets of the regiment before they started were many, such as " The Fighting Fifth," " The Old and Bold," " The Duke of Wellington's Bodyguard," " The only Infantry that Charged Cavalry with Success," but another has since been added, they say, by the 17th, " Never Known to Knock."

Well, to return to the job in hand—in other words to elucidate the illustrations to the uninitiated or the younger generation.

You will observe in the first picture that our worthy friend the Pioneer means to be in at the death; you can see him following a tank which is belching forth devastation on the Hun.

Immediately behind, the " Fighting Fifth " are seen consolidating the day's gains, whilst others, you will observe, bring along the bombs and water, a nasty job at the best of times.

The Crib Bridge, you will notice, has been completed, and as the work was good and the Hun making haste to leave the area immediately in front, there is no maintenance party in the offing and the artillery may safely cross though they have further to go than space permits showing, before they make the passage (a dry one we hope).

Your ubiquitous Pioneer we next find slabbing across vast muddy wastes to enable those gunners the more easily to obtain their daily supply of ammunition with which to strafe the Boche.

Behind we come across others of the battalion busily engaged in running forward a light railway line. Here again we meet the survey party some time before we reach the track layers.

The wiring party, we are quite certain, are hating their job. If the Véry lights had been any nearer it would have been more difficult to illustrate their doings as, generally speaking, it is wiser for the party to lie low in the latter event. You will observe from the moon that a good night was chosen.

Mining is apt to have its drawbacks, but a Lewis gun mounted overhead is a safeguard worth remembering. It is broad daylight, and some of the infantry are resting; one, however, unfortunately stopped part of an " Oil Can," a very objectionable form of missile.

Finally we come to the hard-worked Pioneer passing that rare hour of leisure outside his billet, his thoughts concentrated on the popular game of " House," whilst the air around him resounds with strange sounds such as " Kelly's Eye," " Legs Eleven," " Clickety Click," " Top o' the 'ouse," etc., etc.

Mademoiselle enters the picture at this point. We leave the rest to memories.

THE EDITOR.

PLATE XXVI.

GENERAL VIEWS.

PLATE XXVII.

THE LIFE STORY OF A PIONEER ON ACTIVE SERVICE. (PART I.)

PLATE XXVIII.

The Life Story of a Pioneer on Active Service. (Part II.)

PLATE XXIX.

Range Construction, Bardon Moor.

APPENDIX VII

UNVEILING OF THE WAR MEMORIAL AT YORK, JUNE 14TH, 1924

It seems fitting to close this account of the 17th and 32nd Service Battalions Northumberland Fusiliers (N.E.R.) Pioneers with a reference to the memorial erected by the North-Eastern Railway at York, on which are inscribed the names of so many of those comrades who lost their lives with the 17th Battalion.

Field-Marshal Lord Plumer, G.C.B., G.C.M.G., G.C.V.O., G.B.E., with whom was Sir Charles Harrington, G.B.E., K.C.B., D.S.O., General Officer Commanding in Chief the Northern Command, unveiled the War Memorial on the afternoon of June 14th, 1924. The Memorial, which was designed by Lutyens, R.A., is built of Portland stone, and, as can be seen from the photograph, is in the form of a space enclosed by three screens which are fifteen feet high, having a centrally placed obelisk fifty-four feet high. All the internal faces of the screens are used as panels, upon which are carved the names of the Company's employees who lost their lives during the war.

A large rectangular stone is placed within the three screens on a raised platform flanked on each side by shallow steps.

Under the obelisk there is carved the inscription : " In abiding remembrance of the 2,236 men of the North-Eastern Railway who gave their lives for the Country in the Great War, the Company places this Monument."

The " Great War " stone bears the inscription, " Their name liveth for evermore."

There were several thousand persons who attended the unveiling ceremony, but the space available from which spectators could obtain a view of the proceedings was very limited. Every effort, however, was made to ensure that the relatives of the fallen should be provided with reserved accommodation.

Lord Knaresborough in his opening address made special mention of the 17th Service Battalion Northumberland Fusiliers, and the readiness with which the men came forward in the hour of need. After the service, which was conducted by his Grace the Lord Archbishop of York, Lord Plumer made an appropriate speech, commending the pride with which we hold in memory the sacrifices and achievements of the Great War.

After the ceremony, the Great War stone was heaped round with wreaths and other floral tributes, amongst them being a large laurel wreath of red and white roses surrounding a centre piece representing a " fusil " surmounted with the letters N.F.P.

This was the gift of the N.E.R. Pioneers Association, and was placed on the stone by Major H. S. Cole, Regimental Sergeant-Major Nichols, Sergeant C. Kirkwood and Lance-Corporal MacVeigh.

THE EDITOR.

APPENDIX VIII

CONSTITUTION AND RULES OF THE N.E.R. PIONEERS' ASSOCIATION (LATE 17TH AND 32ND SERVICE BATTALIONS NORTHUMBERLAND FUSILIERS)

Establishment

Patrons:
President:
Vice-Presidents:

Committee of Management

Chairman:
Hon. Treasurer:
Hon. Financial Secretary:
Hon. Correspondence Secretary:
Hon. Auditor:
District Secretaries:

District Officers

Chairman:
Secretary:

Bankers

Midland Bank Co., Ltd.

RULES

1. Name of the Association

The Association shall be called the "N.E.R. PIONEERS' ASSOCIATION" (late 17th and 32nd Battalions Northumberland Fusiliers), with Headquarters at Darlington.

2. Objects of the Association

The objects of the Association shall be:
(a) To have an organization that will enable members to keep in touch with one another.
(b) To keep alive the spirit of comradeship which was fostered during the war.

(c) To hold Re-Union Meetings.
(d) To afford assistance to members finding themselves placed in temporary difficulties.

3. Qualification for Membership

Membership shall be open to any member of the 17th (S.) Battalion Northumberland Fusiliers or of the 32nd (S.) Battalion Northumberland Fusiliers.

4. Subscriptions

The subscriptions of members to the funds of the Association shall be 2s. per annum, which may be paid quarterly, half-yearly, or annually, to the District Secretaries or to the Hon. Financial Secretary.

5. Alteration of Amount of Subscription

The amount of the Annual Subscription may from time to time be increased or decreased by a resolution of the members passed at an Annual General Meeting.

6. Management

The management of the affairs of the Association shall be vested in:

(a) A Committee of Management consisting of: Chairman, Hon. Correspondence Secretary, Hon. Financial Secretary, Hon. Treasurer, and one member elected by each district.
(b) The Committee of Management to be empowered to add to their numbers by co-opting not more than six ex-officers who were connected with the above-named battalions. Seven members of the Committee of Management shall form a quorum.
(c) The members of the Committee shall hold office for one year, but shall be eligible for re-election.
(d) Casual vacancies on the Committee of Management shall be filled by the districts concerned in such a manner as the members of the district may determine.
(e) A Sub-Committee of five shall be appointed by the Committee of Management to deal with all business connected with the Benevolent Fund. Three members to form a quorum.
(f) The Chairman and Hon. Correspondence Secretary shall be ex-officio members of all Committees.

7. Hon. Correspondence Secretary, Hon. Financial Secretary, and Hon. Treasurer

The Hon. Correspondence Secretary, Hon. Financial Secretary, and the Hon. Treasurer shall be elected at an Annual General Meeting, and shall hold office for three years, and shall be eligible for re-election.

The Hon. Correspondence Secretary shall act under the direction of the Committee of Management in calling meetings of the Association and of the Committee. He shall record the minutes of all the meetings, and perform such other duties as are assigned to him by the Association or by the Committee. The Hon. Financial Secretary shall prepare an annual statement of accounts for audit and for presentation to the Annual General Meeting, and be responsible for contributions and finance. The Hon. Treasurer shall receive from the Hon. Financial Secretary all monies due, and make such disbursements out of the Funds of the Association as are authorized by these Rules or by the Committee. He shall keep the Committee informed as to the Association's Funds.

8. District Rules

(a) Each district shall elect annually a Chairman, Hon. Secretary, and Committee to conduct the business arising in their area. Retiring officers to be eligible for re-election.

(b) District Committees shall meet as required and transact all necessary business.

(c) The District Hon. Secretary shall perform the duties assigned to him by the District Committee. He shall forward all monies due to the Association to the Hon. Financial Secretary, and shall render a quarterly return of receipts and expenditure in January, April, July, and October.

9. Annual and Extraordinary General Meetings

An Annual General Meeting of the members shall be held in the month of April in each year, or at such other time as the Committee of Management shall appoint for the purpose of:

(a) Receiving the report of the Committee of Management.
(b) Passing the accounts.
(c) The election of officers.
(d) The transaction of any other business stated in the notice convening the meeting.

Extraordinary General Meetings shall be called by the Committee of Management at their discretion, or on receipt of notice of motion from four or more districts.

Fourteen days' notice of any General Meeting shall be given to the members in such manner as the Committee may from time to time determine.

10. Funds of the Association

The monies of the Association shall be kept in two separate accounts, viz., (a) a General Account and (b) a Benevolent Fund Account. Except as provided in Rules 11 and 12 the income and expenditure of the Association shall be included in the General Account.

11. Benevolent Fund Account

There shall be placed to the credit of the Benevolent Fund Account:

(a) Any special subscriptions or donations.

Appendices

(b) The proceeds of any meeting or function specially promoted on behalf of the Benevolent Fund.

(c) All surplus money from the General Account sanctioned by the Committee of Management.

No amount shall be transferred from the Benevolent Fund Account to the General Account under any circumstances.

12. Payments from the Benevolent Fund

Payments from the Benevolent Fund up to a maximum of £1 may be made at the discretion of the Chairman of the Benevolent Committee, Hon. Financial Secretary, or Hon. Treasurer, any two of these officials to be in agreement as to the amount to be disbursed, provided that such payments shall be reported to the Committee at their next meeting for confirmation.

Payments exceeding £1 but not exceeding £5 may be authorized by the Committee.

Payments exceeding £5 shall only be made on the authority of a meeting of the Association.

Recommendations for payments to be made from the Benevolent Fund in necessitous cases to be reported by the District Secretary concerned to the Hon. Financial Secretary, giving details of the special circumstances for submission to the Benevolent Fund Committee.

13. Monies to be Banked in the Name of the Association

The monies of the Association shall be deposited in the name of the Association in separate accounts, as provided in Rule 10, in a bank approved of by the Committee, namely, The Midland Bank, Ltd.

Cheques shall be signed by the Hon. Financial Secretary and Hon. Treasurer.

14. Audit of Accounts

The accounts of the Association shall be audited annually at March 31st, which will be regarded as the end of the financial year, by the Hon. Auditor appointed at the previous Annual Meeting.

15. Alteration of Rules

These Rules may be altered by a resolution of a General Meeting or an Extraordinary General Meeting duly convened for that purpose in accordance with Rule 9.

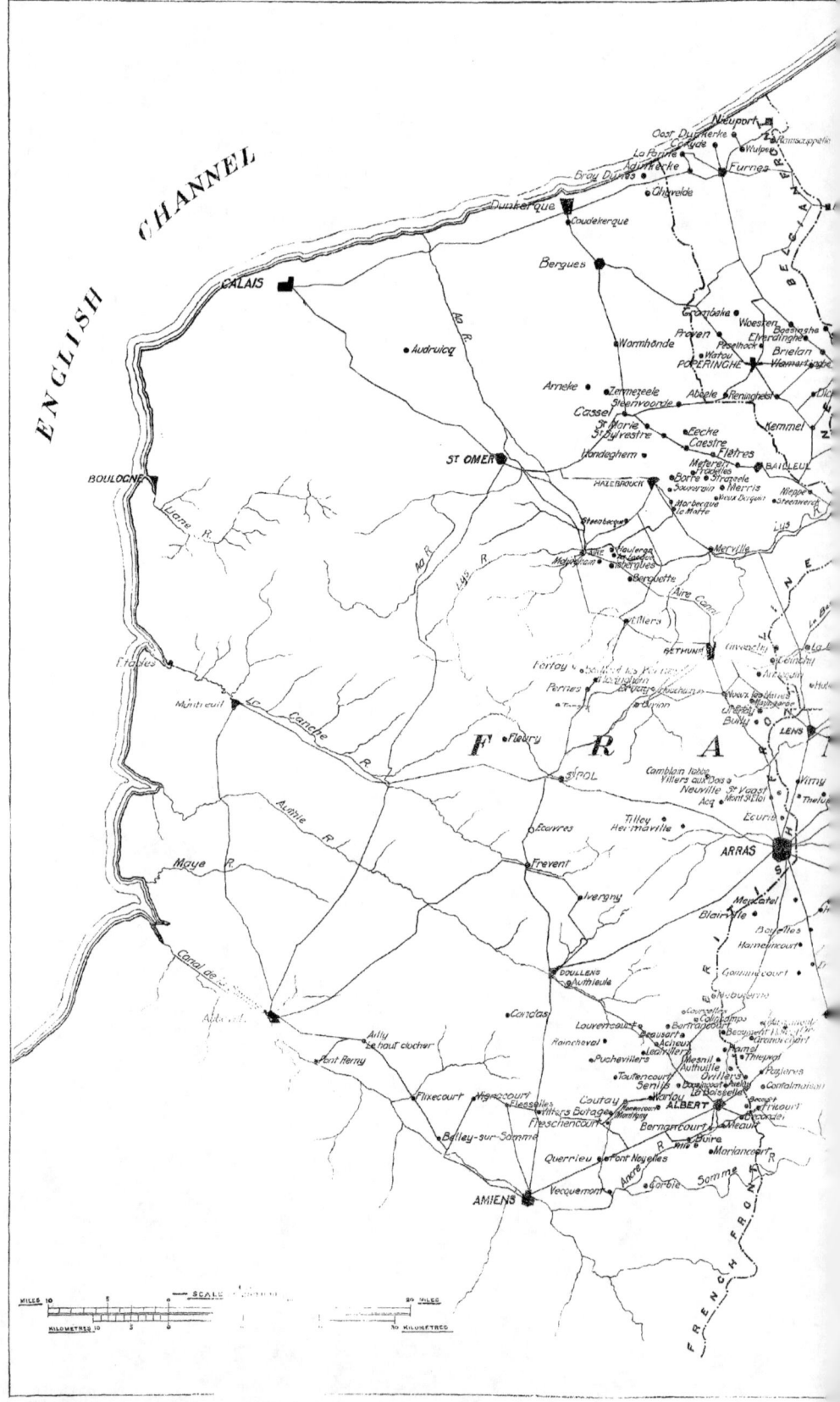

GENERAL PLAN

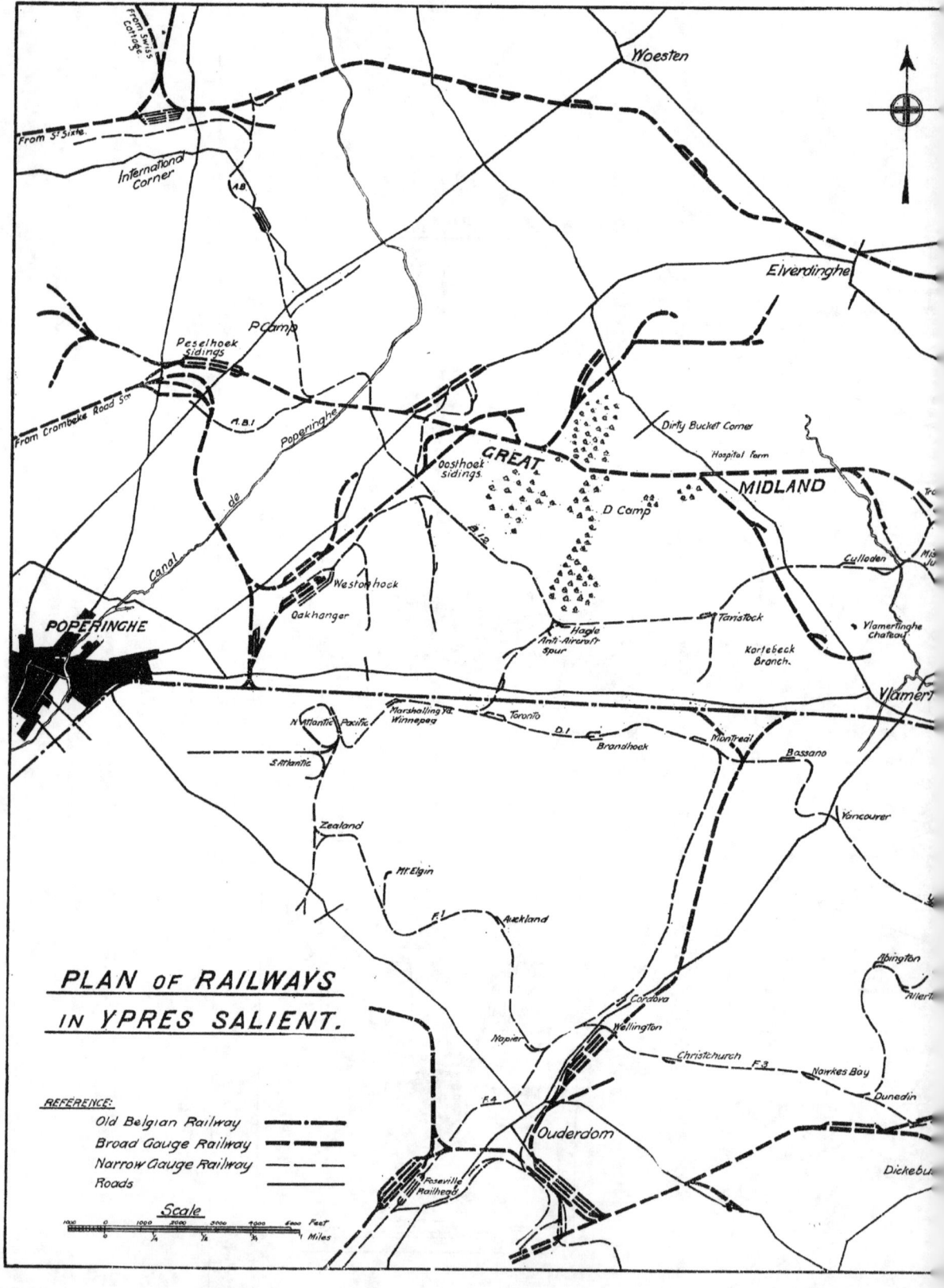

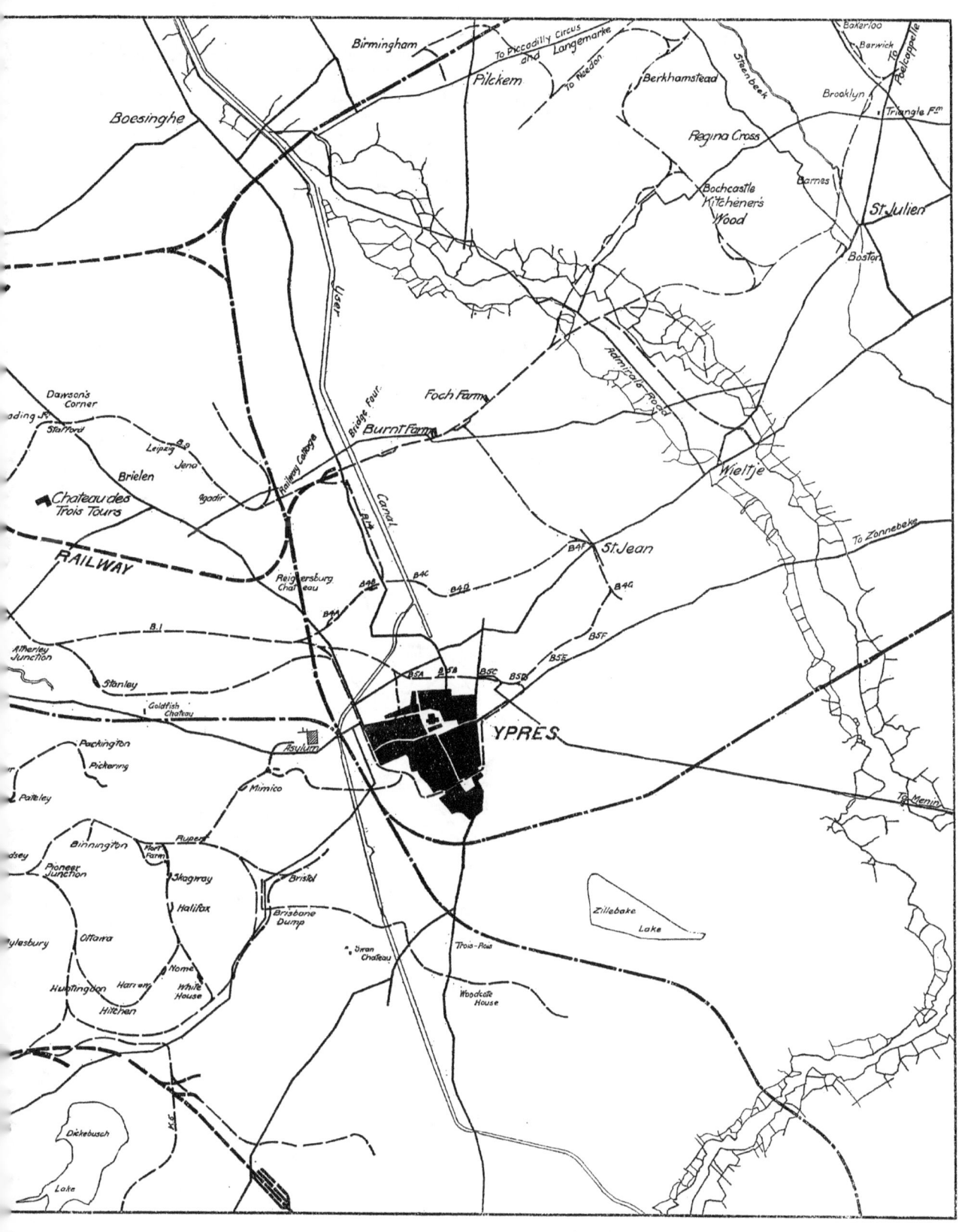

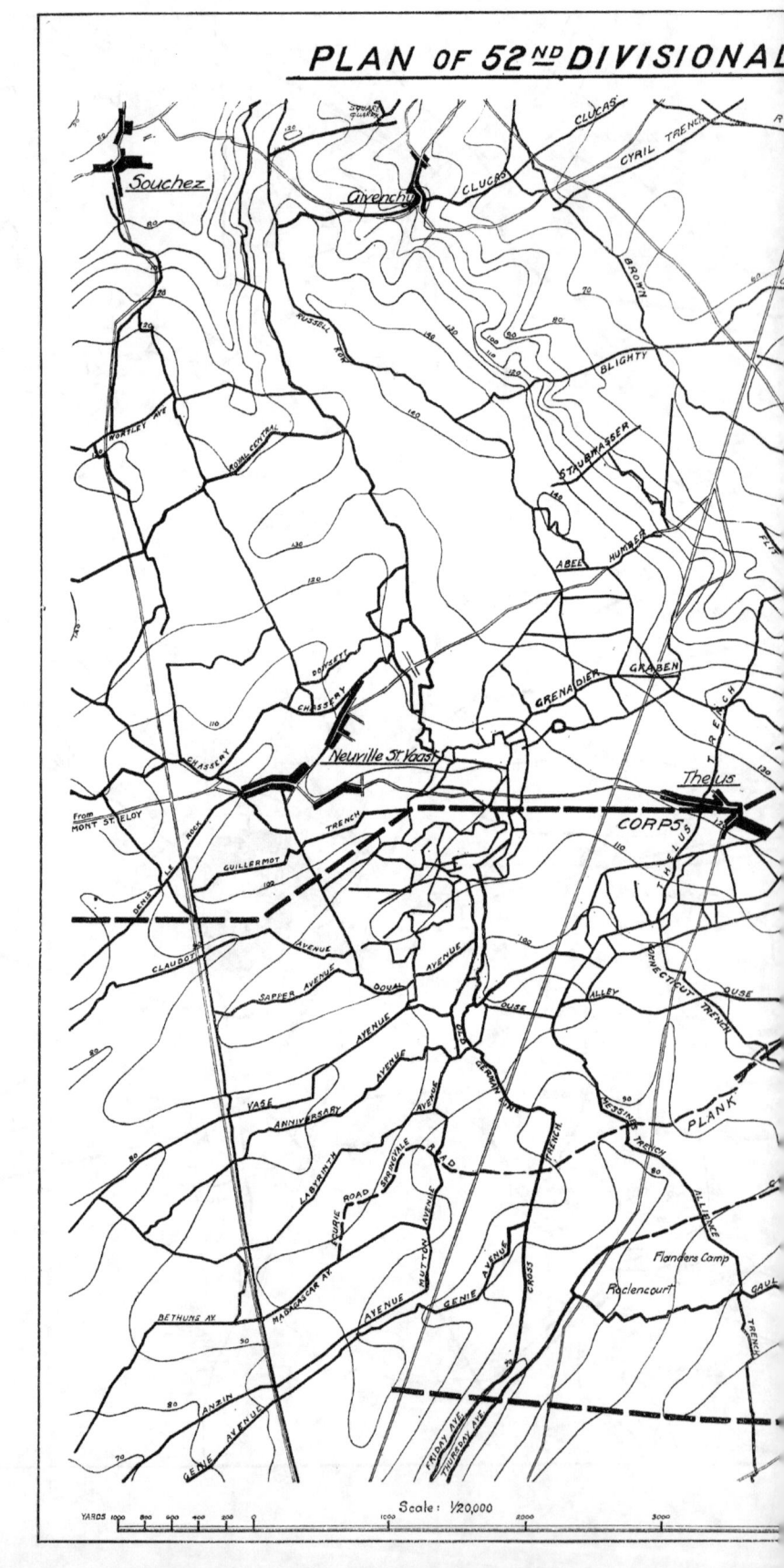

TRENCH SYSTEM — SOUTH OF VIMY.

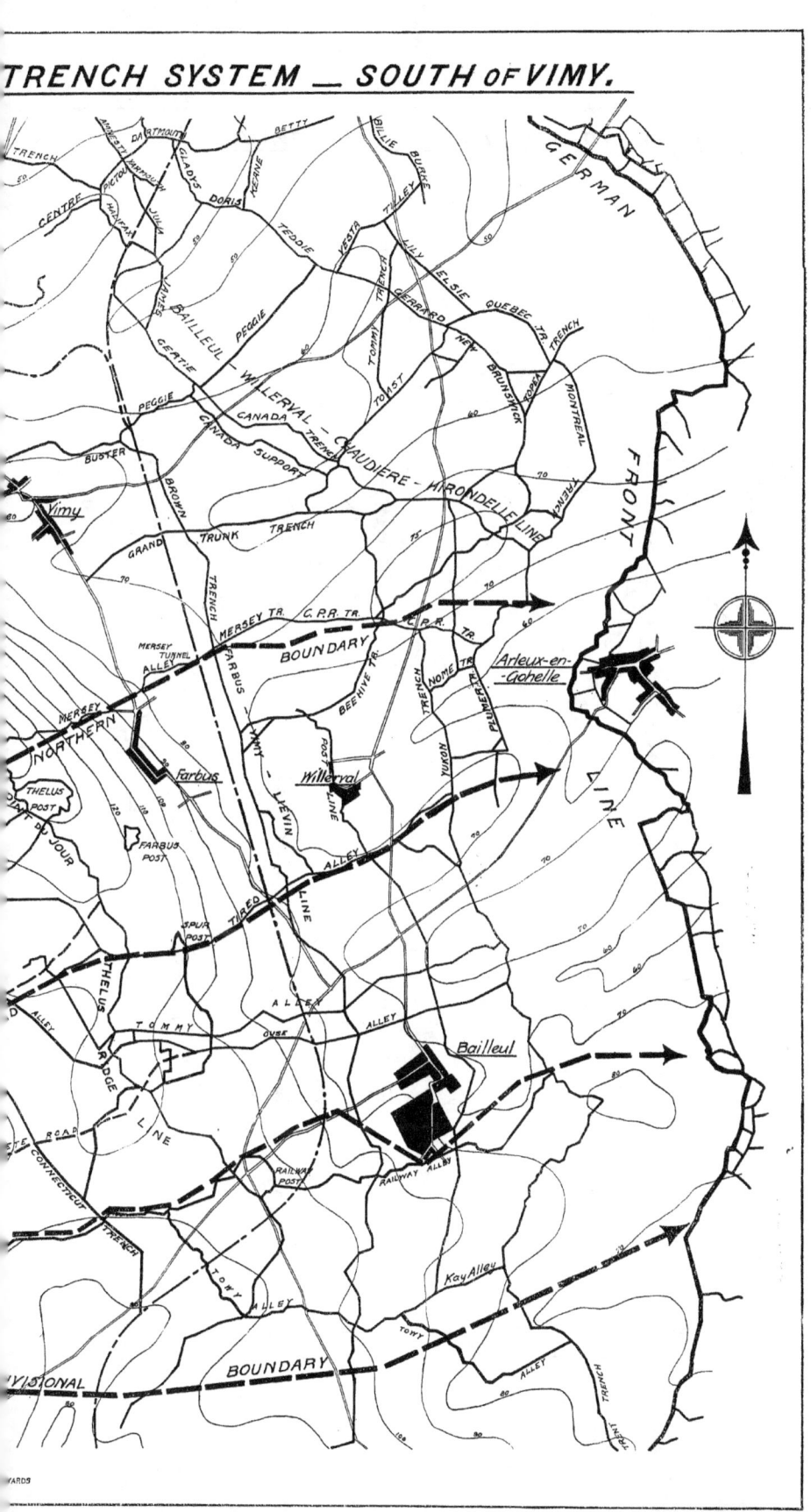

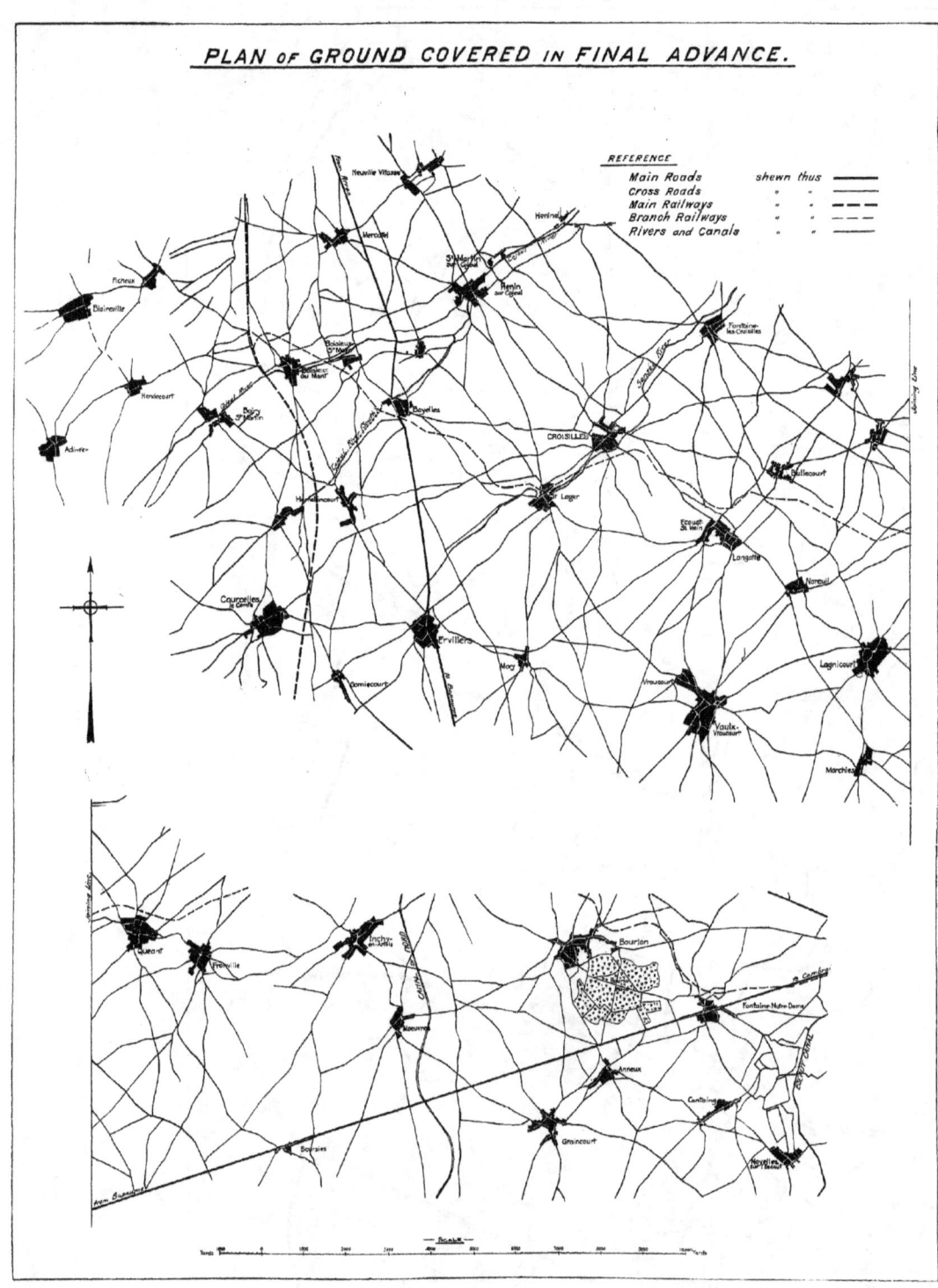

www.ingramcontent.com/pod-product-compliance
Lightning Source LLC
Chambersburg PA
CBHW082038230426
43670CB00016B/2693